Functional Analysis of Information Networks

Business Data Processing: A WILEY SERIES

Editors: Richard G. Canning
Publisher, Canning Publications, Inc.

J. Daniel Couger
Professor, Management and Computer Science
University of Colorado

Personnel Implications for Business Data Processing
Robert A. Dickmann

Design of Sequential File Systems
Thomas R. Gildersleeve

Management Reporting Systems
James M. McKeever in collaboration with Benedict Kruse

A Guide to Packaged Systems
Robert V. Head

Control of the Information System Development Cycle
Robert I. Benjamin

Decision Tables: Theory and Practice
Solomon L. Pollack, Harry T. Hicks, Jr., and William J. Harrison

An Introduction to Data Base Design
John K. Lyon

The Organization of the Data Processing Function
Frederic G. Withington

COBOL Support Packages: Programming and Productivity Aids
Stanley M. Naftaly, Bruce G. Johnson, and Michael C. Cohen

Modular Programming in COBOL
Russell M. Armstrong

Functional Analysis of Information Networks:

A Structured Approach to the Data Communications Environment

Hal B. Becker

A WILEY-INTERSCIENCE PUBLICATION

JOHN WILEY & SONS

New York • London • Sydney • Toronto

Library of Congress Cataloging in Publication Data

Becker, Hal B.
Functional analysis of information networks.

(Business data processing)
"A Wiley-Interscience publication."
1. Data transmission systems. 2. Computer input-output equipment. I. Title.

TK5102.5.B35 001.5 73-14991
ISBN 0-471-06124-7

Printed in the United States of America

10 9 8 7 6 5 4 3 2 1

to
IVAN POPEJOY

a true prophet
who gave freely
the guidance i sought

his death is a loss
to all of us

Preface to the Series

Business Data Processing: A Wiley Series is intended for system analysts, programmers, and managers who desire to improve their competence in business/management applications of the computer. Within each of some twenty subject areas, publications will be provided over a range of technical depth. The objective is to provide a series of publications that will enable readers to gain an understanding in specialized subject areas.

In the face of the growth in depth and complexity of the computer field, practitioners encounter the problems of developing and maintaining technical competence. The junior level practitioner must upgrade his competence to reach the experienced practitioner level. The experienced system analyst/designers and programmers must strive to reach senior levels. The manager must broaden his knowledge to include the new technology that is being employed by his subordinates, but at an appropriate managerial level.

The Series will draw on experienced practitioners in the subject areas to the fullest extent possible, so as to provide useful, practical information.

The Series is designed to address three major areas of interest:

System Analyst Titles. These publications are designed for the practicing system analyst/designers, who already have a knowledge of computer systems, and who desire to learn about and apply new techniques.

Programmer Titles. These publications are designed for the experienced programmers, who desire to improve their competence in program structuring, building, and testing.

Manager Titles. These publications are designed for the active data processing managers who desire to learn ways to improve the operations under their control.

To assist the authors in the preparation of their manuscripts, Wiley has organized a small Advisory Group for providing advice and suggestions on a timely basis to the authors. Experienced system analyst/designers counsel on the System Analyst Titles, practicing programmers on the Programmer Titles, and active managers on the Manager Titles.

Within any one set of titles, say the System Analyst Titles, there will be found a rather wide range of technical content. Some publications will discuss basics, for analysts who have only recently completed their training. Other publications will address the interests of the senior analyst/designers.

Thus Business Data Processing: A Wiley Series addresses the breadth, complexity, and the dynamic characteristics of the computer field. It covers an expanding set of technical subject areas. It addresses the interests of system analyst/designers, programmers, and managers. And it provides basic as well as more advanced information.

Training, updating, and upgrading professionals in the computer field will be a continuing problem. We hope that the Series will be an effective method in helping to cope with this problem.

Richard G. Canning
J. Daniel Couger
Series Editors

Preface

The need for a comprehensive, organized approach to the design and implementation of information networks becomes more obvious every time an attempted configuration fails to reach the design goals or, in some cases, fails to function at all. These failures, particularly the larger ones, are duly noted by various representatives of the trade press and receive nationwide coverage within the computer user and manufacturing communities. These failures are traditionally attributed to faulty or inadequate design, lack of understanding of the problem, or some other nebulous reason.

What we, as users and manufacturers alike, have failed to recognize is that we cannot possibly expect to understand the problem, or any other problem for that matter, until we have an adequate definition of it. It is this definition that we lack.

This book was written as a first step toward the definition of the information networking problem. The functional separation and analysis of information and network processing was chosen as it seemed the only rational, logical way to avoid the pitfalls of the traditional applications-oriented approach to information network design.

It is of value to note that, when approached functionally, the definition becomes independent of any particular manufacturer's equipment, as well as independent of any specific application. Further, the definition of the problem is valid for future as well as currently installed or present generation offerings, thus avoiding the planned obsolescence syndrome.

Having spent the last eleven of my fifteen years in the computer industry exclusively in the data communications environment, I have long since lost all expertise I ever had in the world of information processing. It is to the industry's benefit and my relief that Grayce M. Booth, who has spent her entire fifteen years in the industry exclusively in the information processing environment, believed strongly enough in the functional approach and separation of function concepts to write the companion volume "Functional Analysis of Information Processing," also published by John Wiley and Sons.

The two volumes present comprehensive definitions of information processing and network processing functions which, together, define information networks. This definition does not lead the reader directly to the solution of the design problem. Used as a roadmap or checklist, however, it will go a long way toward assuring that key elements in a design are understood and not inadvertently omitted.

It is hoped that other researchers will evaluate and adopt the approach, initiating the exchange of ideas and experiences necessary to lay the groundwork for the next logical step—that of defining the solution to the problem. The various simulators, models, algorithms, and other analysis techniques must be identified, evaluated, and logically structured before this can be done. Procedures must be developed that will allow network designers to:

1. Identify required hardware and software subsets of the information and network processing functions.
2. Use the appropriate analysis tools and techniques necessary to optimize the configuration.
3. Produce a design modular, flexible enough to be capable of growth and transition into future generation offerings.
4. Insure that the design will operate within acceptable price/performance parameters.

As is always the case with conceptual works such as this, many people contributed to the inception and development of the approach. I am particularly indebted to the late Ivan Popejoy, an early pioneer in networking, who finally convinced me that there was more to information networks than network processors. His thinking and guidance are responsible for the initial intuitive flash of insight that led to the book itself.

Many other colleagues provided additional technical and/or moral support, including:

Robert D. Benson, Leonard M. Call, DuPuy F. Cayce, Robert R. Goerner, and John J. Kucera. Ruth M. Fontenot typed most of the initial draft and Estelle Dombroski the final chapters of it. My special thanks to Grayce M. Booth for her excellent job of editing and typing of the final manuscript.

Phoenix, Arizona

Hal B. Becker

Contents

SECTION IV

Control Functions— The Logical Network

SECTION V
Information Network Example

Appendices

SECTION I

Introduction

CHAPTER 1

Introduction and Scope

Numerous volumes have been written describing the many facets of data communications from a number of different viewpoints. These books provide the system designer of today with a reference source for detailed descriptions, operating characteristics, and general information concerning many of the data communications-oriented devices available. It is possible to explore the intricacies of the various modulation and encoding techniques used in subsets or modems, the reasons for and techniques used in the various levels of line conditioning, the circuit differences and variations between frequency and time division multiplexing, and a host of other similar considerations. Collected and used as such, these books will provide the data communications-oriented system designer with an excellent reference library.

As computer systems evolve and become increasingly dependent on data communications due to the geographical distribution involved, the designer of such systems is faced with an entirely new set of problems of a magnitude previously unknown in the freestanding batch processing world he has been accustomed to. Many new and completely different disciplines must be evaluated and applied to produce the required system. Terminals must be studied and selected, digital subsets or modems specified, common carrier (AT&T, Western Union, etc.) offerings evaluated and ordered, new programming techniques learned and applied, time-sensitive operating systems and associated philosophies studied, and a seemingly endless parade of new problems faced.

This book was written to complement the existing library of data communications reference material by providing a functional, comprehensive approach to data communications independent of specific applications. It will provide the experienced designer of free-standing information processing systems with a bridge or roadmap to the world of information networks. It will also provide an introduction to data communications for the general reader.

A further function is to identify and provide a checklist of hardware and software considerations that should be evaluated in the specification, design, and implementation of information networks. The same considerations apply to networks of all sizes and scales, ranging from those with a few relatively slow remote terminals connected to a single computer complex to those with numerous geographically distributed computers serving hundreds or even thousands of terminals, on a nation- or world-wide basis.

The following chapters define the set of functions to be used by the designer in conjunction with the appropriate analysis tools to configure information networks that provide an optimum information collection, processing, and distribution capability.

A brief history of data communications is provided to acquaint the reader with early approaches to the use of data communications and provide an appreciation of the problems inherent in these approaches. It serves the further purpose of emphasizing the need to abandon these approaches and reverse the philosophy of treating the terminal environment or universe around a computer complex as a subset or peripheral subsystem of it.

A totally new, functional, top-down approach is described, starting with a definition of the six recognized levels of abstraction required in the information network design effort. Hardware and software are separated functionally, discussed, and related to the total network. The hardware elements, discussed in Section III, become the building blocks of the "physical" network. The control functions (software), discussed in Section IV, constitute the "logical" network necessary to control the "physical" network and the flow of information through it. Definitions of concepts presented are provided as necessary to aid the reader in gaining an insight into and understanding of the functional approach to information networks.

This volume is intended to do one thing—provide an introduction to and definition of the functional approach to information networks. The various mathematical network analysis tools and techniques, such as models, simulators, configurators, and other procedures required actually to optimize the network design, are identified and discussed only briefly, as an in-depth presentation of them is beyond this book's scope. Treatment of these subjects at the necessary depth is still in process and will be the topic of a future volume.

Similarly, the functional approach to information processing that is first identified in Chapter 4 is also beyond the scope of this book. The approach is equally valid and important to information processing, however, and a book entitled *Functional Analysis of Information Processing* has been written by Grayce Booth to cover that subject.

Consistent with the emphasis on the functional approach, specific computers (information processors or network processors) terminals, and other network elements are not identified except as necessary for various examples, and then only at a generic level.

It is significant that the material in this book does not require any "Blue Sky" or other futuristic technology or breakthrough, either in hardware or in software. It is, rather, a comprehensive top-down organization of the data communications technologies that have been evolving for over a decade. Everything that is discussed either has been or is currently being implemented somewhere in some system or network.

The functional approach to information networks and network processing leads to an awareness of the basic problem to be solved—that of specifying, designing, and implementing an optimum information collection, processing, and distribution capability. This problem is functionally exactly the same, whether a network of existing or current state-of-the-art computers and network elements is being considered or advanced next generation techniques and equipment are being studied. From this position, it then becomes obvious that, by applying the functional approach to current product line networks, groundwork is laid that will permit a gradual, relatively painless transition in a series of planned steps or phases into the new product lines or next generation offerings.

Further, the approach greatly minimizes the possibility of designing and implementing a network that is capable of growth and expansion up to a certain point but then requires a complete redesign if further growth and extended capability are to be achieved.

Recognizing that there is a distinction between the use of the words "information" and "data," this book uses the word "information" to mean both the "data" that flows in the network and the "information" that is a result of interpreting the "data." The term "data communications" is used when necessary to provide a bridge or link to identify techniques or devices that have, through common usage, come to be identified by or associated with the term.

To aid those readers wishing to pursue the subject further, two related reading lists have been included. The first follows Chapter 16, "The Advanced Research Projects Agency Network (ARPA)," and the second, a more general list, is found in Appendix B.

CHAPTER 2

Evolution and Definition of Information Networks

Information networks existed for years before data communications in the traditional sense appeared. Early computer users developed networks to assure that the information to be processed by their computers would reach the equipment within the desired time frame and in an appropriate form. Reports may have been mailed from their source to the computer location on a daily, weekly, or monthly basis and converted to a machine- or computer-readable form at the central location. Other information may have been telephoned in periodically and collected in files, which were then keypunched at the appropriate time. Many methods, including truck, messenger service, pneumatic tubes, and others, were used to get the information from its source to the location where it was to be processed. The results or output of the computer runs were delivered to the appropriate destination or destinations by similar means.

These early information networks, then, consisted of: (1) information sources—the place or point at which the information first entered the network; (2) a distribution network—the path or route that the information took to get from its source to the computer; and (3) information destinations—the place, point, or points that the output or result of the computer run was to be delivered.

As computers gained acceptance as a management tool and larger companies began applying them, their costs tended to be such that not every location within a company that needed or could use this new tool could justify the expense of owning one. This led to the centrally located computer and the associated networks discussed in previous paragraphs. These networks were used to make the computational power of the centrally located computer available to those who had requirements in addition to the information collection, processing, and distribution functions already mentioned.

These users faced the additional problem of getting their needs defined so that programs could be written and debugged, getting the program and its input information to the computer, and getting the output or results back. Delays due to the mails and other delivery or distribution techniques, problems in getting programs changed or corrected and debugged again, scheduling problems, and other delays all contributed to fairly long turnaround or response time. Techniques were needed that would permit the rapid flow of information from its source to the computer and back to its destination(s).

The first source the early computer pioneers looked to for this capability was the common carriers—the Bell System, Western Union, and others—primarily because they had distribution networks (lines, trunks, etc.) in place and operating. These distribution facilities were available at almost all locations. The common carriers also had terminal devices available that could be used to send written or coded information over the lines and trunks to similar terminals at the other end. These terminals took the form of teletypewriters—essentially a typewriter coupled or connected to the line or trunk. Teletypewriters were a natural outgrowth or improvement on the original telegraph key, an even earlier form of an information source which, when coupled to its sounder, could also be used as a destination.

Since the lines, trunks, and terminals were readily available, all that was required was to provide the computer with an appropriate interface to them. It would then be possible to enter information directly into the computer from its source, which might be tens or hundreds of miles away. Equally needed was the ability to send the output or results back to the originating terminal.

In order to effect this interface, it was necessary to take the computer, which was essentially designed and optimized for its intended task of batch processing, and alter or modify it sufficiently so it could "talk to" the communication line or trunk and the terminal at the other end. This usually required the addition of clocking and buffering circuitry that would be compatible with the particular speed and code set of the terminal, plus an appropriate technique for indicating to the batch processor that a complete unit (bits in earlier years, characters later) of information had arrived or been delivered. It was also necessary to convert the current (electrical) mode of operation of the line to an appropriate voltage mode or level compatible with the circuitry of the computer.

Early systems of this type were usually capable of interfacing with a single line at a time. The interface was accomplished in a way that presented the least amount of disturbance to the existing hardware and software of the batch processor. Batch information processing was still the computer's main task. In fact, frequently the communications interface was used simply to collect information and punch it into card form for use as input to an appropriate batch program run at a scheduled time. Often, the computer would be run in the batch mode during one part of the operating day and then used to collect information from remote locations for later processing during other parts of the day. See Figure 2-1.

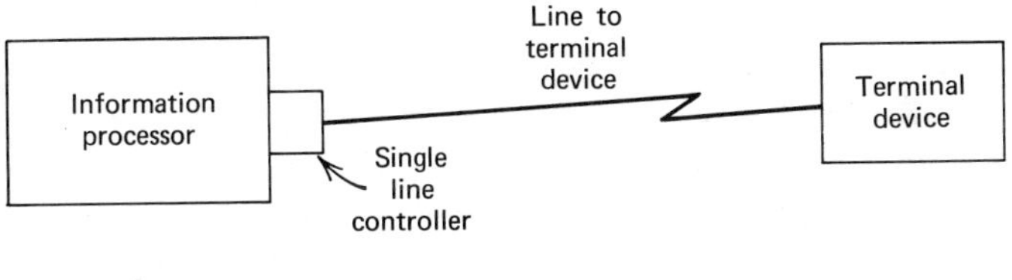

Figure 2-1 **Single line controller**

The effect of this interface was to decrease the delay times previously incurred in the flow of information in the network. Information now flowed at electrical speeds, ten characters a second or so, rather than the speed of the mail, truck, train, plane, or other technique used previously. The resulting decrease in turnaround time produced very favorable reactions and created much interest in the technique. This signalled the start of the data communications revolution that may make the computer revolution that it closely follows seem like an elementary exercise in comparison.

Decreased response and turnaround times, the ability to enter the information into the computer from remote locations, and other benefits all contributed to the belief that computer generated output and reports could be more timely and useful to management. This timeliness could then contribute significantly to obtaining a competitive edge in the marketplace.

The evolution from collecting the information from its sources in an essentially off-line batch mode a single line at a time to the idea of interfacing with several lines and terminals at a time and feeding the incoming information directly to the program in the computer that was to process it was not long in getting under way. The early approach of treating the data communications interface as a subset or peripheral of the batch processor was continued, however, because the batch processor was still considered the center or hub of the network and as such was considered its controlling factor.

With this philosophy firmly in mind, designers turned to the task of providing subsets of hardware that could be coupled to or built into a batch processor, enabling it to control many terminals of, by this time, a rapidly growing variety. The batch system was, of course, still expected to keep up with its primary function of batch processing.

Again, to minimize the effect of this interface on the basic hardware and software architecture of the batch processor, these designs took the form of multiple line controllers that operated in the manner of a peripheral subsystem. These controllers required the execution of instructions in the information processor for their operation. They also placed a memory allocation burden on the processor for the buffering of incoming and outgoing information as well as for storage of needed instructions. See Figure 2-2.

Each time it was desirable to interface a new remote terminal to the network, numerous hardware and software changes were required to accomodate its speed, code set, operating discipline and parameters, and other aspects not previously encountered. Each of these additions produced new programming requirements, more memory space allocated for buffering and program storage, and new hardware interfaces.

As networks grew in size, number of terminals, and complexity, it became obvious that a batch processor with a multiline controller could handle just so many lines and terminals. Beyond that point, the memory and instruction execution overheads began to decrease sig-

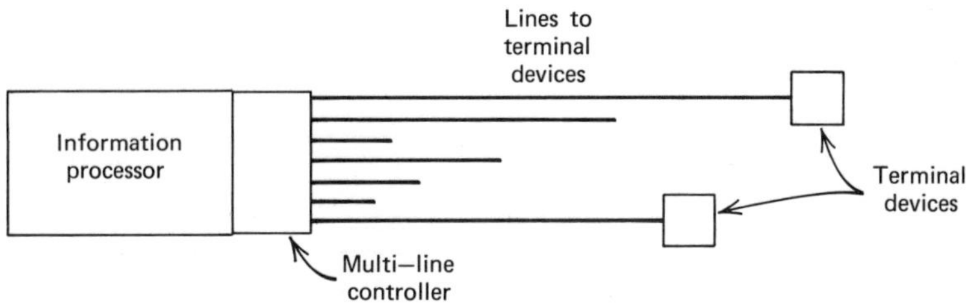

Figure 2-2 **Multi-line controller**

nificantly the percentage of the computer's capability and throughput that remained for processing the information. While not necessarily wrong, this increased overhead was predictable, since a machine designed and optimized for one task—information processing—was being used for a task that has since proven to require hardware of a different architecture and optimization if it is to be performed efficiently.

Although not fully appreciated at the time, it was finally recognized that, if the communications function was to be performed efficiently and the overhead effect on the batch processor minimized, it would have to be removed from the processor and performed elsewhere. This led to the implementation of the early data communications processors. These machines (early 1960's) took two basic forms. Several computer manufacturers started with an existing small-scale batch processing computer, added to it the hardware necessary to interface with the various lines, trunks, and terminals in use, and marketed it as a communications processor. A few others, perhaps with an intuitive grasp of the coming communications revolution, produced computers specifically designed and implemented for the data communications task.

This new approach made it possible to remove much of the data communications overhead from the batch processor and place it in the front-end communications processor. All of the line, trunk, and terminal interface parameters and functions were now executed in a processor implemented for just those tasks. The memory space and execution times previously required in the batch processor for these tasks were now returned to it for use in its specified role of information processing. See Figure 2-3.

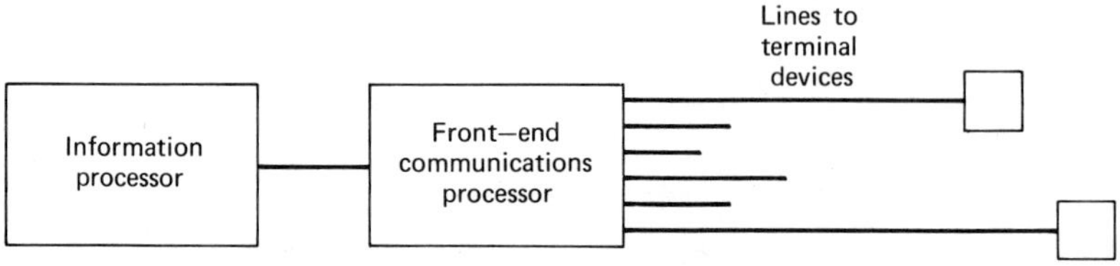

Figure 2-3 **Front-end communications processor**

In addition to the line, trunk, and terminal interface disciplines, the front-end communications processor proved capable of assuming numerous other functions that contributed even further to the reduction of the batch processor overhead. Included in the list are: character or code transliteration, which becomes a significant problem in networks containing a variety of terminal types; preliminary editing of incoming information for proper format and content; error detection and/or correction; a form of queueing and use of a scheduling algorithm for information flowing into the batch processor; and numerous other overhead type tasks.

In addition to providing a front-end capability for batch processors, the communications processors were applied in a free-standing mode to administrative message switching networks. These early networks usually used teletypewriters operating with the 5-level Baudot code at 10 characters per second. At the switching center, electromechanical or manual methods were used to switch incoming information to the appropriate outgoing line or trunk and on to its intended destination(s). Replacing the manual or electromechanical switcher with a communications processor and an appropriate mass storage subsystem (usually disks) for queueing provided previously unknown levels of control and information management. See Figure 2-4. Turnaround times for information flowing in the network were reduced; the lines and trunks were managed more efficiently, permitting greater traffic volumes during the operating day; additional functions such as reroute or alternate destination and intercept became feasible; priority designations could be included; and a host of other similar benefits previously unrealizable were now within reach.

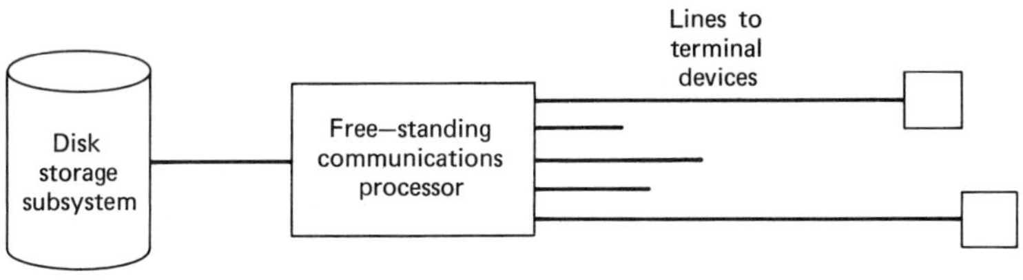

Figure 2-4 **Free-standing communications processor**

The growing use of computers as a management tool, coupled with the possibilities that data communications offered, led to the obvious next step—removing the computer from its traditional batch mode of operation and placing it "on-line." This would produce even faster turnaround times and more timely management information. As mass storage technologies produced subsystems capable of providing tens or hundreds of millions of characters of storage on-line in a random (rather than sequential) access mode, it became possible to realize these goals.

In an effort to extend the computational capabilities of the computer to greater numbers of potential users, sophisticated multi-dimension operating systems dependent to a great extent on data communications began to appear. In addition to the "local batch" processing (jobs entered from the computer's local peripherals) capability, these systems would accept for execution jobs entered from remote locations via the data communications network.

Small-scale batch processors were equipped with single line controllers, enabling them to communicate over ordinary telephone lines with the larger, centrally located system. Symbolic source decks could now be submitted from the remote to the central location, compiled or assembled and (if the appropriate input was included) executed, and the results sent back to the remote processor for conversion to printed reports, punched cards, or other appropriate form.

Further evolution has produced systems capable of supporting concurrent, multidimensional activities including time-sharing, remote batch, transaction processing, direct program access, and, most recently, administrative message switching. These capabilities, all heavily dependent on data communications, serve to make the computational power of the centrally located system available to an ever-increasing community of users.

SECTION II
Functional Approach and Level Definition

CHAPTER 3

Definition of Functional Approach

The increasingly rapid evolution of data communications-dependent computer applications presents today's system designer with an entirely new set of problems of a magnitude previously unknown in the free-standing batch processing world he has been accustomed to. The traditional approach to data communications—that of treating it as a peripheral subset of the central information processing system—is an increasingly frequent cause of: (1) inordinately high system cost; (2) lack of flexibility and growth potential; (3) degraded system performance and a multitude of other associated problems. This approach has typically been one of a "bottom-up" look at the design and implementation problem, where the smallest elements are identified first and an attempt is made to tie them together in an upward direction, with the hope that a workable (even if not particularly efficient) system will result.

The specification, design, and implementation of all classes of information networks must proceed from the highest possible level downward if it is to be:

1. Successful.
2. Capable of orderly growth and transition

to future generation equipment.

3. Within the specified price/performance characteristics range.

Functional analysis of information networks results in the identification of six levels of abstraction or consideration necessary to define the network in terms independent of the applications to be served. These six functional levels proceed from the top down and are discussed later in this chapter.

By following this functional approach and performing the network analysis indicated, the network designer can, by extracting the appropriate subset(s) of the functions provided, configure efficient information networks from the smallest through the very largest scale. Key to the simplicity and success of this approach is the maintenance of a "separation of function" philosophy based on the following assumptions:

1. The manipulation or processing of information in a network is optimally performed by hardware and software designed specifically for the information processing task, hence the term "information processing."
2. The control of the network surrounding the information processor(s) is best performed by hardware and software designed specifically for "network processing."

It has been demonstrated repeatedly by numerous computer manufacturers that it is impossible for a single hardware/software design to do an optimum, or frequently even adequate, job of both. Systems or networks of this architecture are at best a less-than-optimum compromise fraught with the inherent limitations, inflexibilities, lack of modularity and expansion capability, excessive cost and overhead, and poor price/performance of the approach. It should be noted that, when approached from a functional point of view, the networking problems of the current generation of computers are exactly the same as those of the coming future generations of equipment. This point is further emphasized and elaborated in later chapters.

Network analysis tools and techniques have been used for years in the configuration and construction of a variety of different kinds of networks. The petroleum industry applies them to pipeline networks to optimize the cost of construction and capacity; electrical power companies use them similarly to optimize electrical energy distribution networks. The common denominator of all networks is the fact that they are concerned with the flow of something between various points within the network. The petroleum network is used to move crude petroleum from its source at the well to the refinery and on to its destination(s) as a variety of by-products. The electrical network moves electrical energy from its source at the generator at a particular voltage through various switchyards and substations where it is transformed and forwarded to the end users or destinations at various appropriate voltages.

A very close analogy exists between these networks and the growing number of computer systems that are evolving with numerous computers, terminals, and other devices located at geographically separated points around a city, state, or continent. These computer networks are concerned with the flow of information from the entry point through one or more relay points, where it may or may not be modified and sent on to its intended destination.

An examination of the functions to be performed within these information networks reveals that any point or node within the network falls under one or more of the following three node definitions: (1) information source; (2) relay point; and (3) information destination.

Information sources are those nodes at which the information is first entered into the network, and include:

- Remote terminals of all classes
- Information processors of all classes and scales
- Network processors (communications processors configured in the network)

Relay nodes are those points within the network where information is received from a source, possibly altered in form and/or content, and sent on to a destination. Relay nodes include:

- Network processors
- Multiplexors
- Terminal controllers
- Switches

Information destination nodes are those points to which the information is delivered. A destination node may be intermediate in that the information will be sent on to another destination, as in a relay node, or may be final, where the information effectively leaves the network by being presented in an appropriate form to a destination device. Information destination nodes include:

- Remote terminals
- Information processors
- Network processors

Figure 3-1 shows the configuration of some of the types of source/

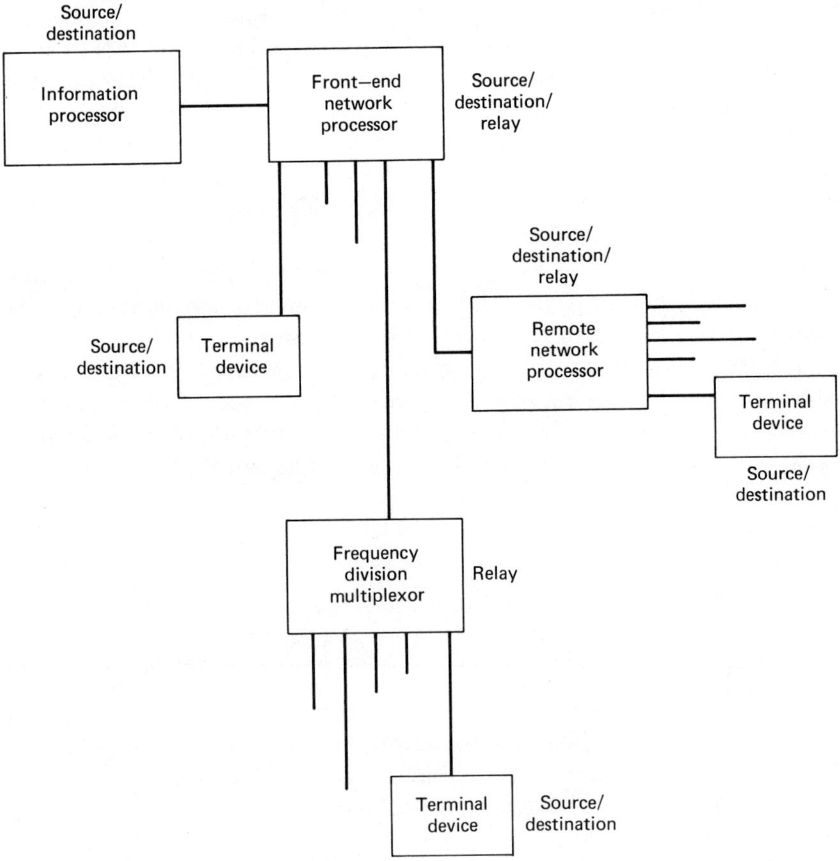

Figure 3-1 **Information network**

destination/relay nodes in an information network. The information processor acts as a source/destination node, as it can enter information into the network (through its front-end network processor) or similarly receive information from the network.

The front-end network processor can enter information originating as the result of some logical process occurring within itself, receive information directed to it as a destination (supervisory control message, for example), and act as a relay node for information flow between the information processor and the surrounding network.

The remote network processor similarly acts as a source/destination/relay node, with the exception that it has a trunk to the front-end network processor rather than a cable connection to the information processor.

The frequency division multiplexor is a relay-node-only device. It cannot originate information or act as a destination, but merely relays information flowing between the remote terminal cluster and the front-end network processor.

The terminal devices shown can enter information into the network (source) or receive information directed to them (destination), but they cannot act as relay nodes.

Information flowing through an information network takes a variety of forms. The most visible and interesting of these, from a user's point of view, is that form required for him to enter at his location (the source) a "message" which is to be delivered to the appropriate location in the network (the destination). The "message" to be delivered is the text that the user wishes conveyed to the destination.

A variety of additional types of information is usually required for use by the network in determining how to route the message to the proper destination. This information takes the form of a "header" which precedes the text of the message and is used by the network itself. All or portions of the header may be delivered to the destination along with the message text.

Message headers typically include various combinations of the following fields:

- The identification code of the sending (source) station
- The identification code(s) of the destination station(s)
- The next consecutive inbound message sequence number of the sending station
- The identification code of the operator entering the message
- The priority level at which the message is to be handled
- A security clearance code if required
- A message type indicator if required

The network processor initially accepting the message checks the "header" fields to insure that sufficient accurate information exists to route the message properly to the intended destination(s). Failure of this check on one or more fields may result in an error response to the entering operator. This response will identify the error so that the operator can correct it and resubmit the message. These conditions are discussed in more depth in Section IV, Control Functions.

CHAPTER 4

Definition of Information Network Levels

The six recognized functional levels of abstraction common to information networks of all classes and scales are defined in the following pages and related to each other in a hierarchical "top down" manner.

The six levels and their names are:

- I Network level
- II Processing level
- III Macro functional level
- IV Micro functional level
- V Element level
- VI Device/technique level

LEVEL I: NETWORK LEVEL

At this, the highest level, the proposed system is analyzed to determine if a network is required. A single, free-standing information processor operating in an essentially off-line batch processing mode, and connected only to its associated adjacent peripheral subsystems (card readers and punches, printers, magnetic tapes, mass random access storage devices, and others) is not considered a network. This type of system is identified at Level II, the processing level.

Any system requiring one or more information processors that are to be interfaced with one or more remote information sources and/or destinations on a full- or part-time basis is, by definition, a network. These remote source/destination devices include anything that is not considered a local or adjacent peripheral subsystem as previously defined. The remote devices may be any of those defined in Chapter 3 as information sources and/or information destinations.

If the system is indeed an information network, it is important that it be recognized as such at the earliest, highest level possible so that proper consideration may be given to identification of the information processing and network processing functions required.

LEVEL II: PROCESSING LEVEL

This level provides the initial separation of the information processing and network processing functions. The applications-related functions are examined to determine if they are better performed in an information processor or in a network processor located at some other node in the network. The lack of recognition of the distinction between the two is primarily responsible for the failure of many systems to achieve the desired price/performance characteristics. Frequently, network processing tasks such as code conversions, formatting, and error checking are done in the information processor, with the result that the overhead imposed reduces its throughput to the point it can no longer process the information flowing in the network within the prescribed time frame.

Ideally, the network surrounding the information processor(s) should be as transparent as possible so that the amount of *non*-information processing work done by the information processor(s) is minimized.

The processing level consists of two separate functions: information processing, or that which occurs within an information processor, and network processing, or that which occurs in the network surrounding the information processor(s).

As mentioned in Chapter 1, this book does not address the functional approach to information processing but concentrates on a complete functional definition of network processing.

LEVEL III: MACRO FUNCTIONAL LEVEL

The network processing function, identified as one of the Level II functions, breaks down into two broad macro functions at Level III, the network functions and the control functions.

A thorough evaluation through Level III of the required network functions leads to the selection or identification of an appropriate set of hardware network elements necessary to meet the specified objectives. Alternate hardware choices can be presented and the advantages and disadvantages of each identified so that the network designer can assure himself that he has a reasonably optimum hardware selection.

Having selected the hardware, it is then necessary to evaluate the control functions to establish or identify an appropriate set of software that is required to insure adequate control of the hardware and of the network as a whole. Depending on the size of the network, it may be necessary to achieve the desired optimization by implementing control function software at more than one node in the network.

At this point, the first three levels may be organized in a tree structure, as shown in Figure 4-1.

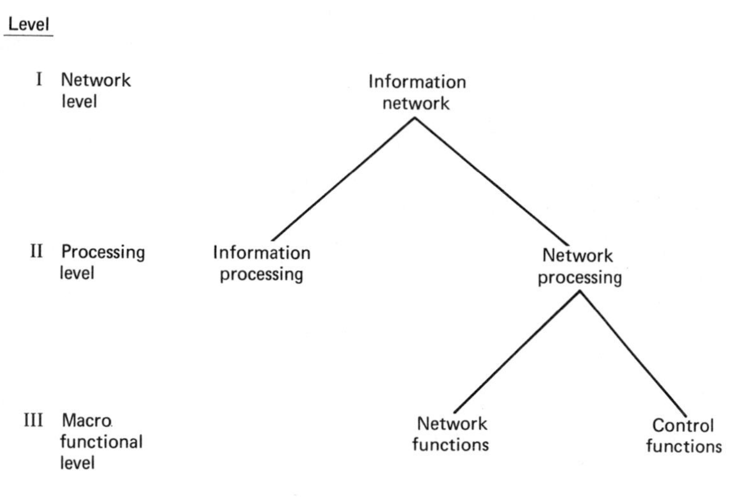

Figure 4-1 **Information networking**

These three levels are sufficient to identify: (1) free-standing information processing systems; (2) free-standing network processing systems; and (3) information networks that include both information and network processing requirements.

Free-standing information processing systems are those that do not interface to a network of any kind as described in the definition of Level I.

Free-standing network processing systems are those that do involve a network under control of one or more network processors but do not include any significant amount of information processing. Any such processing of information required is done by the network processor(s). Systems or networks of this type include administrative message switching, information collection and/or retrieval, and others.

Information networks are those that have an information processing requirement and are to interface with a surrounding network on either a part- or full-time basis. The two basic functions, information processing and network processing, should be separated and performed as optimally as possible through the use of appropriate network elements.

LEVEL IV: MICRO FUNCTIONAL LEVEL

The selection of a subset of the network and control functions necessary to accomplish the desired network capabilities takes place at Level IV. The functions are still fairly general at this level and usually do not require extensive analysis to determine their applicability. The Level IV micro functions are shown and briefly defined here under their appropriate Level III macro function headings for organizational purposes only. Complete definitions and discussion of the lower-level functions are provided in following chapters.

The Level IV micro functions included under the Level III macro function heading "Network Functions" are shown in Figure 4-2.

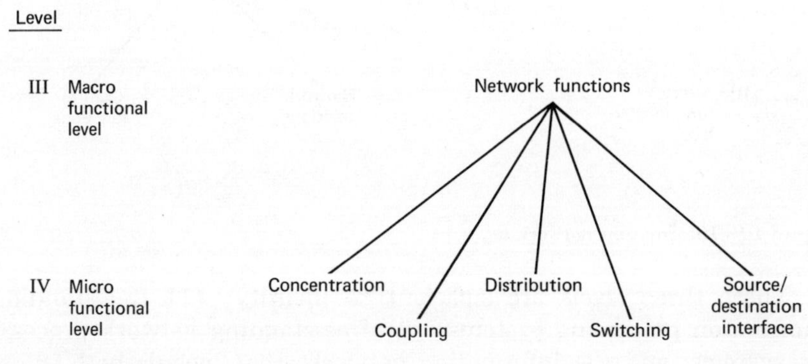

Figure 4-2 **Network functions**

Concentration

The collection/distribution or concentration of information flow from a number of source/destination nodes for transmission to another network node over a smaller number of lines or trunks.

Coupling

The technique or means used to connect source/destination devices and other network elements to the trunks and/or lines of the distribution network.

Distribution

The network of lines and trunks which provides the medium or path over which information flows between nodes in the information network.

Switching

A means of physically establishing or altering the path of information flowing through a node in the network.

Source/Destination Interface

The operating characteristics or disciplines of the source/destination devices used, which must be evaluated to determine their effects on the information network's hardware and/or software elements.

The Level IV micro functions belonging under the Level III macro function heading "Control Functions" are shown in Figure 4-3.

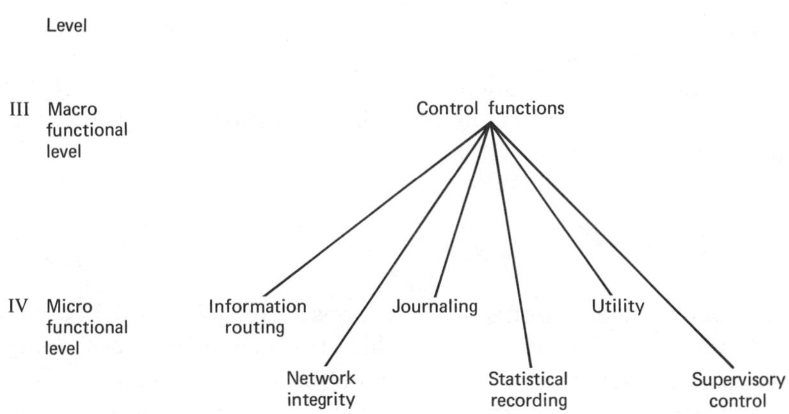

Figure 4-3 **Control functions**

Information Routing

The means or techniques applied to assure that information entered in the network is directed to the appropriate destination(s).

Network Integrity

The controls required to guarantee the integrity and accuracy of the network and the information flowing in it.

Journaling

The controls and/or hardware required to provide the user-specified level of retention for information that has flowed in the network and make this information available for retransmission within a given time frame.

Statistical Information Recording

The accumulation and evalution of statistical information concerning the volumes, response times, delays, and characteristics of the information flowing in the network.

Utility

Those overhead functions required in the network that may possibly be performed more optimally in a network processor than in an information processor.

Supervisory Control

The selection of those manual or external control functions necessary to provide for the handling of exception conditions or those requiring manual intervention.

LEVEL V: ELEMENT LEVEL

At this level, specific forms of the various Level IV network and control functions are identified. Through the use of network analysis tools and techniques, specific forms of these micro functions can be selected and applied to provide the degree of optimization indicated or desired.

The Level V elements are listed and discussed briefly in the following pages, along with the Level VI devices and/or techniques that are applicable. This is done to maintain organization and clarity. Each of the Level V and VI entries is discussed in detail in the following chapters.

The Level V and VI entries belonging under the Level III network function and control function entries include the following, which are shown for clarity under the appropriate Level IV micro function prior to their definition. The network function entries are presented first, followed by the control function entries.

Concentration

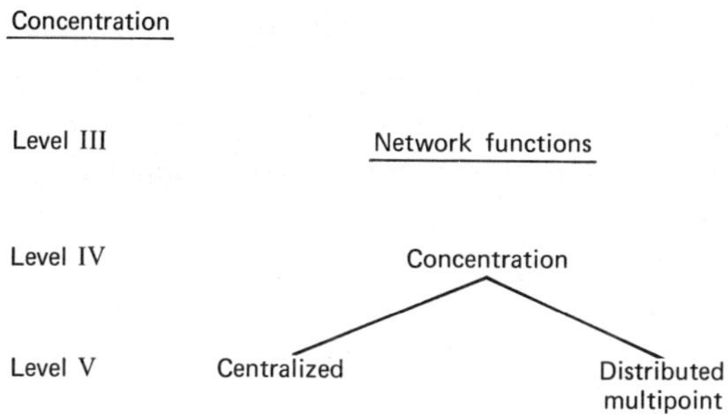

Centralized Concentration. This form of concentration implies the use of a relay node that is located at some optimum point within a cluster of terminals or information source/destinations. Its distinguishing feature is that one end of all the distribution network trunks/lines is connected or coupled to the relay node device. Devices used to provide centralized concentration capability include:

Level VI:

- Front-end network processor
- Remote concentrator
- Remote network processor
- Special purpose terminal controller
- Time division multiplexor (TDM)
- Frequency division multiplexor (FDM)

It should be noted that the first three Level VI entries are all communications or network processors. Ideally, these three devices should be program-compatible variations of a basic building block network processor architecture rather than the proliferation of incompatible, distinctly different devices currently being implemented.

Distributed Multipoint Concentration. Should the cost of distribution network lines/trunks required to provide centralized concentration for a cluster of terminals become prohibitive, or if the level of usage and volume requirements of the cluster are sufficiently low, the distributed multipoint form of concentration may be the optimum design choice. A single line or trunk is routed optimally through a portion of (or possibly all of) the terminals in the cluster and each terminal is coupled to it. Devices used to provide distributed multipoint concentration include:

Level VI:
- Poll and select
- Manual access (Contention)
- Distributed time division multiplexor
- Distributed frequency division multiplexor

The first two Level VI entries usually allow just one of the "N" terminals coupled to the line/trunk to be active at any given time, while the last two frequently permit all connected terminals to be simultaneously active.

Coupling

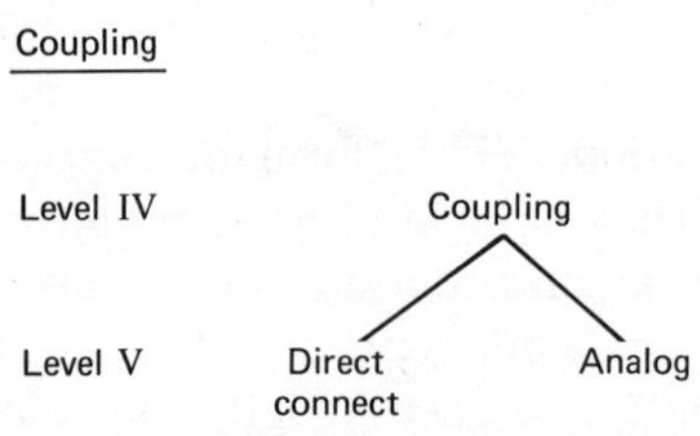

Direct Connect Coupling. This form of coupling is typically used with relatively slow-speed devices (up to 300 bits per second) at fairly short distances. Its identifying feature is that the level or polarity of the direct current flowing in the wire is used to distinguish between zero (0) and one (1) bits. This technique originated in early teletypewriter networks and dates back even farther to the original telegraph key. The most commonly used direct connect couplers include:

Level VI:
- Telegraph adapters
- Mil 188B/C (Military Spec) couplers

Analog Coupling. The need for higher speed devices at greater distances and with increased accuracy and control requires an analog coupling technique where, for example, the information signals of the terminal are converted into audible tones for transmission over voice band trunks or are used to modulate a higher frequency carrier which must be demodulated at the receiving end. A partial list of the commonly used analog couplers includes:

Level VI:

- Subsets (Modems)—all kinds and speeds
- Acoustic
- Radio frequency
- Frequency division multiplexor
- Inductive
- Optical

Distribution

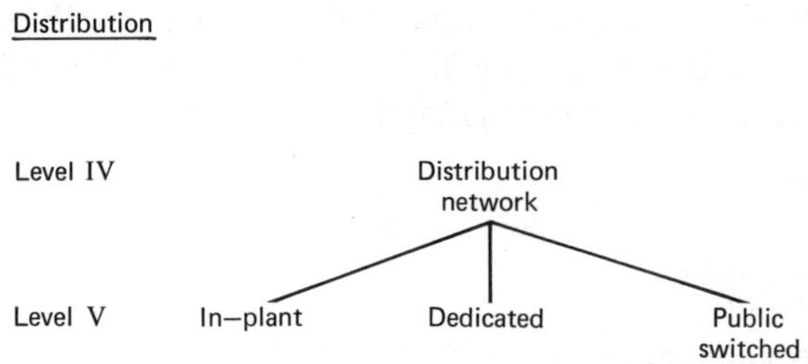

In-Plant Distribution Network. Such networks can be defined when all elements involved—lines/trunks, terminals, switches, etc.—are contained within the boundaries of the surrounding public highways and thoroughfares. Significantly greater design latitudes may be employed in these distribution networks due to the lack of required adherence to the rules of the FCC and other regulatory agencies. In-plant distribution networks take the following forms:

Level VI:

- Hardwire
- Radio frequency
- Optical
- Carrier current
- Cable multiplex
- Combinations of the above

Dedicated Distribution Network. When terminal usage levels and the resulting costs of public switched networks rise above definable thresholds, a dedicated distribution network becomes optimum. These networks are leased from a common carrier (AT&T, Western Union, General Telephone, Microwave Communications, Inc. [MCI], Datran, etc.), configured and installed by them to the user's exact requirements, and dedicated to his exclusive use. Dedicated distribution networks may be:

Level VI:
- Narrow band
- Voice band
- Broadband
- Switched
- Combinations of the above

Public Switched Distribution Network. For relatively low usage frequency and volume requirements, the cost of using the public switched distribution network may be optimum. Use of this network requires only an appropriately coupled terminal or other device and a willingness to pay the specified tariffs or rates in effect. Public switched distribution networks may be:

Level VI:
- Narrow band
  TWX, Telex
- Voice band
  Direct distance dial
  Inbound and outbound WATS
  Foreign exchange
- Broadband
  AT&T and Western Union

Switching

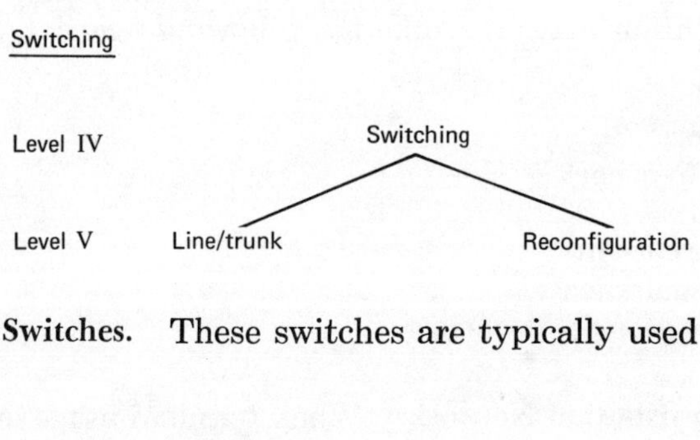

Line/Trunk Switches. These switches are typically used to optimize the cost of providing a given degree or grade of service to a cluster of terminals or other devices at something less than the cost of a separate line/trunk from each terminal to the information processing complex. It usually implies a sharing of "M" lines/trunks by "N" terminals, where "N" is greater than "M." Line/trunk switches take two basic forms:

Level VI:
- Manual access switches
- Automatic communications line switches

Reconfiguration Switches. Reconfiguration switches are used to provide: (1) fail soft or backup capability—the switching of the incoming lines/trunks to an alternate network processor in case of failure; (2) a form of load leveling where excessive volumes in peak periods can be switched to alternate systems; and (3) various reconfiguration requirements that may be necessary as a standard procedure during the operating day. Reconfiguration switches may be:

Level VI:
- Program controlled
- Manual

Source/Destination Interface

The source/destination interface consists of the operating characteristics or disciplines of the devices used in the network. No further breakdown of this Level IV entry is required beyond the following partial list of considerations that should be a part of every network design effort due to their effect on other network hardware and/or software design efforts.

Level V:
- Continuous/intermittent real time
- Source and/or destination
- Fixed/mobile/portable
- Coupling technique
- Buffered/unbuffered
- Single and/or multiple speed
- Single and/or multiple code set
- Error detection and/or correction
- Identification technique
- Programmable and/or operator controlled

Information Routing

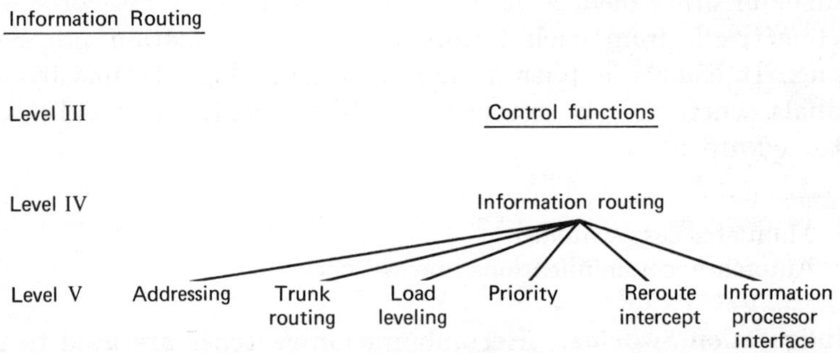

Information Routing—Addressing. Addressing includes the techniques employed to assure that information entered in the network at its source node is directed properly to the specified or desired destination node(s). Addressing techniques include the following:

Level VI:
- Explicit
- Symbolic
- Implicit
- Multiple destination
- Combinations of the above

Information Routing—Distribution Trunk Routing. Various distribution trunk routing techniques are employed to assure that an optimum path through the distribution trunks/lines is used to minimize delay and/or propagation times for information flow within the network. These include:

Level VI:
- Explicit
- Implicit
- Heuristic
- Dynamic

Information Routing—Load Leveling. Load leveling involves the detection of predetermined load and volume and/or maximum delay or propagation thresholds at various network nodes and the selection of appropriate alternate routing methods to decrease the load and/or delay times at such nodes. The alternate routing adopted may produce delays longer than the normal nonpeak period routing, but they will be shorter than those incurred if no load leveling were employed. Load leveling may be:

Level VI:
- Manual
- Dynamic

Information Routing—Priority. Priority schemes may be required to identify various levels of urgency associated with information flowing in the network. Normally, in multiple priority networks, information with the highest priority or urgency is delivered first and that of lower priority is delivered after all higher levels for that destination and/or trunk have been delivered. Priority considerations include:

Level VI:
- Single level
- Multiple level
- Information aging
- Queue size

Information Routing—Reroute/Intercept. Reroute/intercept involves the interruption of normal network addressing and/or trunk routing and/or priority designations due to an abnormal or exception condition. Rerouting implies a change in the information destination designation due to inoperative terminals and/or trunks or other conditions. Intercept indicates that the network must retain, in appropriate intercept queue(s), for later delivery, information that cannot be delivered to its destination because the terminal is inoperative, or down for the evening, or requires a paper change, or other similar condition. Reroute/intercept considerations include:

Level VI:
- Manual
- Automatic (under program control)

Information Routing—Information Processor Interface. The interface between an information processor and the surrounding network is frequently accomplished through the use of a front-end network processor. The method of interfacing these processors should be carefully designed to avoid the network bottleneck that frequently occurs here. Information processor interface considerations include:

Level VI:
- Single information processor
- Multiple information processors
- Fixed routing
- Variable routing
- "Y" configuration
- "I" configuration
- "Delta" configuration

See Chapters 5 and 10 for definition and discussion of these configurations.

Network Integrity

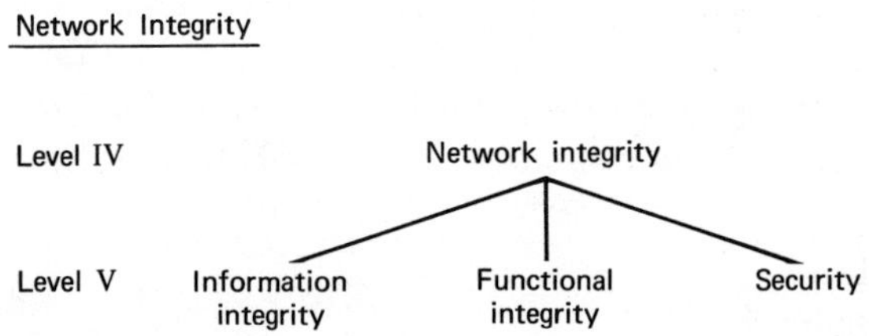

Information Integrity. This entry concerns those control functions necessary to maintain the desired level of accuracy and validity of information flowing in the network. Information integrity considerations include:

Level VI:
- Error detection/correction
- Retransmission
- Continuity

Functional Integrity. This element involves the maintenance of the specified level of availability of the various network devices and/or hardware elements. Functional integrity involves the following:

Level VI:
- Fail soft/backup requirements
- Restart/recovery techniques
- Test/diagnostic

Security. Security in an information network is required to prevent unauthorized access to the various data bases being maintained. It may involve several levels in large networks or consist of a simple terminal identification procedure in smaller ones. A partial list of security considerations includes:

Level VI:
- Terminal identification and validation
- User or operator identification
- Access code validation and data base clearance

Journaling

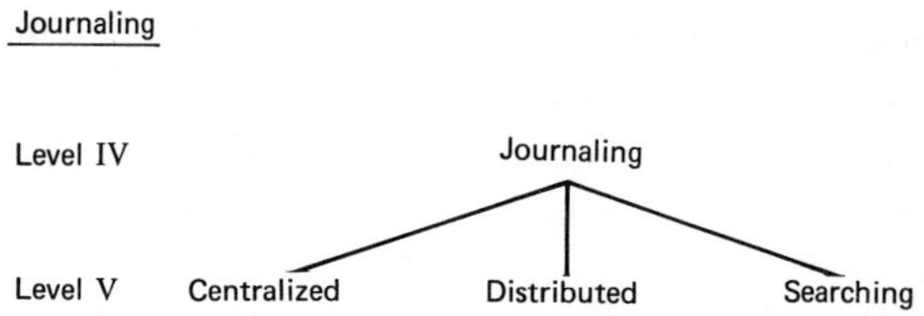

Centralized Journaling. In smaller networks or in larger ones where necessary the journal of information that has flowed in the network may be maintained at a single (usually the central) location. All information flowing anywhere in the network must be sent to the central location for entry in the journal.

Distributed Journaling. In large networks where line/trunk costs and information volumes necessary to maintain a centralized journal become prohibitive, a distributed journal may be the optimum choice. Journals are maintained at selected regional, district, or other network nodes for all information flowing through them.

Journal Searching. The techniques employed to identify the information desired, locate and search the appropriate journal(s), initiate the retransmission when it has been found, and log a record of the activity are some of the considerations involved in journal searching. The following Level VI considerations apply to all three of the preceding Level V Journaling elements:

Level VI:
- Tape journals
- Random access mass storage journals
- Response time requirements
- On-line journals
- Off-line journals

Statistical Information Recording

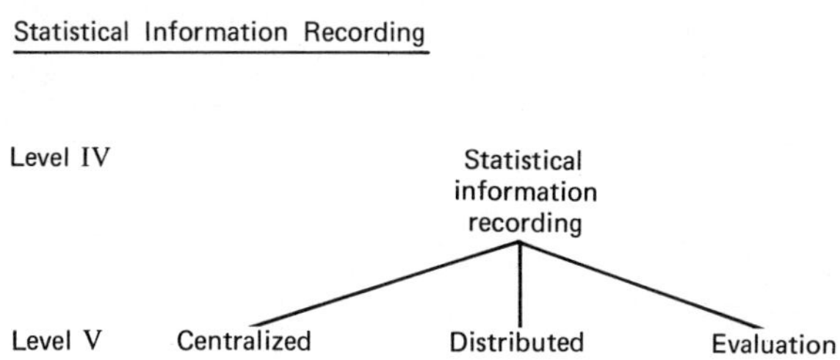

As in journaling, the statistical information recording function may be centralized or distributed with the information recorded on magnetic tape, mass storage devices or, if small enough, in the core memory of a network or information processor.

Statistical Information Evaluation. A partial list of Level VI evaluation results and considerations includes:

Level VI:
- Line loading
- Volume analysis
- Queueing delay
- Response time
- Billing

Utility

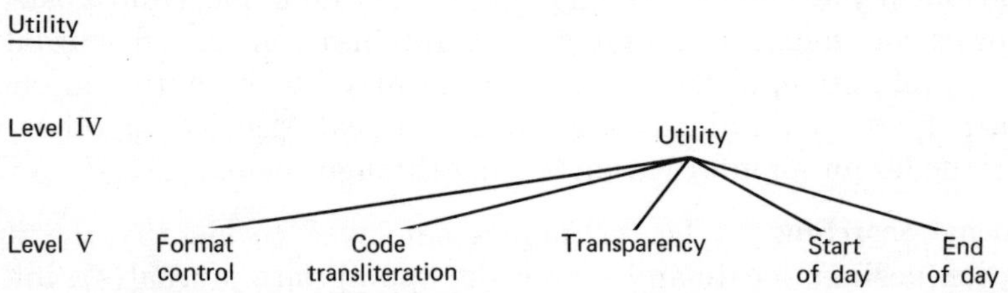

Format Control. Numerous controls and/or manipulations of information flowing in the network may be necessary to assure that it is in the most acceptable form possible for the destination hardware and/or software. A partial list of level VI entries includes:

Level VI:
- Carriage return/line feed insertion
- All numeric field verification
- Blank insertion and/or compression

Code Transliteration. The various code sets employed by terminals and other source/destination devices are not always the set(s) employed in the information processor(s) of the network. The transliteration to the appropriate set is an overhead function that is normally performed more efficiently by a network processor than by an information processor. A partial list of commonly used code sets includes:

Level VI:
- ASCII
- Four out of eight (4/8)
- EBCDIC

- 5-Level baudot
- 6-Bit transcode
- 6-Bit Binary Coded Decimal (BCD)

Transparency. The transmission of format-free binary information, such as a program being sent to a remote processor that has requested a restart or reboot operation, requires the inclusion of specific control character and parameter sequences to assure that the various hardware and/or software elements in the network do not examine or respond to bit sequences within the information. There are no Level VI entries identified at this time for transparency.

Start of Day. Numerous initialization functions are required at the start of each operating day for those networks that do not operate around the clock. Similar functions are required at midnight or some other selected time for those networks that do operate continuously. These functions include: setting the time of day clock and date, initializing sequence number sets, initiating the transmission of undelivered information left from preceding day(s), and numerous other procedures. Start-of-day functions may be required at either or both of the following Level VI entries:

Level VI:
- Network
- Terminal or other source/destination

End of Day. A similar set of activities may be required at the close or end of the operating day or period. Queues of undelivered information must be repacked and initialized, hourly and/or summary statistical information reports must be prepared and delivered, intransit information must be completed, and other similar functions must be performed. End-of-day functions may be required at:

Level VI:
- Network
- Terminal or other source/destination

Supervisory Control

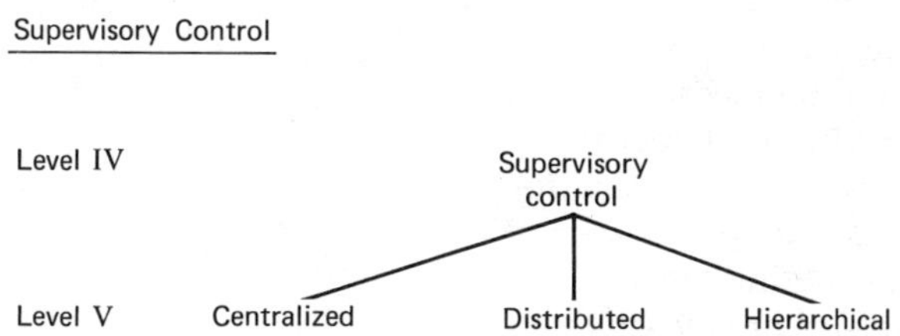

Centralized Supervisory Control. Smaller networks may require only a single, possibly centrally located, supervisory control station or terminal for the entry of various types of control information. The station may be a single terminal on which all control information is entered and to which all log information generated by the network is delivered. Larger centrally controlled networks may use one terminal for entering control information and one or more destination-only terminals for the output of statistical reports and/or logging.

Distributed Supervisory Control. Larger networks spread over large geographic areas may find it less than optimum to maintain centralized supervisory control due to large volumes of control information, propagation delay in effecting the control, and other similar considerations. For these networks, a multiplicity of supervisory control stations at geographically optimum locations is required. The single versus multiple terminal considerations discussed in centralized supervisory control apply also.

Hierarchical Supervisory Control. Various levels of supervisory control may be required to maintain effective control of the network. Terminals, for example, may be allowed to request to be placed on intercept, while the central supervisory station is the only one allowed to enter a request for reroute. At another level, distributed control stations may accept and execute reroute requests while the predetermined "master" or central station is the only one permitted to request a statistical information report.

Larger networks, using a form of distributed and/or hierarchical supervisory control, may require the ability to subset this control on the basis of corporate divisional or regional boundaries due to differences in their operational characteristics and usage of the network. Other networks used or shared by entirely different corporations may require similar supervisory control subsetting capability. The following partial list of control functions applies to all three of the preceding Level V elements:

Level VI:

- Initiate start of day
- Initiate end of day
- Place on intercept
- Remove from intercept
- Add new source/destination node
- Delete source/destination node
- Change routing table
- All stations broadcast

- Add new distribution trunk/line
- Delete distribution trunk/line
- Request journal search
- Request statistical information report
- Alter poll/select sequence and/or frequency
- Initiate reconfiguration
- Initiate restart and/or recovery
- Add new relay node
- Delete relay node
- Enable/disable message type
- Alter send/receive limit
- Initiate test/diagnostic procedure
- Clear circuit
- Change error threshold

SECTION III

Network Functions– The Physical Network

Chapters 5 through 9 in this section treat the five Level IV network functions in sufficient depth to provide the network designer with an identification and understanding of the hardware elements involved in the design, specification, and implementation of information networks. Examples are included to identify the various alternatives available for the optimization of the network. Used as a guide or roadmap, this section can serve further to identify, functionally, the considerations that should be evaluated to insure that some element or aspect of the network is not being ignored.

The network functions discussed in this section can be considered as those hardware elements that, when properly configured, constitute the "physical" network. These elements are capable of little, if any, movement of information through the network. The control functions discussed in Section IV are necessary to control the physical network and the flow of information through it. These control functions, when properly selected and implemented, constitute the "logical" network.

Discussion of the network functions at extreme depth has been purposely avoided, as it tends to detract from the relative simplicity of the separation-of-function philosophy. Numerous books already in print provide detailed explanations of the inner workings of the various network processing hardware items described in this section. (See related reading lists in Chapter 16 and Appendix B.)

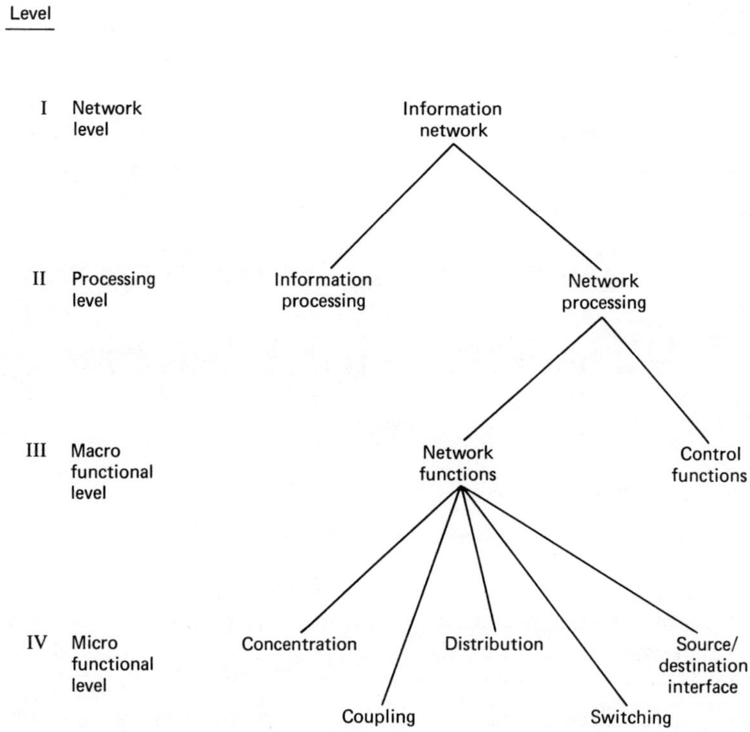

Figure 5-1 **Network functions**

A portion of the tree structure, through Level III, for information network is provided in Figure 5-1 to identify the location of the network functions relative to the overall information network architecture.

CHAPTER 5

Concentration

The following definition of micro function concentration, from Chapter 4, is repeated here to provide a frame of reference and starting point for the discussion of the Level IV micro function concentration: "*The collection and/or distribution or concentration of information flow from a number of source/destination nodes for transmission to another network node over a smaller number of lines or trunks.*" Figure 5-2 gives the tree structure through Level V, showing concentration and its subsidiary functions.

Concentration is a technique used to reduce or optimize the line and trunk costs involved in connecting the remote source/destination devices to the appropriate information processing center or centers. Frequently, the cost of providing a single line or trunk between each device and the center is prohibitively expensive. Many factors, including the number and speed of the terminals, the distance of the cluster from the center, the desired level of service or availability to be provided, and others must be evaluated to determine if concentration can be applied and, if so, in what form.

Frequently, remote terminals and other source/destinations occur in logical or geo-

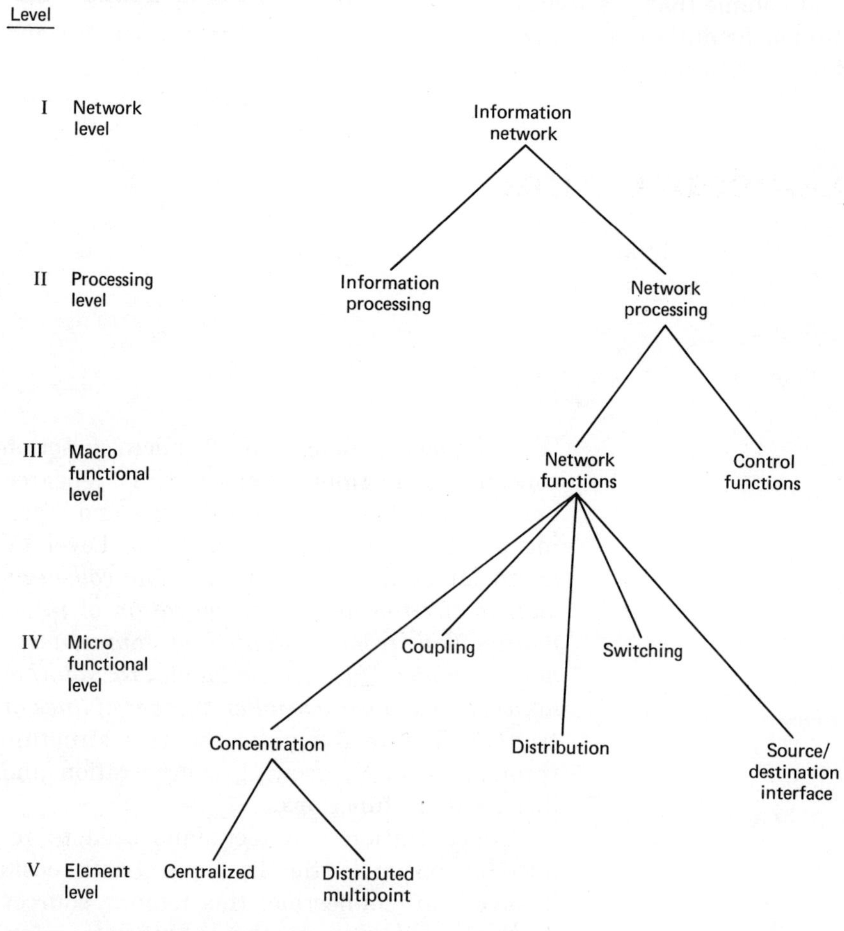

Figure 5-2 **Concentration function**

graphic groups or clusters. Examples of such clusters include: all the terminals in the same room, on the same floor, or in the same building; all the terminals in the same city or state; all the terminals contained in an area bounded on all sides by public highways or thoroughfares; and other similar geographic or logical groupings.

As an illustrative example of concentration, assume a cluster of 30 terminals operating at 10 characters per second, all located in the same city and all having a need to interface with an information processing complex located in another city 300 miles away. Assume further that each of the 30 terminals has a sufficiently high usage and volume that it essentially must be connected to the network continuously during the operating day. Schematically, the cluster and information processing complex appear as shown in Figure 5-3.

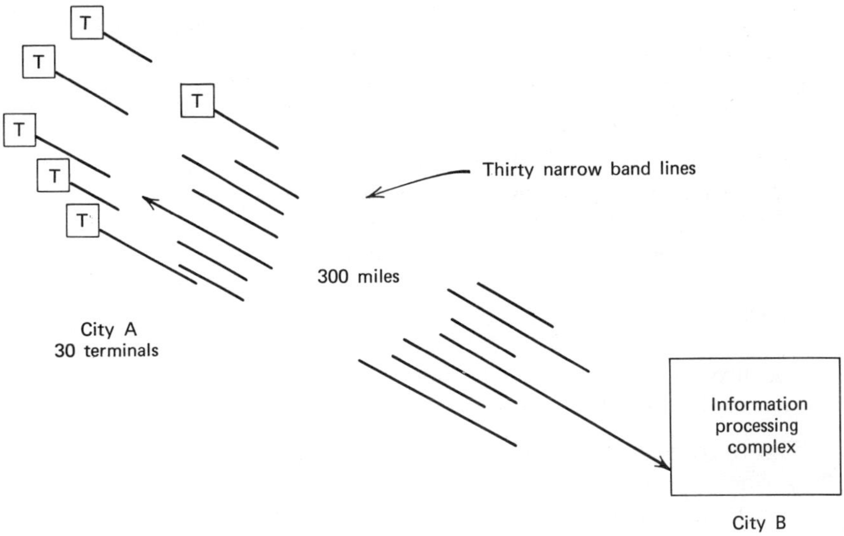

Figure 5-3 **Example of need for concentration**

The cost of a single narrow band line (type 1006) capable of operating at the indicated speed from one of the terminals 300 miles to the center is derived as follows from the Bell System tables:

The first 100 miles are $1.75/mile/month;
the next 150 miles are $1.23/mile/month;
the last 50 miles are $ .70/mile/ month;
therefore;
the first 100 miles cost $175.00/month;
the next 150 miles cost $184.50/month;
the last 50 miles cost $ 35.00/month;
resulting in a total monthly cost for a single line of $394.50.

This figure multiplied by the 30 lines required gives $11,835.00 per month for line costs alone. These figures assume that the lines are interstate—i.e., cross state lines—as the intrastate rates for the same lines may be different. These figures are line costs only and do not include any terminal or other station charges.

The 30 terminals each operating at 10 characters a second are capable of sending a theoretical maximum of 300 characters a second into the center. A type 3002 voice band trunk with an appropriate subset or modem is capable of handling 300 characters per second. By running such a voice band trunk the 300 miles between the city where the cluster of terminals is located and the city where the information processing complex is and by providing the appropriate concentration devices, exactly the same grade or level of service and availability can be provided to the terminal cluster. The cost of a voice band trunk of this type is:

$3.30/mile/month for the first 25 miles;
$2.31/mile/month for the next 75 miles;
$1.65/mile/month for the next 150 miles;
$1.15/mile/month for the next 50 miles;
therefore;
the first 25 miles cost $ 82.50/month;
the next 75 miles cost $173.25/month
the next 150 miles cost $247.50/month;
and the last 50 miles cost $ 57.50/month.

The total cost for the single voice band trunk which replaces the 30 narrow band lines is $564.75/month, which represents a savings of $11,270.25 per month in line costs and provides exactly the same degree of service. This example is used to show the relative line cost savings only. The cost of the concentration devices and other common carrier imposed charges must be calculated before an exact determination of the savings can be made. These charges are not included here due to the local variations that occur in different parts of the country. The application of the concentration function produces the schematic representation shown in Figure 5-4.

This single example is presented only to show the relative magnitude of the savings to be realized through the application of the concentration function. The various types of concentration techniques and devices are discussed in following pages of this chapter.

5-1 CENTRALIZED CONCENTRATION

Centralized concentration implies that the terminals in the group are clustered around some geographic location that can be identified as a logical concentration point, as in the example used to introduce this chapter. In the example, the terminals in the cluster are all located someplace within the boundaries of City A, which is 300 miles from the information processing complex. This does not mean that the

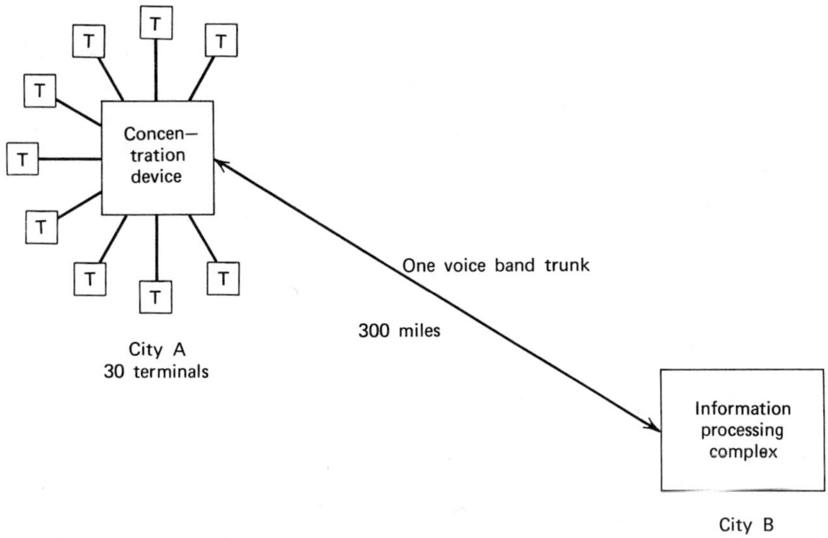

Figure 5-4 **Concentration installed**

cluster must always be within a city, however, as one terminal in each of several cities within a state or other geographic area may be a more appropriate and logical definition of a cluster. Various parameters, including the number and speed of the terminals, the distances involved, the grade of service required, and others, must be analyzed to determine the cluster definition and boundaries and to establish the degree of optimization possible.

The main identifying feature of the centralized concentration function is that one end of all the lines and trunks in the cluster is terminated at a concentration device that is centrally located within the cluster. Many different kinds of devices are utilized to provide the centralized concentration function. Those devices most commonly used are discussed in depth later. While some of these devices have not traditionally been considered as concentrators, they are shown when viewed functionally to be performing a centralized concentration function. Included in the list are:

- Front-end network processor
- Remote concentrator
- Remote network processor
- Special purpose terminal controller
- Time division multiplexor
- Frequency division multiplexor

Front-End Network Processor

That class of information processors having a moderate to large data communications or network interface requirement frequently uses a data communications or "network processor" as a front end to handle the communications load. This is done to relieve the information processor of those tasks that are essentially overhead and can be more efficiently performed in a processor specifically designed for them. In this way, the information processor is free to spend a greater percentage of its time doing the thing it was designed for, namely, information processing.

Chapter 10 also discusses the use of front-end network processors. That discussion concerns the problem of routing the information flow to the appropriate information processor(s) of the complex from a control function point of view. This chapter covers the use of a front-end network processor as a form of centralized concentration and its relationship to the terminal cluster surrounding it.

Front-end network processors may be configured in a variety of way, depending on the network design and implementation philosophies that are adopted.

The "I" Configuration. This is the most frequently used configuration and includes a single information processor cable-connected to a single adjacent front-end network processor, as shown in Figure 5-5.

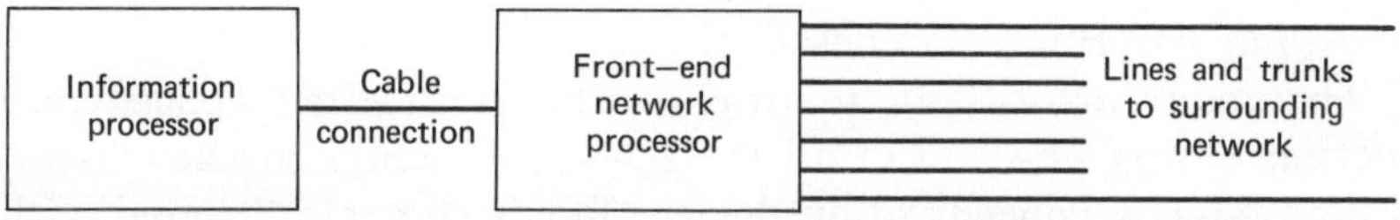

Figure 5-5 **"I" configuration**

In this configuration, the front-end network processor assumes all the responsibilities for handling the interface to the various lines, trunks, and source/destination devices included in the network surrounding the information processor. The various line and trunk speeds, characteristics, source/destination device parameters, disciplines, and other communications-oriented tasks are removed from the information processor, thus increasing its throughput potential.

The front-end network processor is a programmable computer

performing a centralized concentration function, since one end of all the lines and trunks involved, including the cable to the information processor, is connected to it. The information processor now appears to the front-end network processor as an information source and/or destination. Information is exchanged via the cable connection, which provides a medium or path for the flow between them.

New or additional source/destination devices or lines and trunks can be added to the network and interfaced to the front-end network processor with a minimum of disturbance to the information processor. The hardware and software flexibility and modularity typically found in network processors further aids in the reduction of the problems involved in implementing these additional network elements.

Some types of information processors are equipped with multiple-line controller options that are used to provide them with an interface to the surrounding network, as shown in Figure 5-6. These controllers

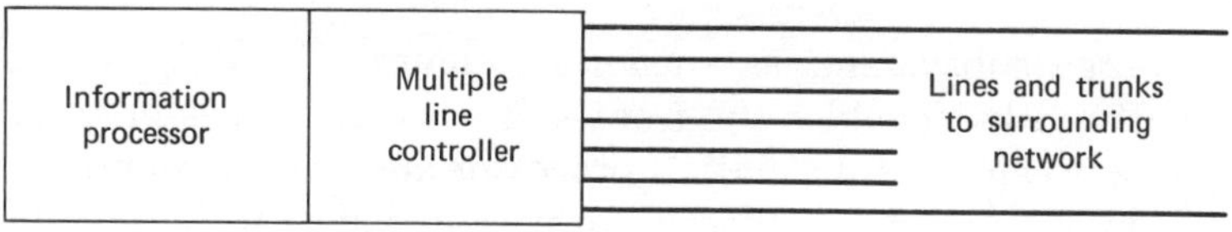

Figure 5-6 **Multi-line controller**

are an integral part of the information processor hardware and, as such, must rely on it for direction and control. Memory space and processor time are required to perform the tasks involved in interfacing with the lines, trunks, and source/destination devices included in the network. These time and space requirements frequently detract from the throughput potential of the information processor to the point that the price/performance characteristics of the complex fall below acceptable limits. As the quest for optimum price/performance characteristics in information networks assumes greater importance, there is a noticeable trend away from the integral multiple-line controller approach and toward the use of front-end network processors. These front-end network processors are computers designed specifically for the communications tasks and, as such, can significantly reduce the communications overhead on the host information processor.

The "Y" Configuration. Frequently, to provide for a smoother, more manageable method of presenting information to the information processor, the network processor is configured with a random access

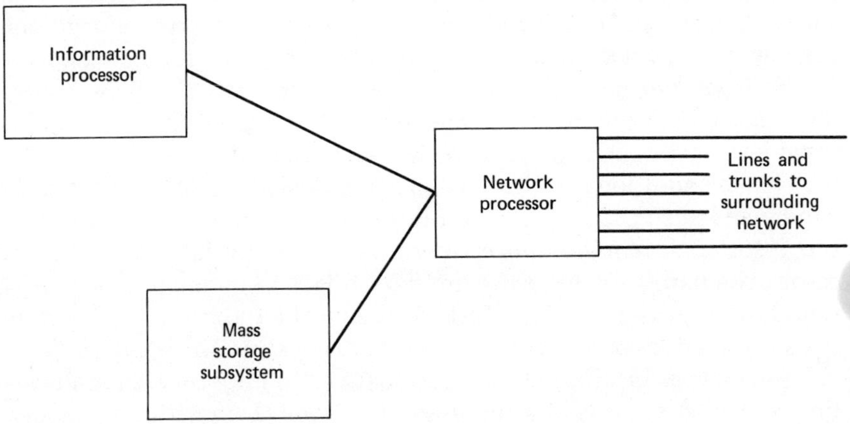

Figure 5-7 **"Y" configuration**

mass storage subsystem, as shown in Figure 5-7. This subsystem (frequently disks) enables the front-end network processor to act as a buffer between the information processor and the surrounding network. It may be used to collect information that is to be sent to the information processor and build it into queues in logical blocks or segments for processing rather than simply forwarding it and forcing the information processor to build the queues before it can process them. This avoids interrupting the information processor every time another block or record that must be added to the queue being constructed appears. Similarly, information generated by the information processor to be sent to the front-end network processor for distribution to the appropriate network destinations can be sent to the network processor and placed in queues on the mass storage subsystem. The network processor can then send the information to its destination when the appropriate line or trunk is available. Since the information is usually generated at speeds in excess of the line or trunk and destination device capabilities, it is desirable to move it out of the information processor at the highest possible speed for forwarding by the network processor at the slower speed. This frees the information processor for other tasks by removing the associated overhead and placing it in the network processor. In essence, the mass storage subsystem moves the network-associated queue management function and overhead for information flowing in and out of the information processor from itself to the front-end network processor.

The front-end network processor can also use the mass storage subsystem for the building and maintenance of queues associated with information flowing from source to destination through and under its control, but not associated with or aware of the presence of the information processor. An example would be the use of the front-end network processor as an administrative message switcher in addition to its other information processor-associated network functions. This approach produces significant savings due to the elimination of the requirement for one system to handle the information processor-associated tasks and another separate system to perform the message switching function.

In addition to information flow queue management capability, the mass storage subsystem can be used for the storage of source/destination, user, operator, and other identification tables and codes. The front-end network processor can then perform many validity checking and identification functions, thus insuring that only valid, acceptable information and/or users are permitted access to the information processor and its files. This represents a further decrease in the communications overhead functions that must be performed by the information processor.

The "Radial" Configuration. Some large-scale information processing networks include multiple information processors at a single location, with several or perhaps all of them having a requirement to interface with the surrounding network. An example of this type of configuration is shown in Figure 5-8.

The front-end network processor may be used in this configuration to direct the incoming flow of information to the appropriate information processor if each is performing separate kinds or types of processing. The front-end network processor programs can include the logic necessary to identify the incoming information as to type and determine which information processor it should be directed to. Information flowing from the information processors outbound is examined by the front-end network processor and directed to the appropriate network destination.

Another application of this configuration is that of providing a fail soft or backup capability in the event that one of the information processors should fail or be taken out of service. The front-end network processor can then redirect the incoming information flow to the designated backup information processor. A variation of this technique can be used to provide a load-leveling capability, where the front-end network processor directs the incoming information flow to

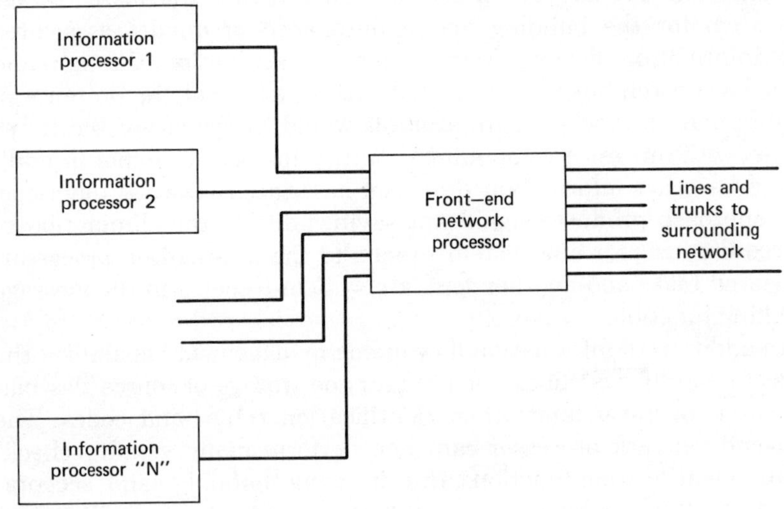

Figure 5-8 **"Radial" configuration**

the information processor with the lowest load or level of activity.

As described earlier, the front-end network processor may have a mass storage subsystem associated with it which can further improve its performance in the radical configuration.

The "Delta" Configuration. This configuration is similar to the "Y" discussed earlier, with one important difference. The mass storage subsystem associated with the front-end network processor is also accessible by the information processor, as shown in Figure 5-9. This configuration provides several significant advantages over the "Y"

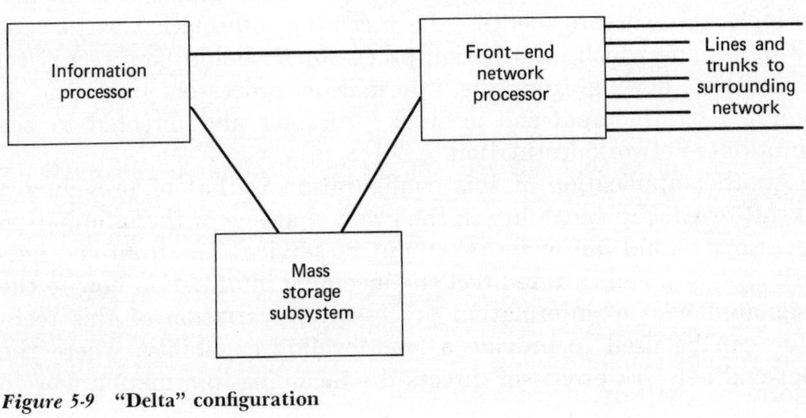

Figure 5-9 **"Delta" configuration**

configuration. The queues built in the mass storage subsystem by the front-end network processor can be structured in the exact form required by the information processor. When they are complete or when the information processor is ready to process them, it can access them directly through its own channel to the mass storage subsystem. This avoids the necessity of having the front-end network processor handle the information twice—once when it receives it from the source device and places it in the queue, and again when it retrieves it from the queue and sends it to the information processor. Similarly, information generated by the information processor can be placed in outbound queues and retrieved for transmission to the appropriate destination by the front-end network processor when the queue is complete or the destination's line is available.

The "shared access" capability of this configuration further reduces the information processor overhead by eliminating the interrupts, memory space, and processor requirements usually incurred when all of the information flow is directed through the interface between the two processors. Again, the net result of decreasing the information processor overhead is to increase the throughput potential for its primary function, information processing.

Should any portion or all of the information processor's data base be maintained in the shared mass storage subsystem available for remote inquiry and/or update capability, further reductions in overhead may be achieved. The front-end network processor can be given the limited logic and processing capability necessary to perform the inquiry and/or update function. This eliminates the need to send the request for the inquiry to the information processor, schedule it, interrupt its information processing task, execute the inquiry or retrieval, send the response back to the front-end network processor, and then resume its information processing.

In all of the preceding discussion of the shared mass storage subsystem, the effect has been to reduce the amount of information flowing between the two processors via the direct cable connection. By using this interface primarily for the exchange of control information—e.g., notice that a logical input file is complete and ready for processing, an output file is complete and ready for distribution to its destination—significant reduction of queue and file management overhead may be achieved in both the information and front-end network processors.

From the preceding discussion of front-end network processors in their various configurations, it can be seen that they are performing a form of centralized concentration. One end of each of the lines, trunks, mass storage subsystem channels, and cable connection(s) to information processor(s) is connected to or terminated in the centrally located front-end network processor.

Remote Concentrator

Again, the example used to introduce this chapter, presents a situation where a form of centralized concentration can be economically applied. The "centralized" location and its terminal cluster, however, are 300 miles away from the information processing complex. Many devices can be used to perform the remote concentration function, ranging from small, relatively inexpensive multiplexors (discussed later) to the more capable remote concentrator. A remote concentrator is a programmable device very much like the front-end network processor, with its own memory and processing capability. An example is shown in Figure 5-10.

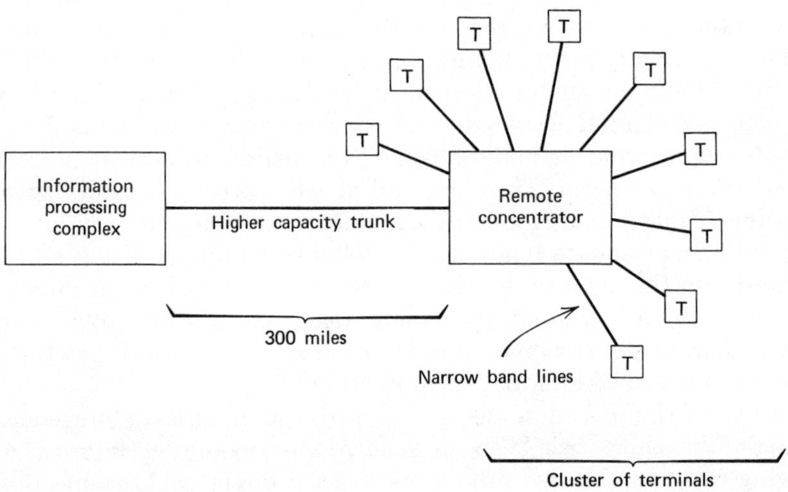

Figure 5-10 **Remote concentrator**

The cluster of terminals is shown 300 miles distant from the information processing complex. The number of terminals in the cluster, their speed, and the desired grade of service or availability determine how many of what type the trunk(s) between the remote concentrator and the information processing complex should be. If the terminals number 30 or less and operate at 10 characters a second or less, a single voice band trunk operating at 2400 bits per second (300 characters per second) is sufficient to permit all of the terminals simultaneous, continuous access to the information processing complex.

The terminals may be permanently connected to the remote concentrator via leased or dedicated narrow band lines. This would usually be the case if the level of usage and the volume of information exchanged are relatively high. If, however, the usage and volume are very light, the terminals may gain access to the remote concentrator by dialing in and using the public switched voice band lines (see Chapter 7-3) and suitable couplers (see Chapter 6-2).

In the example, the remote concentrator is provided with 30 ports to which the incoming calls from the terminals are switched. The remote concentrator is then capable of handling the first 30 terminals that dial in to request access. Since it is a dial-in arrangement and the level of usage and volumes are relatively light, the remote concentrator is capable of providing a given grade of service to considerably more than the 30 terminals it can handle simultaneously. So long as it has available ports, it can answer incoming calls; but when all ports are busy, additional incoming calls receive a busy signal and must try again later.

The advantages of a programmable remote concentrator over other nonprogrammable devices must be evaluated by the network designer to determine if the usually higher cost can be justified. A number of these advantages and capabilities are discussed in following paragraphs.

Frequently, the terminals in the cluster include several different speeds and code sets. The remote concentrator can be programmed to recognize which of these a terminal is using and convert to a common code set prior to forwarding to the information processing complex. Information coming from the complex to the terminals in a common set is then converted to the appropriate set for forwarding to the terminal. Moving this function out to the remote concentrator relieves the information processing complex of the overhead involved and increases its throughput potential accordingly.

The remote concentrator is also capable of identifying many forms of invalid information received from the terminals in the cluster. These include, to name a few, parity and other transmission errors, incorrect header information, invalid format such as numerics in alpha fields, alpha in numeric fields, etc., and other errors that, were they allowed to remain, would cause the information to be rejected by the information processing complex. The remote concentrator can reject the information and request an appropriate correction or retransmission from the terminal, thus providing a further decrease in networking overhead at the information processing complex.

The remote concentrator can be used to provide for the exchange of information between terminals in the cluster it is servicing. In this fashion, it performs a message switching type of function on a "local" basis rather than sending the information all the way to the information processing complex, where it would be turned around and sent back for forwarding to the appropriate destination. It may be necessary for journaling purposes to send a copy of the message to the information processing complex, but this still represents a savings in overhead as the information flows between the two locations (information processing complex and remote concentrator) only once instead of twice.

While most frequently used to concentrate information flow between teletypewriter-like source/destination devices and an information processing complex, remote concentrators can be applied to other devices with equal ease and reduction of cost and overhead. Assume, for example, that the cluster of terminals shown previously in Figure 5-10 are small-scale information processors rather than teletypewriters as indicated. These information processors might normally be used in a free-standing mode for information processing at the local site. For certain classes of processing—i.e., those requiring a larger information processor—or for those programs requiring access to a data base not available locally, it might be desirable to enable these small-scale information processors to access (through an appropriate interface) the larger, centrally located information processing complex. This mode of operation is frequently referred to as "Remote Batch" or "Remote Job Entry."

Due to the larger volumes of information involved, a narrow band line as used for teletypewriters operating at 10 characters a second or so is not sufficient. A higher capacity line operating at 300 characters per second, for example, is required to reduce the time involved in moving this information. Depending on the number of remote job entry terminals, the frequency of usage and volumes involved, the response times desired, and other considerations, the trunk between the remote concentrator and the information processing complex may be a voice band or, if necessary, a broadband trunk. Broadband trunks capable of 5000 or more characters per second may be required for the larger configurations.

Remote concentrators generally forward information to the central information processing complex in some logical or incremental block size. Whether or not this is done depends on memory size, number and speed of the terminals in the cluster, information volume, and other considerations. These blocks may be as small as a single character at a time, a single teletypewriter line, a single card image, or other intermediate possibilities up to a complete message or transaction. Information flowing in the other direction is usually similarly blocked at the information processing complex for transmission to the remote concentrator. This is essentially a form of time division multiplexing, which is described later in this chapter (see Chapter 5, pg. 64).

The ratio of terminals in the cluster being served and the speed or capacity of the trunk between the remote concentrator and the central information processing complex is not determined by speed alone. The 30:1 ratio used in the introductory example is a theoretical maximum ratio. In reality, the number of terminals that could be served simultaneously by the single trunk at 300 characters per second is somewhat less than 30. This is a result of the need to utilize a portion of the trunk capacity for header and terminal identification information, block check and error control information, and other similar control functions. As mentioned earlier, this ratio defines the number of terminals in the cluster that can be active *simultaneously*, which is not necessarily the maximum number of terminals that can be adequately serviced within the cluster by the remote concentrator.

Ideally, since a programmable remote concentrator is performing a function (centralized concentration) that is very similar to the task of a front-end network processor, it is desirable, in the selection of processors to perform these tasks, to choose a single machine with an architecture sufficiently modular and flexible so that it can be configured to do both jobs. This eliminates the need for programmers trained in one language for the front-end network processor and programmers trained in another language for the remote concentrator. Unlike systems are frequently the case today, which leads to a less-than-efficient interface between the two due to the dissimiliarities involved.

In the larger networks being designed and implemented today, a remote concentrator may not interface directly with the information processing complex. Network analysis may indicate that one or more intermediate concentrators are required to produce the desired optimization (see Figure 5-11).

Notice that remote concentrator "A" is performing a centralized function for the cluster of terminals surrounding it and that concen-

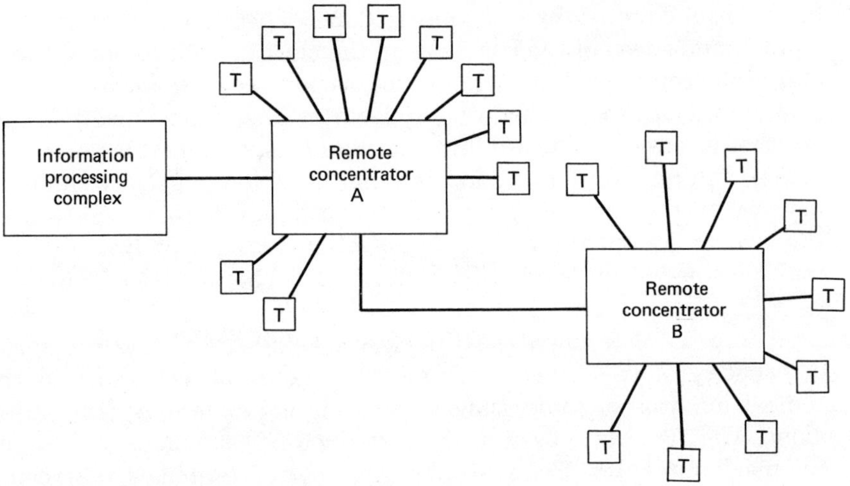

Figure 5-11 **Multiple concentrator configuration**

trator "B," which may be hundreds or thousands of miles from "A," is performing the same function for the cluster of terminals surrounding it. By providing remote concentrator "A" with sufficient capability and a sufficiently high capacity trunk between it and the information processing complex, it may be more economical to route the information from remote concentrator "B" through "A" rather than running the trunk from "B" all the way to the complex.

Remote concentration can also be used to provide two or more geographically separated information processing complexes with the concentration function (see Figure 5-12). In this configuration, the single remote concentrator identifies the appropriate information processing complex to which to direct the information flow from a specific terminal and similarly forwards outbound information to the appropriate destination.

It should be noted in the two figures used as examples that each of the information processing complexes may have included in the configuration a front-end network processor performing a local centralized concentration function in addition to the remote concentration shown.

Remote Network Processor

A remote network processor is essentially a remote concentrator—i.e., a programmable network processor—which is used to perform centralized concentration with a few added capabilities. The most

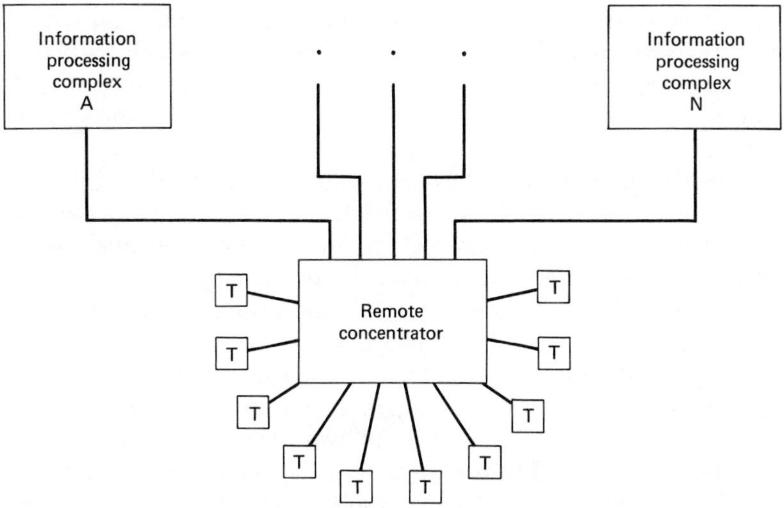

Figure 5-12 **Remote concentration**

common of these is the inclusion of a mass storage subsystem that can be randomly accessed. The storage that this subsystem provides is used as an extension of the processor's memory and enables it to perform numerous additional functions that contribute to the reduction of overhead at the information processing complex as well as to extend its own capabilities.

Should the trunk between the remote network processor and the information processing complex fail, the incoming information from the terminals in the cluster can be queued in the mass storage subsystem. This enables the terminals to continue to send inbound information rather than shut down and face the retransmission task when the trunk has been repaired. Similarly, outbound information passing through the remote network processor to a terminal that is out of service or not available can be queued in the mass storage subsystem for retrieval and forwarding at a later time. This capability is particularly useful when the remote network processor is servicing terminals or other source/destination devices that are in different time zones and shut down at a given local time of the operating day. Information destined to such terminals is placed in an intercept queue for delivery the next day when the terminal indicates it is up and running and ready to receive.

Another use of the mass storage subsystem is to provide storage space for terminal and/or user identification tables. These tables are used to assure that only previously validated terminals and users are allowed access to the network, particularly in networks with dial-in capability. This is another overhead function that is more efficiently performed in the network rather than in the information processor complex.

Historical journals of all information flowing through the remote network processor (which is essentially a relay node) may also be kept in the mass storage subsystem. Requests for retransmission of earlier information may be handled at the remote network processor rather than being forwarded to the information processor complex, which again adds to its network overhead.

The mass storage subsystem may also be used for queueing of administrative message switching information that the remote network processor is handling within its own terminal cluster.

In general, the addition of a mass storage subsystem to a remote concentrator gives it significant queue management and buffering capability that can be used to maintain an optimum flow of information through the relay node and make utilization of the lines and trunks under its control as efficient as possible.

In other networks where a remote network processor is required to handle the network processing at the node and it is desirable to provide some limited degree of peripheral input/output capability, card readers, punches, printers, and other devices may be included in the configuration. While this may seem to verge on information processing in a network processor, which is contrary to the separation of function philosophy defined earlier, it is, in some instances, the only reasonable approach.

For example, in a large, nationwide parts distribution network consisting of dozens of warehouses around the country, each of which services the dealers in the surrounding area, a remote network processor is required at each warehouse location. Each network processor accepts incoming parts orders from the terminals located in the dealers' facilities and forwards them to one of several regional centers for processing and disposition. Thus, each remote network processor is performing a centralized concentration function. When the regional information processing center determines from which of the warehouses within its control the parts are to be shipped, it directs the shipping and billing information to the remote network processor within the warehouse. This information must then be printed (invoices and shipping documents) and punched (picking tickets for stock clerks to use in locating and assembling the parts orders) at the warehouse. Card readers may be desirable to accept parts orders that arrive at a warehouse by mail or are phoned in and converted to punched card form for entry into the network.

Ideally, the remote network processor used primarily for centralized concentration should be of an architecture that provides for the inclusion of these input/output devices. They do not necessarily have to be high performance—e.g., 1000-line-a-minute printers and 1000-card-a-minute readers are not required as the volume of information is usually not great.

The three preceding centralized concentration devices (front-end network processor, remote concentrator, and remote network processor) are all communications or network processors performing varying forms of the same basic task. Frequently, in networks being implemented today, equipment manufacturers supply a machine of one architecture as a front-end network processor, another different one for the remote concentrator, and perhaps a third still different one for the remote network processor. The software design and programming problems inherent in this mixture of equipment are obvious. Since all three devices are performing essentially the same task, it is hoped that future generations of network processors will be sufficiently modular and of a building block architecture that will permit one basic machine to be configured to perform any or all of the three tasks with equal ease.

The few examples given illustrate the flexibility and active program control of the information flowing through them which remote network processors provide. Other more passive, less flexible centralized concentration devices that are usually less expensive are discussed in following pages.

Special Purpose Terminal Controller

Another form of centralized concentration is performed by a class of devices known as special purpose terminal controllers. Some types of terminals, such as cathode ray tube displays, frequently occur in a cluster which is connected to the network via a single trunk (see Figure 5-13). This controller accepts inbound information from the cathode ray tube terminals and sends it in some logical or blocked form to a network processor or other device at the other end of the trunk. Similarly, outbound information is received by the controller, identified, and sent to the appropriate cathode ray tube. Very little control or manipulation of information other than acting as centralized concentrators is performed by these types of controllers.

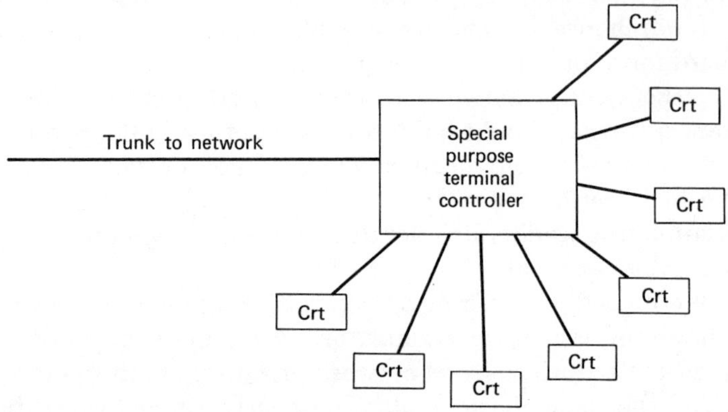

Figure 5-13 **Special purpose terminal controller**

These controllers may include some form of memory—delay line, core, or other—and are capable of acting as a buffer between the terminals and the network trunk. In this mode, the sum of the information flow rate from the terminals in the cluster may exceed the capacity of the trunk, but the buffering capability of the controller overcomes this problem.

The centralized concentration function provided by the special-purpose terminal controllers produces significant savings in trunk costs by eliminating the need to run a separate trunk from each source/destination device in the cluster all the way to the information processing complex or other network node.

Time Division Multiplexor

Time division multiplexing is a technique used to concentrate the flow of information from some number of source/destination or terminal devices located in a definable cluster onto one (or more) higher speed trunk(s) for transmission to the information processing complex. The centralized concentration devices discussed previously in this chapter generally use a form of time division multiplexing in their operation. These devices, with the exception of the special purpose terminal controller, are programmable network processors capable of considerable latitude and flexibility in their application of time division multiplexing to the task of centralized concentration.

For those networks where a centralized concentration node is indicated but where this latitude and flexibility are not required, a class of essentially passive devices, known as time division multiplexors (TDM's), is available. These multiplexors accept inbound information from the source/destination devices, place it on the trunk to the information processing complex in a time division multiplex fashion, and perform the reverse procedure for outbound information (see Figure 5-14). Using as an example the same configuration shown

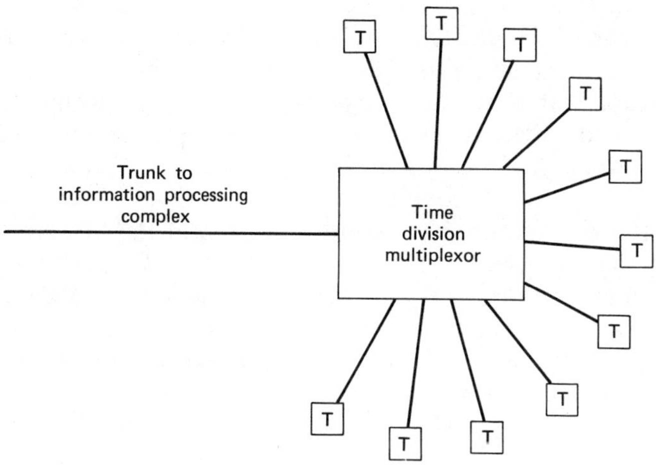

Figure 5-14 **Time division multiplexing**

in Figures 5-3 and 5-4 at the beginning of this chapter, this section next describes the use of a time division multiplexor as a centralized concentration device.

The 30 terminals in the example cluster operate at a maximum of 10 characters per second and all have a requirement to be on-line at all times during the operating day. A narrow band line capable of handling the 10 characters per second rate is installed between each terminal and the time division multiplexor. From the time division multiplexor to the information processor complex or other network node, a higher capacity voice band trunk capable of handling 300 characters per second is installed.

The time division multiplexor divides the passage of real time on the voice band trunk into increments, with each increment representing the time required to transmit one character on the trunk, as shown in Figure 5-15. The sum of the speeds of the narrow band lines then equals the speed of the voice band trunk as opposed to concentration, where the sum may exceed that of the voice band trunk.

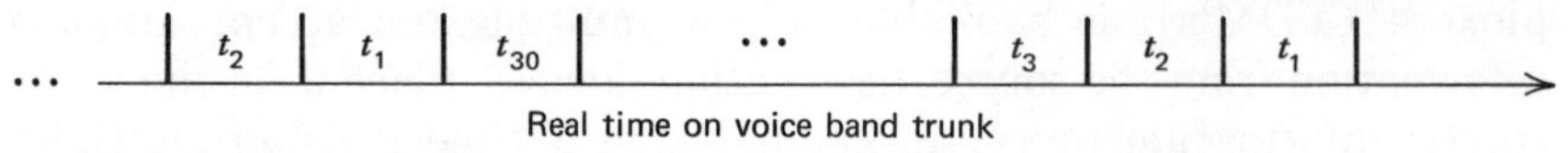

Figure 5-15 **TDM technique**

Each time increment, t_1, t_2, . . . t_{30}, is assigned to a particular terminal in the cluster and is used to transmit the character, if there is one, from that terminal to the information processing complex at the other end of the trunk. Thus, t_1 is used for terminal one, t_2 for terminal two, and so on to t_{30}, which contains the character from terminal 30. This procedure is repeated 10 times each second, which is exactly the rate required to assure that each of the 30 terminals can run continuously at its rated speed of 10 characters per second. For those terminals running at less than rated maximum speed, as would be the case if the information were being entered by an operator on the terminal's keyboard, the time division multiplexor enters a "null" or "fill" character in the terminal's time increment when no character is present.

The receiving device at the other end of the trunk, usually a network processor, must demultiplex the character stream it receives from the time division multiplexor. This involves unpacking the incoming character stream, appending the characters to the appropriate individual character strings, and, when the end of the message or other appropriate indication is received, passing the string on for processing and disposition by the network processor software. This procedure is shown in Figure 5-16. Notice that the characters being

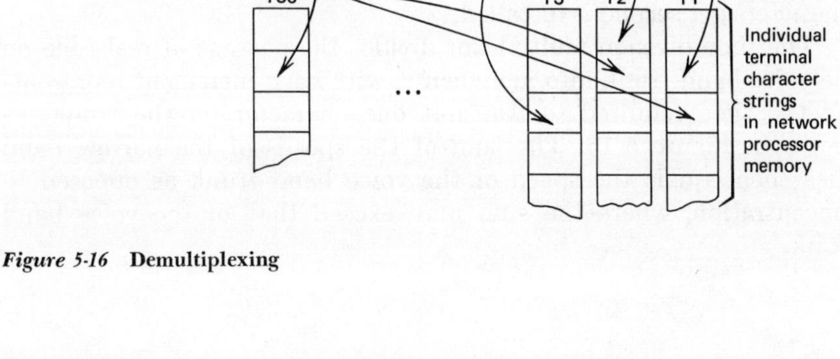

Figure 5-16 **Demultiplexing**

placed in the individual terminal strings are not necessarily in the same relative position. This is to be expected because the terminals do not necessarily start entering characters at the same time, operators type at different rates, messages of various lengths are entered, and so forth, all of which affect the relative arrival rates of the characters from the time division multiplexor. It is the network processor's responsibility to assure that the incoming characters are placed in the proper terminal string.

As discussed previously, the 30:1 ratio shown here is a theoretical maximum. Some relatively small portion of the time on the trunk is required for terminal identification, block checking or error control, and other related control types of information.

Since it is not reasonable to expect that all of the terminals in the cluster will be sending or receiving at the same time, provision must be made to handle information flowing in both directions simultaneously. This can be accomplished by specifying a "two way simultaneous" or "full-duplex" trunk between the time division multiplexor and the network processor. This capability allows 300 characters per second of information flow in both directions simultaneously, which permits either a combination of transmitting and receiving terminals or, if the terminals are so constructed, all 30 terminals sending and receiving simultaneously at their maximum rated speed of 30 characters per second.

This relatively simple example was used to illustrate only the basic mechanics of time division multiplexing. Many variations in technique exist among the numerous time division multiplexors being manufactured today. Differing speeds, code sets, line and trunk types, and other characteristics influence the basic design and capabilities of these devices. However, they all perform the basic function, that of centralized concentration, which is applied to produce a level of optimization in the network costs. The choice of this form of time division multiplexing versus other methods of centralized concentration is a function of extensive network analysis, which is beyond the scope of this book.

Frequency Division Multiplexor

Frequency division multiplexing is another form of centralized concentration that differs in several respects from time division multiplexing. Like time division multiplexors, frequency division multiplexors (FDM's) are essentially passive and exert little if any control over the information flowing through them.

The terminals or other source/destination devices in the cluster to be served by the frequency division multiplexor are each connected to it by a line of sufficient capacity to handle the device operating at its rated speed; then a trunk is installed between the frequency division multiplexor and the central information processing complex.

Rather than dividing the passing real time on the higher capacity trunk into a single string of character positions, as in time division multiplexing, frequency division multiplexors operate quite differently. The higher capacity trunk, of whatever class, voice band or broadband, is of a predetermined bandwidth as defined by its supplier. This bandwidth is expressed in terms of cycles per second or hertz. For example, a public switched voice band trunk has a nominal bandwidth of 3000 hertz.

This bandwidth is divided by the frequency division multiplexor into some appropriate number of subchannels, and each of these subchannels is assigned to one of the terminals in the cluster. Each of these subchannels then uses the frequencies within its range to transmit and receive the information from its assigned terminal to and from the information processing complex (see Figure 5-17). Viewed

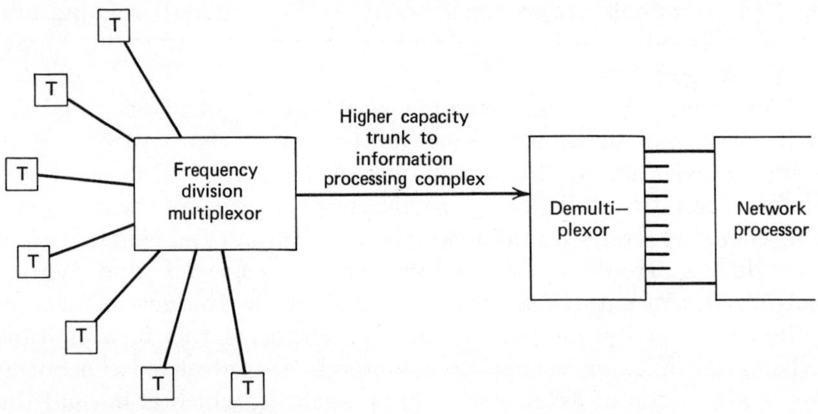

Figure 5-17 **Frequency division multiplexing**

schematically, the information flow placed on the higher capacity trunk by the frequency division multiplexor appears as shown in Figure 5-18. The bandwidth of the higher capacity trunk is shown divided into "N" subchannels, each of which is assigned to a single terminal for its exclusive use.

The number of subchannels available through frequency division multiplexing on a higher capacity or bandwidth trunk is a function of numerous factors, including the capacity and conditioning of the

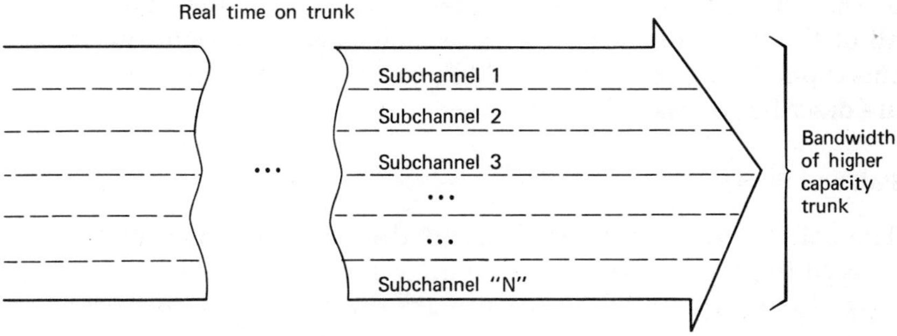

Figure 5-18 **FDM technique**

trunk (see Chapter 7, pg. 101), the number and speed of the terminals or other source/destination devices, and other similar considerations. These factors are also used, along with others such as distances involved, to establish whether time or frequency division multiplexing is the more optimum choice for the network.

Notice that a "demultiplexor" is required and is shown adjacent to the network processor in Figure 5-17. This device demultiplexes the "N" subchannels on the higher capacity trunk and presents them to the network processor as individual channels, each operating at the speed of the associated terminals. The network processor is not even aware of the presence of the multiplexor, which is essentially transparent to it. No software is required to sort out the incoming character stream as is the case with time division multiplexing.

The demultiplexor may be a free-standing device adjacent to the network processor or may be integrated or "built into" it, much as modems or other coupling devices are built into terminals and other source/destination devices.

5-2 DISTRIBUTED MULTIPOINT CONCENTRATION

Distributed multipoint concentration implies that the terminals to be serviced do not necessarily occur in clusters, as is the case in centralized concentration. If the cost of separate lines or trunks for each terminal is execessive and if similar costs involved in attempting to apply centralized concentration are too high, distributed multipoint concentration may produce the degree of performance and optimization desired.

All of the forms of centralized concentration previously described in this chapter can be configured to provide simultaneous service to all of the connected terminals or other source/destination devices. Not all of the forms of distributed multipoint concentration can provide this capability. The devices used to provide this form of concentration are described on the following pages.

Poll and Select

The poll and select form of distributed multipoint concentration can be used to provide service to a group of terminals where the volumes, usage frequency, and message size are sufficiently low so that simultaneous service to all of them is not a requirement. In effect, the terminals alternate usage of the trunk between them on a predetermined basis. A typical configuration is shown in Figure 5-19.

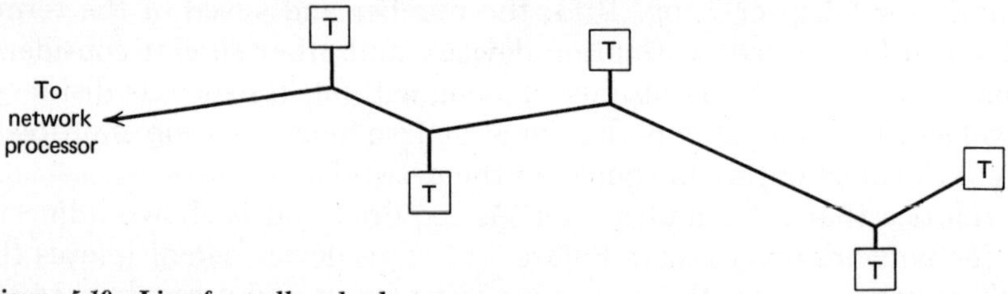

Figure 5-19 **Line for poll and select use**

The single trunk is shown routed through several terminals, which may be tens or hundreds of miles apart. Each terminal is connected to the trunk and can, under control of the network processor at the other end, use the trunk to interface with the network. In poll and select configurations, the capacity or speed of the trunk is usually equal to the maximum information rate of a single terminal, which is adequate since it is not necessary that all terminals be operative simultaneously.

In most poll and select configurations in use today, the trunks are under control of a network processor or other programmable device (e.g., information processor with multiline controller). This network processor may be controlling several such poll and select trunks in addition to performing a host of other network processing tasks. Poll and select capability originated in manual and electromechanical administrative message switching systems long before the advent of computers. Many of these systems are still in use today. This section, however, discusses only those poll and select configurations that are part of an information network.

Polling is a function performed by the network processor and involves the interrogation, by means of a coded character sequence, of each of the connected terminals in a predetermined order to determine if any of them have any information to be entered into the network. The network processor maintains tables identifying the terminals connected to each trunk and cycles through these tables in the designated order.

If a terminal has information to enter into the network when it is polled, polling of the other terminals on the trunk is suspended while the information is entered. If the polled terminal has no information to enter when polled, it responds with a "No Traffic" reply, and the network processor proceeds to poll the next terminal on the trunk as indicated by its tables.

Selection is essentially the converse of polling and involves the forwarding of information to a specific terminal on a poll and select trunk. When all inbound information has been received, the network processor determines whether it has any information to be sent out to a particular terminal. If it does, it sends that destination's specific "selection code" out on the trunk. This selection code sequence "blinds" all the other terminals on the trunk and enables the selected terminal to "copy" or print the information being sent.

It is possible on some poll and select trunks to select more than one terminal to receive the information at one time. This is accomplished by sending the desired set of "select" codes prior to the information or by sending a "group" code which causes all of the stations in the predetermined group to respond to the select code. "Group" selection allows a more efficient utilization of the trunk by permitting several terminals to "copy" the information at the same time rather than sending a complete copy of the information to each terminal on the trunk that is to receive it.

Poll and select trunks may be operated in either a two-way alternate (half-duplex) mode or a two-way simultaneous (full-duplex) mode. In the half-duplex mode, the information flows from the terminal to the network processor or the network processor to the terminal, but not in both directions at the same time. In the full-duplex mode, information may be flowing in both directions simultaneously, with one terminal receiving information from the network processor (selected) while another is sending information (as a result of being polled) to the network processor.

As mentioned previously, the poll and select form of distributed multipoint concentration originated in electromechanical administrative message switching systems. Since many companies have these systems in place and operational, it is only logical that they be considered for inclusion in a planned information network so long as they are capable of handling the necessary volume of information in an acceptable form.

Contention

Like poll and select, the contention (sometimes called manual access) form of distributed multipoint concentration involves a single trunk with a number of source/destination devices connected or coupled to it in a cluster (all in the same room, building, or geographic area) or geographically distributed (see Figure 5-19). Contention differs from poll and select in that, rather than being polled and selected by the controlling network processor, the terminals (under control of an operator) indicate when they have information to be entered into the network.

Like poll and select, only one terminal on a contention trunk can be active at a given time. To gain access to the network, the operator depresses a "bid" or access key on the terminal. The terminal's contention logic or circuitry then determines if the trunk is already in use by one of the other terminals on it and displays a busy light or gives other suitable indication if such is the case. If the trunk is not already in use, the requesting terminal puts a signal on it indicating to the others that it is now busy and to the operator that he is free to initiate his interaction with the network.

The contention scheme provides an optimum form of access for those terminals and other source/destination devices that do not have heavy volume and/or frequency requirements. It is somewhat less complex than a poll and select trunk in that the poll and select logic or software requirement in the network processor at the other end of the trunk is eliminated. It is ideal where a delay of several minutes or a "try again in a few minutes" level of access is sufficient for the terminal's needs.

Once access is gained through this method, it is necessary that the terminal identify itself to the network processor. This can be provided by the terminal hardware in the form of an "answerback" drum or message automatically sent in prior to actual information flow, or it can be entered in some suitable form by the terminal operator. This identification is used not only to tag the information entered at the terminal but also to allow the network processor to examine its outbound queues and determine if there is any information to be sent to the terminal.

It is desirable on contention systems, and poll and select as well, to include some means of disconnect capability in both the terminal and network processor. It is necessary in the terminal so that the network processor can disengage the terminal and free up the trunk in the event that an operator requested access and then failed to respond when it was granted. It is also necessary in the network processor so that the terminal operator can "bust" or "break" an unwanted outbound message being received but known to be invalid or unnecessary. There is no point in this case in tying up the trunk any longer.

Obviously, in contention systems as described, it is impossible for a terminal to receive any information from the network unless the operator requests and is granted access. It may be desirable, if the relative amount and frequency of outbound information significantly exceeds inbound, to merge the "select" portion of the poll and select scheme with the contention system. In this manner, the terminal operators can request access via the contention key when desired while the network processor can select the terminals when outbound information is to be directed to them.

Distributed Frequency Division Multiplexor

When the terminals in the cluster to be served are widely separated, the trunk costs involved in centralized frequency division multiplexing are excessive, and it is necessary that all the terminals be active simultaneously, a distributed frequency division multiplexor may be the optimum choice. A single higher capacity trunk is routed optimally through the terminal cluster as in poll and select and contention, as shown in Figure 5-20.

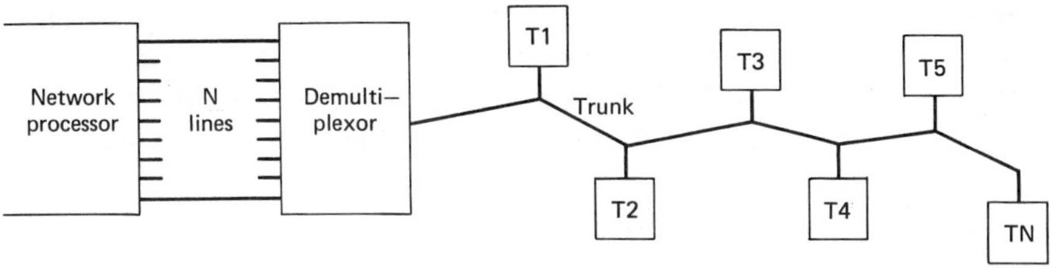

Figure 5-20 **Distributed FDM**

Rather than a single, centrally located, frequency division multiplexor of "N" subchannels as described in previous pages, one subchannel is built into, or provided with, each of the "N" terminals.

This single channel, perhaps in the form of an optional plug-in circuit board, is assigned its specific frequency range and behaves exactly as it would in centralized frequency division multiplexing. As before, a demultiplexor is required at the network processor, either free-standing as shown or integrated into it.

It is possible to service more terminals than the "N" subchannels of the trunk can accommodate, if desired. If it is only a requirement that some (but not all) of them ("M," for example) be active simultaneously, each terminal can be equipped with an "N" position switch. When the terminal operator desires access to the network, he rotates this switch and searches the "N" subchannels for a vacant one which he can occupy. He must return later and try again if he finds they are all busy. In this way, "N" subchannels can provide a specified degree of service to a larger number of terminals at a more optimum cost. This feature can be applied to centralized frequency division multiplexing as well and can produce similar savings there.

Another variation of this type of frequency division multiplexing involves a trunk that is continuously transmitting various types of information, a different type on each subchannel. A terminal operator desiring to examine a specific type of information need only rotate his switch to the appropriate subchannel of the trunk and copy the information flowing on it. In this way, all "M" of the terminals could be receiving information simultaneously from the "N" subchannels. This type of service may be provided by stock brokerage houses or by the stock exchange itself; by news services with various types of local, national, and international news on the various subchannels; or by other similar organizations with a requirement for the simultaneous dissemination of various types of information. Obviously, the subchannels used for outbound information cannot be interrupted to be used for inbound information flow. If inbound traffic is a requirement, some of the subchannels in the trunk could be reserved for it. The terminal operator would then turn his selector switch to those subchannels and search for a vacant one on a contention-type basis.

Distributed Time Division Multiplexor

This form of distributed multipoint concentration is very similar to distributed frequency division multiplexing except that the demultiplexor at the network processor is eliminated (see Figure 5-21).

The network processor now receives a time division multiplexed character stream, which it must demultiplex and sort into appropriate character strings for the active terminals. This technique is generally

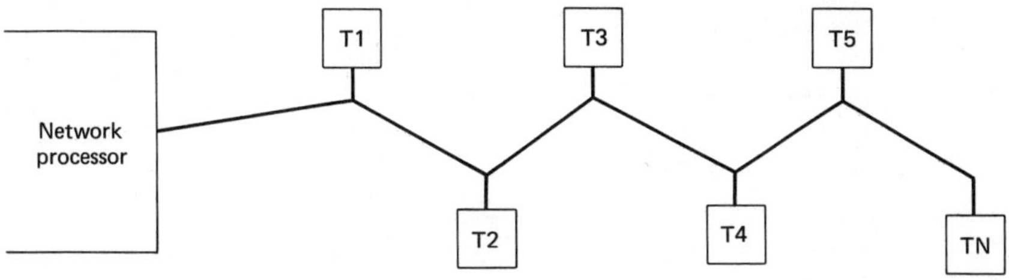

Figure 5-21 **Distributed TDM**

more involved and requires more sophisticated hardware in each terminal due to the inherent intricacies of timing. Each terminal essentially contains a complete TDM that utilizes just one of the "N" time slots available. While most of the capabilities of distributed frequency division multiplexing could be implemented, the added cost of the more expensive (due to complexity) hardware would have to be weighed against the greater number of terminals that can usually be handled with time division multiplexing (as contrasted to frequency division multiplexing) and the possibility of two or more trunks that the terminal could be switched between. The number of terminals to be serviced, their speed, and the relative distances involved would also be used as evaluation parameters.

CHAPTER 6

Coupling

The coupling function involves the method of physically connecting the source/destination devices at the various nodes in the network to the associated lines and trunks of the distribution network. Since most source/destination devices (excluding information and network processors) do not generate information signals in a form that can be directly interfaced to a network processor, some form of coupling is required. Further, many source/destination devices do not generate information signals in a form that can be transmitted directly on the lines and trunks, which again requires some form of coupling device. Two basic forms of coupling have evolved and are in use today; direct connect and analog. The tree structure through Level V, showing the position of the coupling function, is given in Figure 6-1.

6-1 DIRECT CONNECT COUPLING

Direct connect is perhaps the earliest form of coupling used to interface remote source/destination devices to a computer over distribution network lines. The terminal devices most frequently chosen in earlier systems were teletypewriters because they were available, they

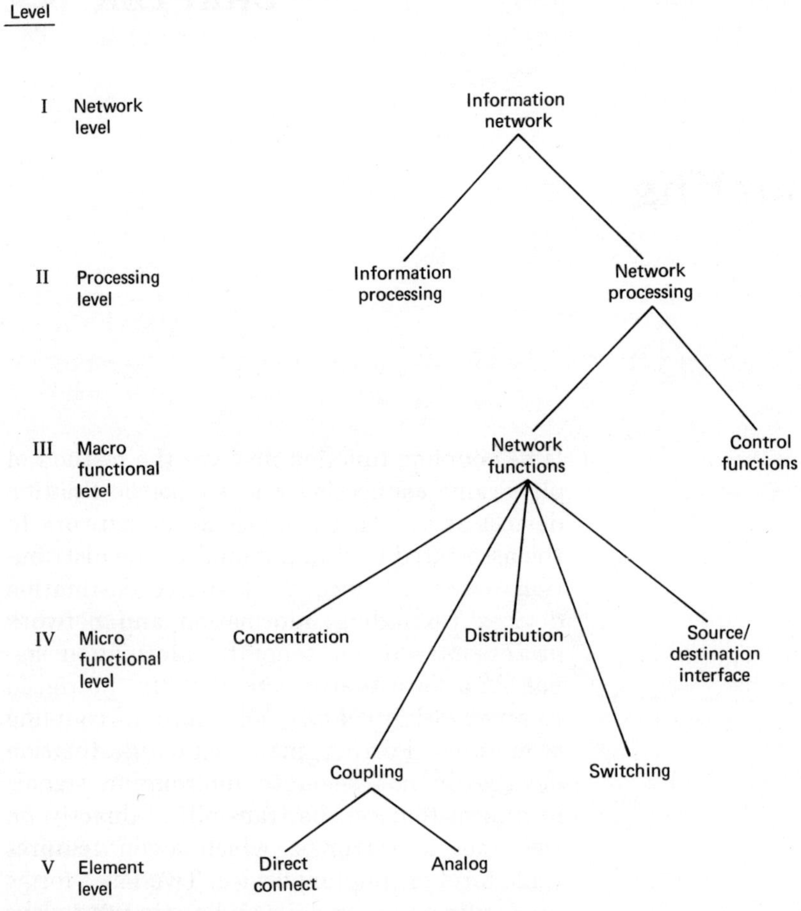

Figure 6-1 **Coupling function**

worked, and the required lines were also readily available.

Voltage Current Adapters

Teletypewriters were originally designed to provide point-to-point communication between two identical devices, one at each end of the interconnecting line. For this use, signalling techniques that would represent the information flow were developed to support the needed rate (5–10 characters per second) at the required distance (up to tens of miles).

Depression of a specific key on a teletypewriter caused an electromechanical device to translate the indicated character into a series of "zero" and "one" bits which were placed directly on the line. The one bits were represented by a specified electrical current flowing in one direction, and the zero bits were represented by current flowing in the opposite direction (or not at all, in some cases). The electromechanical device in the receiving teletypewriter examined the incoming electrical current variation, decoded it to identify the character, and caused it to be printed. This form of information representation became known as "current signalling," and the terminals themselves were said to present a "current interface" to the distribution line.

Network processors, like information processors, usually represent zero and one bits with a form of voltage variation, a zero bit being zero volts and a one bit being some positive voltage, say five volts.

In order to interface a teletypewriter or other "current" signalling device to a network processor operating in a "voltage" mode, a device is required to convert the current flow representing a zero bit to zero volts and the current flow representing a one bit to five volts. The device that evolved became known as a Voltage Current Adapter or simply VCA. The VCA was placed between the network processor and the distribution network line and thereby coupled the processor to the line.

Voltage current adapters, like other direct connect coupling techniques discussed in following pages, are limited in maximum information flow rate by the following general rule: The maximum information flow rate is inversely proportional to the length of the distribution network line. In other words, the closer the source/destination devices are to each other, and thus the shorter the interconnecting line, the higher the flow rate between them can be. As the line becomes longer and the interference, noise, and distortion become greater, the maximum flow rate that can be accurately maintained decreases. Through the use of repeaters in these lines (every so many miles, depending on the total distance involved and the speed desired), a given signal rate could be propagated across the country or even across oceans, as required. These repeaters would amplify the incoming weak signal and transmit it at full strength on to the next repeater, where the process would repeat.

Early teletypewriters operating at 75 bits per second could be tens of miles apart and still maintain sufficient accuracy. Higher speed devices within 100 feet or so of a network processor can maintain rates of several thousand bits per second in the direct connect mode.

Electronic Industries Association Standard Interface

As the requirement to connect newer types of source/destination devices to computers grew, the need for some form of standard interface appeared. This resulted in the preparation by the Electronic Industries Association (EIA) of an interface standard called EIARS232C.

This standard defines "the interface between data terminal equipment and data communication equipment employing serial binary data interchange." A standard 25 pin connector is identified, with the function of each pin clearly specified and the voltage limits associated with it defined. In addition to those pins used for the data signals themselves, other pins are used to pass specifically identified control signals across the interface. These control signals are used by the devices on both sides of the interface to initiate, control, and terminate the flow of information across the interface. EIARS232C has become known as a voltage interface.

The EIARS232C interface specification recommends that the line length between the connectors not exceed 50 feet. Each pin in the connector is attached to an individual wire in the cable, which is in turn connected to the same pin in the connector at the other end. The EIARS232C interface standard indicates that, within the specified parameters, a nominal maximum information flow rate of 20,000 bits per second can be maintained.

The MIL188b/c Interface Specifications

There are government interface specifications (b is one version, c another) that perform a function similar to that of the EIARS232C. The primary difference is that the voltage and current limitations, impedances, and other parameters are specified and limited in such a way as to make detection of the information flow by electronic means difficult if not impossible. This is very important in some secure government installations. The MIL188b/c interfaces will permit information flow rates up to several thousand bits per second at distances of several hundred feet.

Parallel Interfaces

Frequently in an in-plant environment, source/destination devices are used that generate information in a bit-parallel, character-serial fashion. Examples of this include employee badge readers, low-speed card readers, factory feedback devices, and others. Typically, these devices are directly connected to a cable containing the specified number of parallel data lines plus some number of control lines, with distances limited to 1000–2000 feet.

The network processor interfacing to these lines may include a port or channel capable of accepting the parallel input and placing it in memory or may use a form of coupler that makes a parallel-to-serial conversion and then presents the information flow to a standard serial port or channel.

6-2 ANALOG COUPLING

The need for higher information flow rates at greater distances—hundreds or thousands of miles—plus the need for increased configuration flexibility led to the development of several forms of analog couplers. Analog coupling is distinguished from direct connect by two main characteristics.

An analog coupler is always placed between the source/destination device at each end of the interconnecting line or trunk, as opposed to the single coupler used at the network processor end of the line in direct connect coupling. Secondly, the information signals are altered in form and used to modulate a higher frequency carrier on the line or trunk rather than being placed directly on it. The resulting modulated carrier is analagous to, or represents, the information flow generated by the source/destination devices.

Analog coupling techniques for use in information networks are still evolving at a rapid rate. The more commonly used forms and some of the newer ones are discussed in following pages.

Digital Subsets

The most commonly occurring form of analog coupling in use today involves the use of digital subsets or modems (modulation-demodulation). Traditionally, due primarily to tariff regulations, these couplers were supplied by the common carriers and were contained or packaged in free-standing cabinets. The connections between these modems and the network element with which they interface will usually conform to the EIARS232 interface specification previously mentioned.

Fairly recent relaxation of these regulations now makes it possible to interface the common carrier trunks with modems supplied by noncommon carrier producers. Users of these couplers are still required to obtain a device from the common carriers known as a Direct Access Arrangement (DAA), which is placed between the trunk itself and the noncommon carrier supplied coupler. This DAA acts as a filter to assure that no out-of-tolerance signals or voltages are placed on the trunk.

With network element producers now free to supply couplers of their own manufacture for use on common carrier trunks, the next logical step is to integrate the coupler physically into the source/destination device or other element to be coupled to the trunk. The use of the newer integrated circuit technologies to produce such integrated couplers should result in significant cost savings to the users.

The following list of free-standing couplers is not all-inclusive but is presented to illustrate the range of capabilities and functions performed. The Bell System designations are given, as they are the most commonly used and recognized. Other carriers provide similar or equivalent classes of couplers.

Bell System 103 Series (Asynchronous-Bit Serial). The following variations are available within the 103 Series:

- 103A Couples low-speed elements, such as teletypewriter, to the switched voice band trunks. Maximum range=300 bits per second, half- or full-duplex.
- 103E A rack-mounted version of the 103A which greatly compresses the space required when many modems are needed. Maximum rate=300 bits per second, half- or full-duplex.
- 103F Couples low-speed elements to dedicated narrow band or voice band distribution network trunks. Maximum rate=300 bits per second, half- or full-duplex.

Bell System 201 Series (Synchronous-Bit Serial). The following types are available within the 201 Series:

- 201A Couples medium speed elements operating at 2,000 bits per second (half-duplex) to a switched voice band or a dedicated (half- or full-duplex) voice band distribution network trunk.
- 201B Couples medium speed elements to a dedicated voice band distribution network (half- or full-duplex) trunk at 2400 bits per second.

Bell System 202 Series (Asynchronous-Bit Serial). The following variations are available within this series:

- 202C Couples medium speed elements to a switched voice band network or a dedicated voice band distribution network trunk, most commonly on the former, at speeds up to 1200 bits per second in half- or full-duplex.

202D Couples medium speed elements to a dedicated voice band distribution network trunk—half- or full-duplex. With special conditioning of the trunk, it can be operated at speeds up to 1800 bits per second.

Bell System 203 Series (Synchronous-Bit Serial). This newly announced series couples medium speed elements to the public telephone network or to a dedicated voice band distribution network trunk at speeds higher than possible with the 201 Series. When coupled to the public telephone network, the maximum speed is 3600 bits per second—half- or full-duplex. On dedicated distribution network trunks, speeds of 7200 bits per second (or possibly higher) are attainable.

Bell System 300 Series (Synchronous-Bit Serial). The following couplers are provided within the 300-Series:

301B Couples high-speed devices to a dedicated broadband distribution network trunk. This modem operates at 40,800 bits per second (full-duplex) and is the equivalent of 12 voice band trunks (known as a "group" in the Bell System).

303B Couples high-speed devices to a dedicated broadband distribution network trunk. This modem operates at 19,200 bits per second (full-duplex) and is the equivalent of 6 voice band trunks (known as a "half group" in the Bell System).

303D Couples even higher speed devices to a dedicated broadband distribution network trunk. This modem operates at 230,400 bits per second (full-duplex) and is the equivalent of 60 voice band trunks (known as a "super group" in the Bell System).

Bell System 400 Series (Asynchronous Bit-Parallel Character-Serial). Various modems in this series are used to provide a network processor with an interface to the public telephone network for the purpose of answering incoming calls originating at TOUCH-TONE telephones. The network processor may cause the modem to send a specific tone to the caller, indicating that it has responded to the call and is ready to accept information. The caller then depresses the TOUCH-TONE buttons in any predetermined sequence, and the network processor receives the corresponding string of characters (made up of 10 numbers, 0–9, plus # and *) which it can interpret and then takes appropriate action.

Limited amounts of numeric and/or coded alphabetic information can be entered into networks in this manner. Some of these modems are specified to include a voice response unit interface, which allows the network processor to send spoken responses to the caller (constructed as a result of information entered by the caller) in addition to the tone(s) previously described.

Acoustic Coupling

An acoustic coupler permits a source/destination device to be connected to a switched voice band trunk directly through a telephone. This coupler is cable connected to the source/destination device on the one side and acoustically coupled to the telephone handset on the other by two openings provided, one each for the mouthpiece and earpiece (transmitter and receiver). The coupler converts the signals generated by the source/destination device into a series of audible tones, which are then passed to the mouthpiece or transmitter of the telephone and then onto the switched voice band trunk.

Information coming in the reverse direction is converted into audible tones at the earpiece of the telephone, detected by the acoustic coupler, and converted into the appropriate electrical signal for use by the source/destination device. The most significant advantage provided by acoustic coupling is that small portable terminals can be carried from place to place and used to access the information network anywhere a telephone capable of reaching the desired information processing complex is available.

Radio Frequency Coupling

Radio frequency couplers are used primarily with mobile terminals accessing the information network through a form of radio frequency distribution. (For more discussion of radio frequency facilities, see Chapter 7, pg. 89.) These couplers consist of a small transmitter-receiver connected to the source/destination device and are capable of converting the information signals to some specified radio frequency and broadcasting it to an associated antenna system.

Radio frequency couplers used in an in-plant environment where the antenna is a grid in the ceiling may be quite small and capable of transmitting only the few feet between the terminal and the antenna. If the mobile terminal is a teletypewriter in a vehicle that may be miles from the antenna, the coupler must obviously be larger and more powerful.

Frequency Division Multiplexing

Frequency division multiplexing can be considered a form of coupling. Currently limited to use with dedicated trunks, the multiplexor performs the function of converting the information signals from the source/destination devices into a form suitable for transmission on the specified subchannel of the dedicated trunk. The multiplexor is connected directly to the trunk, and no intervening subset is required.

Inductive Coupling

Inductive coupling is another technique that can be used to interface remote source/destination devices to a switched distribution network trunk. This type of coupling is used today to permit tape recording of both sides of a telephone conversation. The coupler itself consists of a coil of wire embedded in a pad placed under or near the telephone instrument. This coil is connected to a cable that plugs into the tape recorder. Signals generated by the voice conversation produce a magnetic field around the telephone, which is picked up by the coil of wire and sent to the recorder over the connecting cable.

A suitable coupler could be added to the coil of wire in the pad to convert the induced signals into a form capable of driving a source/destination device. Current technology and the operating characteristics of the telephone mouthpiece or transmitter would limit a source/destination device so coupled to a destination-only mode of operation. It is not possible to induce signals in the telephone from the coil of wire in the pad, thus allowing the device to act as a source also.

Optical Coupling

If some form of optical distribution network is chosen (see Chapter 7, pg. 91), it is necessary to couple the various source/destination devices to it. The optical trunks in the network may be configurated with a single source/destination device on each or may be used in a centralized concentration form with a suitable multiplexing technique.

The optical coupler's function is to convert the information signals from the source/destination device into a form that can be used to modulate the light beam that constitutes the connecting trunk. For information flowing to the source/destination device, the coupler must convert the modulated light beam into the signal form necessary for use by the device.

Optical trunks are capable of supporting flow-rates in the range of millions of bits per second, and it is expected that they will be most frequently used with the higher speed source/destination devices or for the multiplexing of large numbers of slower speed devices.

CHAPTER 7

Distribution Network

It is the function of the distribution network to provide a path or means for the information to flow between the various nodes in the network. While many forms are currently in use, the most frequently thought of are the various lines and trunks supplied by the common carriers—American Telephone and Telegraph, Western Union, and others—that were an early and obvious choice for data communications applications due to their ready availability.

The flow of information in distribution networks is regulated by numerous agencies. When lines or trunks cross state boundaries, the Federal Communications Commission (FCC) is the controlling agency. If the lines and trunks of a network are all contained within a state's boundaries, various state agencies are involved. Some large cities maintain municipal agencies. It is the function of these agencies to regulate, control, and establish rates for the use of the various distribution network facilities. The rates established for a given grade of service may vary considerably from state to state or from city to city, which presents an additional aspect of network design to be considered.

The various types of distribution networks

available to the designer may be grouped into three broad classifications—in-plant, dedicated, and public switched—each of which is discussed separately. These discussions are at a functional level only and do not include detailed cost comparisons and evaluations. The complexities of the various tariffs filed by the regulatory agencies place such discussions beyond the scope of this book. The position of the distribution function within the tree structure is shown in Figure 7-1.

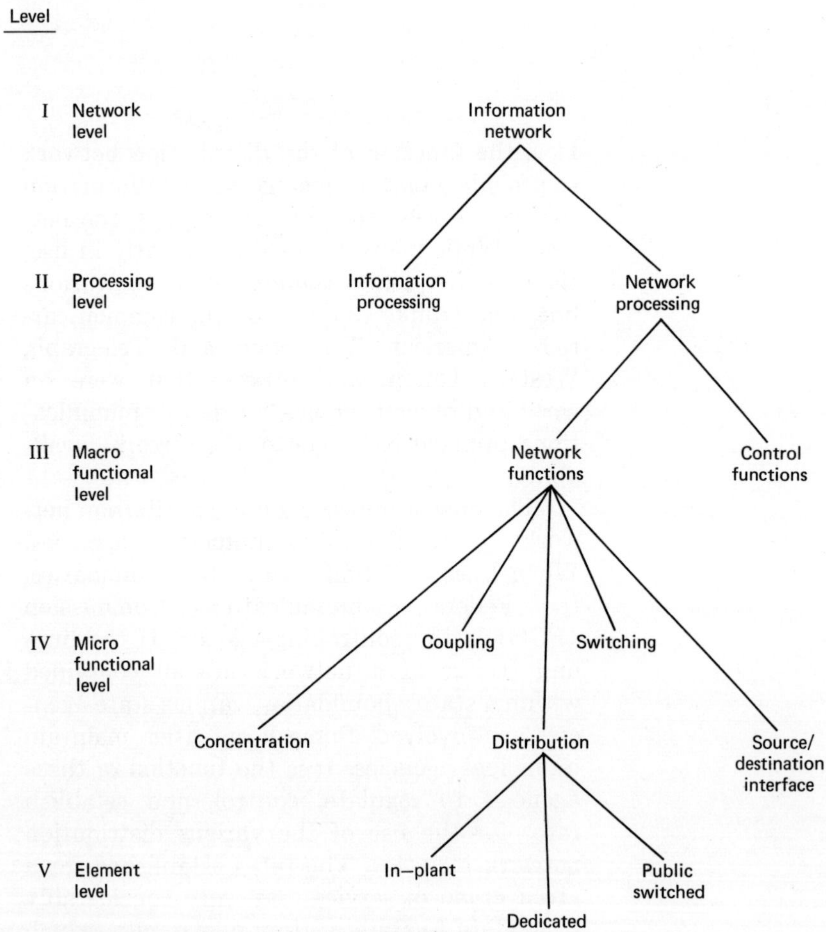

Figure 7-1 **Distribution function**

7-1 IN-PLANT DISTRIBUTION NETWORK

An in-plant distribution network is typically considered as being contained within the physical boundaries or confines of a single building or factory. This definition should be expanded or broadened to include a network that extends beyond the building or plant so long as the lines or trunks involved do not cross public highways or thoroughfares.

As long as the network is contained within the geographic area bounded by public highways or thoroughfares, the FCC tariffs and regulations do not apply and significantly greater latitude is available to the designer. Optical and certain forms of radio frequency trunks, however, are not controlled by tariff and may cross public highways and thoroughfares. The following types of in-plant distribution networks are included to illustrate this flexibility but do not necessarily represent all the available possibilities.

A significant feature of in-plant distribution networks is that they need not necessarily be supplied by a common carrier such as the Bell System or Western Union and so they are not covered by their tariffs and other regulatory policies.

Hardwire

The hardwire in-plant distribution network is perhaps the simplest of all in concept. It consists of lengths of wire that are routed between the various source/destination or relay nodes of the network. Various types of wire may be required, depending on the distances involved, desired speed or information flow rate, shielding requirements, and other similar considerations. These types may range from a simple pair of twisted wires for a 10 character per second (well below capacity) teletypewriter operating in a half-duplex mode up through shielded coaxial cable used for much higher speed devices and information flow rates.

Radio Frequency

Another form of distribution network involves the use of a radio frequency transmission and reception technique. The advantages of this approach are the extreme flexibility and portability of the terminals used, the lack of wires and cables, and the relative ease with which the network can be expanded or reconfigured. Each terminal to be used in this type of environment requires its own specific radio frequency coupler (see Chapter 6, pg. 84), which it uses to interface with the radio frequency trunk. This coupler is in the form of a device that: (1) converts the terminal's signals into a form that can be transmitted by the coupler to the antenna of the network; and (2) receives information from the antenna and converts it into a form suitable for the terminal's use.

Terminals used in this fashion are extremely portable and are free to move anywhere within the range of the antenna. They may be entirely self-contained and operate on battery power or may be plugged into a wall receptable to obtain their electrical power.

The antenna system may be in the form of a grid placed overhead in the ceiling of the building, in which case the terminal needs only a coupler capable of transmitting a few feet. Portable time-sharing terminals, for example, could be wheeled around anywhere in a building, plugged into an electrical power receptacle, and used without tying up telephone lines, instruments, and facilities as required when other forms of coupling—e.g., acoustic and inductive—are used.

Instead of being a grid in the ceiling of the building, the antenna may be placed on the roof of a centrally located building in the network. With more powerful couplers, the network can be extended to include mobile terminals that are perhaps in the form of teleprinters located in vehicles driven around within the network. Note that in this case there is an overlap from a strictly in-plant situation into a wider area. The radio frequency trunk itself is then a specified or assigned portion of the radio frequency spectrum controlled by the Federal Communications Commission. To this extent, in-plant distribution networks are controlled by a regulatory agency, but under a different set of laws than those governing the use of common carrier lines and trunks.

The bandwidth of the portion of the radio frequency spectrum assigned to a specific network may be used in a number of ways. It may be subdivided into a number of identical channels for use by individual terminals. Each terminal's coupler is then wired or coded to use its assigned subchannel when interfacing with the network. Should there be an insufficient number of subchannels available and if it is not necessary that all terminals be active simultaneously, the terminals may be equipped with a coupler than can, either automatically or manually, examine all the subchannels looking for one that is not in use. If none are found, the operator will try again at a later time.

The assigned bandwidth may also be divided into a number of

different subchannels for use by devices having various speeds. If great distances are involved, it may be more economical to use a larger subchannel as a path between the antenna and a remote radio frequency concentrator. This concentrator can, through its own antenna, interface with the cluster of terminals surrounding it, since their couplers are not powerful enough to cover the distance to the processing complex. The concentrator can then retransmit the information through its more powerful transmitter by assigning the active terminals to subchannels of its assigned channel. In this way, the same degree of service can be provided to the remote cluster of terminals without incurring the cost of equipping each of them with a coupler large enough to span the distances on its own.

Radio frequency coupled terminals do not necessarily have to be concentrated by using a radio frequency concentrator. If a remote concentrator that utilizes either dedicated or public switched trunks is nearby, this may be the optimum choice. The terminals can interface with the antenna at the concentrator, which can, through an appropriate coupler, present the information flow to it for forwarding to the information processing complex.

Optical

In areas where difficulty of terrain, excessive radio frequency interference, or other similar conditions prohibit the use of hardwirc, radio frequency, or other types of distribution network, an optical trunk may be a practical choice. The information is moved between nodes by modulating an optical beam through the use of appropriate couplers at either end.

The optical trunk may be in the visible portion of the spectrum—i.e., visible to the unaided human eye—or may be outside it in the infrared or ultraviolet range. The selection is a function of many factors, including the desired information flow rate, the distances involved, number of subchannels required, atmospheric interference considerations, and others. For shorter distances of up to a few miles, the infrared spectrum has been used successfully at speeds up to several million hertz, which is sufficient to multiplex many slow-speed devices like teletypewriters. Greater distances will require the application of laser or other technologies, which will not only cover the required distance but will provide even higher information flow rates.

Another relatively inexpensive form of optical trunk uses fiber optics. This technique involves the use of small transparent plastic or glass fibers that can transmit light energy at relatively high efficiencies. These bundles of fibers can be strung or routed like wires between network nodes where line-of-sight optical techniques are impossible or impractical. This form of optical trunk is obviously not subject to the same atmospheric interferences—rain, snow, fog, birds, etc.—that the other forms are.

Like radio frequency distribution trunks, the optical trunks can be divided into subchannels through the use of an appropriate multiplexing technique which permits a single trunk to service a number of terminals or other source/destination devices.

Carrier Current

Another form of in-plant distribution network involves the use of the electrical power lines in the building as a path for information flow between terminals and the information processing complex. The terminal or other source/destination device is plugged into the wall socket that supplies it with electrical power. Through an appropriate coupling device, perhaps built as an integral part of the terminal, the terminal impresses its signals on the same wires from which it receives its power. At the other end of the wire, a suitable decoupler is provided to remove the signals and present them in an appropriate form to the network processor (see Figure 7-2). The inbound information

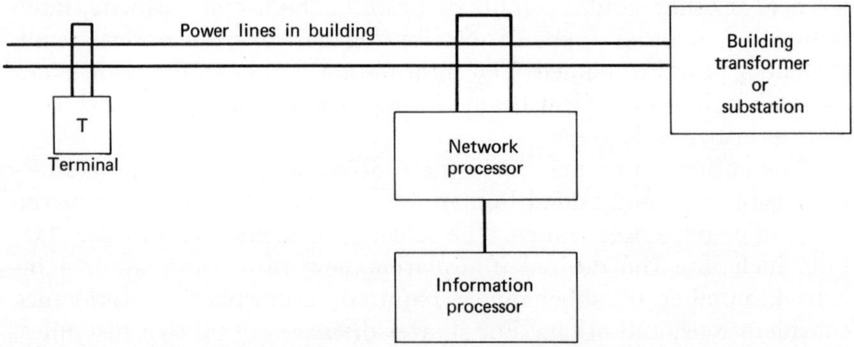

Figure 7-2 **Carrier current distribution**

flow must be decoupled from the power lines prior to their entry into a transformer or power substation within the building, as the signals cannot be transmitted through these devices.

Due to the relatively high amount of noise, switching transients, and other types of interference usually found on power lines, it is not practical to use them for terminals with speeds much above the teletypewriter range of 10–30 characters per second.

This form of in-plant distribution network provides several advantages. It is not necessary to run additional wires between the terminals and the information processing complex. Terminals are extremely portable and may be used any place in the building where electrical power is available, so long as an appropriate decoupler is included on the power line.

Cable Multiplex

Cable multiplex is a form of in-plant distribution network used to provide simultaneous access to a number of terminals in a given building or area. The terminals may be of the teletypewriter class, 10–30 characters per second, or higher speed devices such as cathode ray tube terminals operating at 100 characters or more per second.

The configuration involves one or more higher capacity lines—coaxial cable, for example—routed through all areas in the building where terminals are or will be located, as shown in Figure 7-3. Ter-

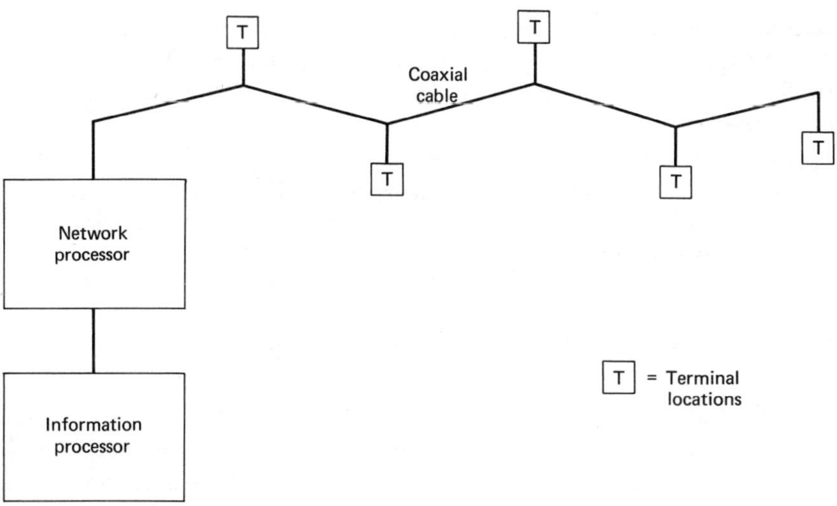

Figure 7-3 **Cable multiplex distribution**

minals or other source/destination devices are coupled to the trunk in a time or frequency division multiplexing mode, and may be added or deleted as necessary. If the sum of the information flow rates of the terminals does not exceed the capacity of the trunk, then all may be active simultaneously. A greater number of terminals may be connected to the trunk and each provided with a switch to examine the subchannels to find a vacant one. In this case, not all terminals can be simultaneously active (see Chapter 5, pg. 73).

Numerous cable multiplex trunks may be required to handle the number of terminals and different information flow rates and to provide the desired grade of service to the terminals. The trunks may be configured with one trunk handling all of one terminal type and one handling all terminals in a given area, or some other logical arrangement.

Combination

Many in-plant networks are impossible to configure or optimize by using a single type of distribution network line or trunk. For example, those with a centralized concentration function requirement may use narrow band hardwire lines from the terminals to the concentrator but higher capacity voice band hardwire trunks between it and the network processor.

The use of optical trunks may be necessary, also, with several terminals connected via hardwire to the optical coupler, which transmits to its associated remote or distant coupler, at which point the traffic may revert to hardwire trunks for entry into the network processor.

Many combinations of types of in-plant distribution network trunks may be required in a given network. Examination of the numerous parameters involved is required to select the appropriate subset necessary to obtain the desired grade of service and optimization.

7-2 DEDICATED DISTRIBUTION NETWORK

A dedicated distribution network (sometimes called leased) is one that is leased from a common carrier, configured to the user's specifications or configuration requirements, and dedicated to his exclusive use. As such, it is under control of the appropriate intra- or interstate tariffs and is maintained by the common carrier. The charges for such networks are generally a function of the number of terminals and clusters involved, the distances between the clusters and other network nodes, the type of lines or trunks required, and other related factors.

Dedicated distribution networks may be completely in-plant, may extend out of the in-plant category to intra- and/or interstate, or may be a combination of all types and controlled by the appropriate tariff or tariffs in effect at the time.

Two broad designations cover the dedicated distribution network —point-to-point and switched. The various types available are discussed in the following pages and are identified as to the category in which they belong.

Dedicated Narrow Band Distribution Network

Dedicated narrow band lines are usually configured in a point-to-point mode and are used to provide a path for information flow between terminals and other network nodes at rates up to 300 bits per second. They are most commonly used with teletypewriter and other similar low-speed devices. This should not be confused with the use of low-speed devices on wider band trunks, as in the common use of teletypewriters on public switched voice band trunks.

Narrow band lines can be separated into two major classifications —telegraph grade (direct current) and carrier (analog)—with the difference being the type of coupling involved and the corresponding mode of information flow.

In direct current narrow band, the information signals from the terminal are transmitted directly on the line in a direct current form and may or may not be converted at the other end of the line by an appropriate coupler (see Chapter 6). An example is the use of an AT&T Model 28 Teletype on a telegraph-grade narrow band line connected to a network processor at the other end through a tele-

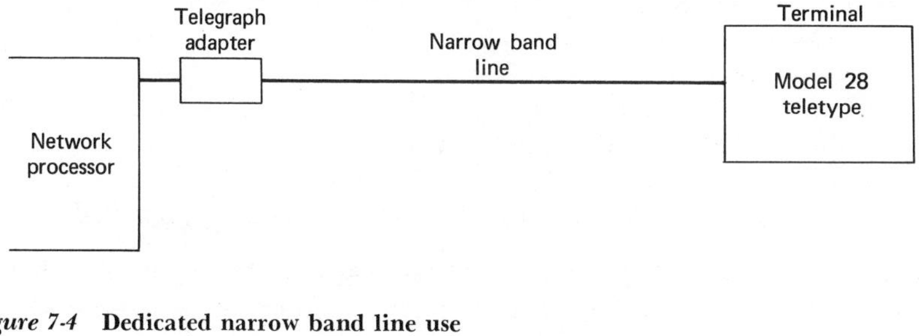

Figure 7-4 **Dedicated narrow band line use**

graph adapter coupler, as shown in Figure 7-4. The information signals from the terminals are transmitted in a direct current mode over the line to the telegraph adapter, which converts them to an appropriate voltage mode interface for the network processor.

A narrow band line may be used with a single terminal or other device that is connected and is on-line all the time, or it may be connected to a number of terminals in a distributed multipoint form and controlled by a network processor using poll and select logic or manual access (contention) mode.

Numerous distributed narrow band offerings have been or are available from the common carriers. Many of these were installed originally in administrative message switching systems, and the network designer who finds them still operational should consider integrating them into the network he is designing. This is particularly advantageous if the line and terminal configuration is reasonably optimum and still capable of providing the necessary grade of service.

The more commonly occurring versions of these offerings are listed below.

- *Bell System 83 Series*
  Model 28 Teletype equipment
  Speeds up to 75 bits per second
  Half-duplex mode
  5-level Baudot code
- *Bell System 81 Series*
  Similar to the 83 Series, but operates in a full-duplex mode.
- *Bell System 8A1*
  Model 35 Teletype equiment
  Speed of 110 bits per second
  Half-duplex mode
  8-level ASCII code
- *Bell System 8B1*
  Similar to the 8A1 Series, but operates in full-duplex mode.
- *Bell System 86A2*
  Model 37 Teletype equipment
  Speed of 150 bits per second
  Half-duplex mode
  8-level ASCII code (upper and lower case)
- *Bell System 86B2*
  Similar to the 86A2 Series, but operates in full-duplex mode.

Other Bell System offerings are available using the equipment listed above. These offerings vary in the control sequences utilized and the optional features that are available.

A variety of comparable offerings, using the same types of equipment, is available from Western Union. Due to the similarity of equipment and procedures, they will not be listed here.

The administrative message switching systems that the above offerings were used for include the following types, which are not discussed in depth as they are beyond the scope of this book.

- Manual torn tape switching system
- Semi-automatic switching system
- Automatic switching system

Western Union currently offers a service called DATACOM, which is a system for multiplexing several lower speed channels over a single dedicated voice grade channel. The maximum number of lower speed channels attainable ranges from 24, operating at 75 bits per second, to 3, operating at 1200 bits per second.

With an analog type narrow band line, the information signals from the terminal or other source/destination device are converted or modulated into a form suitable for transmission over the line and demodulated at the other end into a form suitable for the receiving device. This narrow band analog form is generally used where the terminals do not generate information signals in a direct current form; and further, it usually provides a higher grade of service over greater distances than can be achieved using the direct current mode.

Dedicated Voice Band Distribution Network

When speeds greater than possible with narrow band lines are required, the use of voice band lines and trunks should be considered. These facilities were designed originally for use in voice communication between two points but with suitable couplers may be used for interfacing a variety of source/destination devices to an information network.

The bandwidth of a voice band line is approximately 3000 hertz, which is suitable for transmitting voice generated signals and reproducing them at the other end in a humanly recognizable form. While the frequency response does not reproduce the human voice exactly in full fidelity, the loss or distortion incurred is not sufficient to render the voice unintelligible to the listener.

When used for voice traffic with a telephone, the handset containing the earpiece and mouthpiece (receiver and transmitter) can be considered the coupling device. Its function is to couple the human voice to the line by altering it to a form suitable for transmission on the line to the other end, where it is decoupled and presented to the listener.

A voice band trunk is capable of supporting an information flow rate considerably greater (in excess of 10,000 bits per second) than is possible on narrow band facilities. It becomes the optimum choice when the toll charges for the use of the public switched voice band (dial-up) facility exceed the cost of a dedicated trunk. Network analysis will indicate at what level of usage (frequency and volume of information) at the specific distance involved the switch to dedicated lines should occur.

If the terminal or other source/destination device has a very low usage frequency and transmits limited amounts of information, the long distance or local toll rates may be the least expensive way to provide the desired grade of service. For the higher usage and volume devices or where it is necessary that they be on-line continuously, the dedicated facility is required.

Terminals and other source/destination devices are usually coupled led to a dedicated voice band line or trunk in an analog form (see Chapter 6), with the appropriate couplers at each end.

Depending on the information flow rate required, terminal or other device operating characteristics, and other considerations, the trunk is operated in a synchronous or asynchronous mode. In the synchronous mode, the coupling devices at each end of the trunk provide a timing signal or clock that is used to establish the information flow rate, usually in bits per second, and enable the terminals to identify the appropriate character frame. In some systems, this timing is provided by the terminal or other source/destination device, and the coupler's clock is not used.

In either case, with or without the coupler's timing clock, before information flow can begin, the transmitting and receiving devices must establish synchronization between themselves. This is done by the transmitting device preceding the information with a series, two or more, of synchronization or "synch" characters. These synch characters are the same code level (bits per character) as the information flow and have a unique configuration of zero and one bits. The receiving device examines the incoming bit stream one bit at a time until it recognizes a synch character. On receipt of two or more consecutive synch characters, the receiving device confirms that it has identified the proper character frame and is now ready to receive the information flow.

The flow of information on a trunk operating in a synchronous mode is illustrated in Figure 7-5. Included in the diagram are the synch characters which precede the information and are used by the receiving device to establish synchronization and identify the character frame.

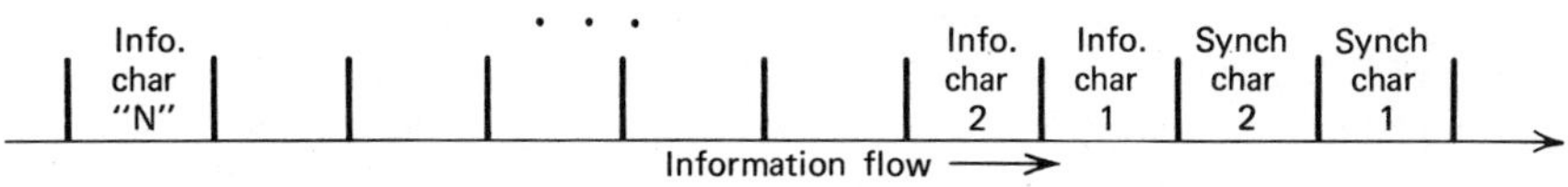

Figure 7-5 **Synchronous transmission**

Each of the characters on the trunk, including the synch characters, contains the same number of bits. The most frequently used character size today is eight bits, usually in the ASCII format, although others are possible.

Synchronization of the transmitting and receiving devices is necessary each time a transmission is initiated or has been interrupted. If the trunk is operating in a half-duplex two-way alternate mode, the synchronization must be performed each time the trunk is turned around and the transmitting device becomes the receiver, and vice versa. It is frequently a requirement that additional synch characters be included or inserted in the information flow periodically to maintain synchronization during the transmission of long messages. This is done to prevent the receiving coupler and terminal device from "drifting" and losing the established character frame.

Information flow rates in excess of 10,000 bits per second can be achieved through the use of appropriate couplers on dedicated voice band trunks.

Asynchronous transmission on dedicated voice band trunks preceded the synchronous form. This was due primarily to the fact that most of the early terminals and other source/destination devices operated in the asynchronous mode.

In the asynchronous mode, the need for the synch characters as a means of establishing the character frame is not present. The only timing requirement is one of establishing and maintaining the specified information flow rate in bits per second.

Two states are recognized on the trunk itself: a one bit, sometimes called a "mark," and a zero bit, sometimes called a "space." When no information is flowing on the trunk, it is placed in a marking condition, which is essentially a continuous one bit.

When the transmitting device wants to start transmitting information, it frames each individual character to be sent with "start" and "stop" bits. Start bits are always a zero and stop bits are always a one (see Figure 7-6).

The receiving device takes no action so long as the trunk remains at a continuous mark or stop bit status. As soon as the zero start bit

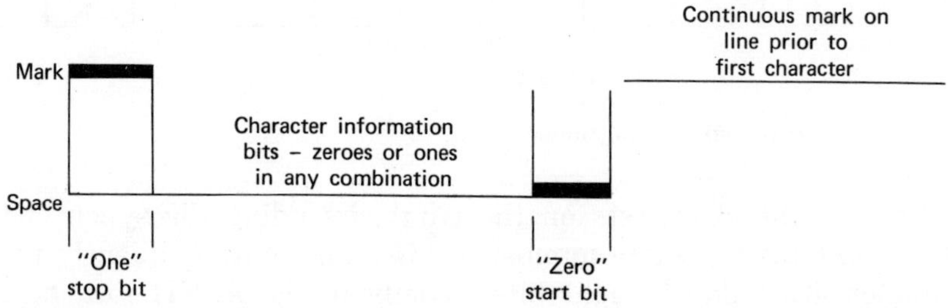

Figure 7-6 **Asynchronous transmission**

arrives and the transition from mark to space is detected, the receiver prepares to receive the following character information bits. Early model teletypewriters use a single start bit, five data or information bits, and one or more stop bits. Later model teletypewriters use one start bit, eight data bits, and one or two stop bits. Code levels of six and seven information bits per character are also in use.

Following receipt of the information bits, the stop bit or bits (always a one) return the trunk to the marking or idle condition. The receiving device is then ready to start looking for the zero or start bit, which signals the arrival of the next character.

With the start and stop bits framing each set of character information bits, the transmitting device is not required to send each character within a given, specified time interval, as is the case in the synchronous mode of operation. Devices with keyboards that are used by human operators or other devices that generate character streams in an irregular manner require the asynchronous mode of operation unless a suitable buffer is provided between the keyboard and the trunk. This buffer collects the characters from the keyboard asynchronously and then transmits them synchronously on the trunk by preceding them with the appropriate synch characters.

Asynchronous transmission on dedicated voice band trunks usually occurs at speeds up to 1800 bits per second. Beyond that speed, the synchronous mode of transmission is used. Some manufacturers' equipment uses dedicated voice band trunks in the synchronous mode for anything over 600 bits per second.

Prior to 1969, the common carriers would not authorize the use of couplers not of their own manufacture on the facilities. In 1969, that restriction was altered to permit the use of "foreign" couplers manufactured by others on the common carriers' lines and trunks, provided these were interfaced through a common carrier supplied Data Access Arrangement (DAA). This device (DAA) insures that the foreign coupler does not place signals on the lines or trunks that exceed predetermined levels. This decision made it possible for equipment manufacturers to integrate or build the couplers into their terminals, network processors, and other source/destination devices.

The standard dedicated voice band trunk as supplied by the common carrier is capable of speeds up to about 1200 bits per second. To obtain the higher rates, special "conditioning" of the trunk is required and must be supplied by the common carrier. This conditioning involves additional equipment on the trunk, and an additional monthly charge is made for its inclusion.

Three types of conditioning are available from AT&T that provide for successively higher information flow rates on their dedicated voice band trunks. These are designated C1, C2, and C4. Western Union's corresponding conditioning is called Class E, F, and H. For example, C2 conditioning is required on an AT&T supplied dedicated voice band trunk if it is to be operated at 2400 bits per second using a 201B subset (coupler) in the synchronous mode.

A complete discussion of voice band trunks and their numerous options, costs, coupling techniques, conditioning, and modes of operation is beyond the scope of this book. Other books are available for an in-depth treatment, and detailed literature is available from the common carriers themselves. Additional information is also available in the FCC tariffs governing their use.

Dedicated Broadband Distribution Network

When a requirement for information flow rates above that possible with dedicated voice band trunks (about 10,000 bits per second) is indicated, a wide band or broadband trunk is used. These dedicated trunks, supplied by the common carriers, may be used to provide information flow rates of 19,200–500,000 bits per second and above, if desired.

This type of trunk may be used with its appropriate coupler as a single trunk operating at its rated speed or may be divided into a number of subchannels each operating at a slower speed. A single broadband trunk divided into several voice band subchannels may prove more economical than the same number of dedicated voice band trunks configured between the network nodes.

Broadband trunks are frequently specified as being equivalent to some number of separate voice band trunks. The most familiar broadband trunks were the AT&T TELPAK series in use between the late 1950's and 1967, which were classified as follows:

Designation	Equivalent full-duplex voice band trunks
TELPAK A	12
TELPAK B	24
TELPAK C	60
TELPAK D	240

TELPAK A and B were eliminated in 1967 after the FCC ruled that their associated rates were discriminatory in that a larger user could obtain a group of voice band trunks via TELPAK at a lower cost per voice band than a small user who could not take advantage of the bulk rate. An alternate broadband trunk is now available that replaces the discontinued TELPAK A. This trunk may be used as:

1. A single 48,000 bit per second trunk.
2. Two 24,000 bit per second trunks.
3. Twelve voice band trunks.
4. Combinations of the above, not exceeding the 48,000-bit-per-second maximum.

In general, TELPAK voice band subchannels or trunks may be further subdivided into a maximum of twelve narrow band trunks or channels.

The regulations, tariffs, and rules governing the use of TELPAK and other broadband offerings are very complex. Network designers intending to specify their use should consult their local common carrier representatives for guidance.

Dedicated Switched Distribution Network

When it is not necessary that the terminals or other source/destination devices in the network be connected or on-line continuously, a switched distribution network may be more economical than point-to-point. An in-house time-sharing system with a capacity for 30 simultaneous users is an example. The system may serve 100 or more terminals, but since each requires connection for only a portion of the operating day, 30 available ports are adequate. To gain access, the terminal users dial the number of the system; if one of the 30 ports is available, access is granted.

The switched distribution network used to gain access to the time-sharing system may be dedicated solely for its use; or more likely, it may be included in an existing in-house or in-plant switched distribution network. Such a network is almost always of voice grade quality, and it may or may not be possible to gain access to the public switched voice band distribution network through it.

If such an in-plant switched voice band distribution network exists, it should be considered as a source of distribution network trunks in the information network design. Use of these trunks with appropriate couplers on the terminals or other source/destination devices may prove more economical than the installation of a separate facility, even if some expansion is required to provide the desired grade of service.

Access to the public or other switched voice band distribution networks is possible in some dedicated networks by first dialing an access code (usually a single digit) which, if a trunk on the desired network is available, results in a second dial tone. The desired number is then dialed, and the source device is connected to the desired destination if the latter is available.

An example of this occurs in a large nationwide corporation with dozens of divisions. At each plant location, a dedicated switched voice band distribution network is provided for voice communication within the plant. The common carriers provide means for dialing directly between individual telephones in separate locations through an extension of this capability. A user in one plant desiring to call a telephone in another plant across the country simply dials the appropriate access digit, waits for the second dial tone, and dials the desired number; if the destination phone is not busy, he is connected to it.

In this manner, the company is provided with a nationwide dedicated switched voice band distribution network that, with the appropriate coupler (acoustic or inductive, for example) can also be used to provide part of the distribution function in its information network.

The ability of a network processor in such a complex network to dial out to a destination device via the common carrier-supplied Automatic Call Unit (ACU) is currently hindered by the problems involved with multiple dial tones in the switched networks. It is anticipated that these problems will be overcome and the dial-out function used to provide even greater alternate routing, fail soft, and/or backup capabilities.

Combination Dedicated Distribution Network

Selection of the optimum configuration and form(s) of dedicated distribution network required is a result of the network analysis performed by the designer. For many relatively small information networks, a single form of distribution suffices; larger, more complex networks require several if not all of the available forms.

A free-standing administrative message switching network consisting of a network processor and a number of remote teletypewriters, for example, may require just an appropriate number of dedicated narrow band distribution trunks. A large multiple-dimension information network capable of remote job entry, time-sharing, administrative message switching, information collection and/or retrieval, and other tasks involving information processing complexes located around the country may require a number of different types of lines and trunks.

The remote job entry terminals or devices may use dedicated switched voice band trunks normally, resorting to public switched voice band in the event of a failure. Time-sharing terminals with the appropriate couplers may do the same. The administrative message switching terminals may be on dedicated narrow band trunks. Dedicated broadband trunks may be used between concentration nodes. The in-house time-sharing terminals may use the dedicated switched voice band, while the remote ones use the public switched form.

7-3 PUBLIC SWITCHED DISTRIBUTION NETWORK

The public switched distribution network is usually considered to include only the voice band trunks—the whole world and all of its telephones. While the greatest percentage of the public switched network is indeed voice band, the popular conception is somewhat erroneous, as it encompasses everything from narrow band through voice band and includes broadband as well.

For those networks where the terminals, or perhaps a single cluster of many terminals, are close enough to the information processing complex and usage and volume requirements are minimal, some form of public switched distribution may be more economical than a dedicated network.

The public switched distribution network can be structured into three distinct forms or classes, each of which is discussed in the following pages. They are: (1) narrow band; (2) voice band; and (3) broadband.

Public Switched Narrow Band

The two most commonly used forms of this facility are the TWX Teletypewriter Exchange Service, formerly owned by AT&T, and the

Western Union TELEX service, to use their original names. AT&T agreed to sell the TWX network to Western Union, and the transfer was completed in 1971.

The TWX service provides for direct dial-up connection between any two teletypewriter terminals in the network. Two classes were originally offered, one operating at 45 bits per second using the 5-level Baudot code, and the other operating at 110 bits per second using the 8-level ASCII code. Terminals operating at the two different speeds can communicate with each other via speed and code conversion equipment located at the common carrier's switching office. The information flow rate, however, is limited to the slower speed.

Terminals or source/destination devices other than teletypewriters can be interfaced with the TWX network through the use of an 811B subset or coupler. With this capability, called TWX CPE (Customer Provided Equipment), a network processor can interface to the TWX network and the 50,000 plus TWX terminals located in the U.S. and Canada. If TWX service is already being utilized within a company, it should be examined to determine if its continued use in the network via CPE will contribute to the network's optimization.

The most commonly used terminals in the TWX network are the Teletype Model 28 KSR (Keyboard Send and Receive) or ASR (Automatic Send and Receive) at 45 bits per second and the Teletype Model 33 KSR and ASR at 110 bits per second.

A TWX terminal may or may not be equipped to answer incoming calls and send its own identification code back to the network processor for verification. For those terminals not so equipped, an operator must press an "Answer" key to accept the incoming call and either type in the firm's name and identification or depress the "Here Is" key, which automatically sends out the identification code.

The Western Union TELEX network is very similar to TWX except that the transmission speed is limited to 50 bits per second using the Model 32 Teletype and the 5-level Baudot code. The service extends to the U.S., Canada, Mexico, and through the international carriers around the world.

Western Union provides the TELEX Computer Communications Service (TCCS), which is a computer system linked to the TELEX network, permitting the transmission of information from a TELEX terminal to another TELEX terminal or to a TWX terminal operating at 45 or 110 bits per second.

All of the above services are, of course, in addition to Western Union's traditional telegram service.

Public Switched Voice Band

For those distribution networks requiring a higher information flow rate than is available with narrow band but having a usage frequency and volume requirement that does not justify a dedicated voice band trunk, the public switched voice band trunk may be the optimum choice. The maximum information flow rate on these trunks is somewhat less than is possible with dedicated voice band at this time. However, AT&T, the Bell System and the independent modern manufacturers are working toward higher rates through the design and introduction of newer coupling devices.

Since this type of voice band trunk is switched, a dialing function is necessary to establish the connection between the appropriate source and destination devices. If the device is a terminal and is the originator or source, the dialing is usually accomplished manually by the operator. If a network processor is the originator or source, however, it must use a common carrier supplied Automatic Call Unit (ACU) in order to initiate a call on the trunk. Two versions of this ACU are currently in use—the Bell 801A, which is used in areas having rotary dial switching office equipment, and the Bell 801C, which is used when TOUCH-TONE switching office equipment is available.

Automatic Call Units are configured with varying numbers of dial-out channels dependent on the frequency and length of connect time required. Each dial channel in the ACU is connected permanently to a specific voice band trunk. Thus, a network processor with a requirement for ten dial-out voice band trunks needs an ACU with ten dial-out channels—one per trunk.

The number of dial-out channels required in a network processor is a function of the number of terminals to be reached in this manner, the frequency of dialing, the length of time (a function of information volume), and other factors. In networks where the number of dial-out channels required is greater than one but the average connect time is fairly long, it is desirable from a cost optimization viewpoint to provide a single dial channel that can be assigned to any of the voice band trunks. It remains coupled to that trunk long enough to complete the dialing function and establish the connection and then, under control of the network processor, is assigned to a different trunk to repeat the procedure. Such "floating" automatic call units are not currently available from the common carriers but are under investigation by numerous equipment manufacturers.

Terminals and other source/destination devices are usually connected to voice band trunks by analog couplers of some form (see Chapter 6).

The public switched voice band distribution network is available in a variety of forms, each with its own characteristics and rate structure. Network analysis is again required to establish which form or forms are necessary to provide the optimum grade or level of service. The more common of these are discussed briefly in the following pages.

Direct Distance Dialing (DDD). This service permits the direct dialing between any two nodes in the public switched voice band network—to or from terminals, network processors, or other source/destination devices. The charge for the service (over and above coupler and installation costs) may be a fixed monthly fee (assuming that no long distance calls are made), a message unit basis (number of calls and connect time), or a fixed fee plus any long distance charges incurred.

Foreign Exchange. This service provides a means of serving a remote cluster of terminals on a dial-in basis at something less than the cost of direct distance dialing. When a sufficient number of terminals exists in the remote cluster and the calling frequency and connect time result in long distance charge above a specified threshold, a foreign exchange trunk or trunks may be the optimum choice (see Figure 7-7).

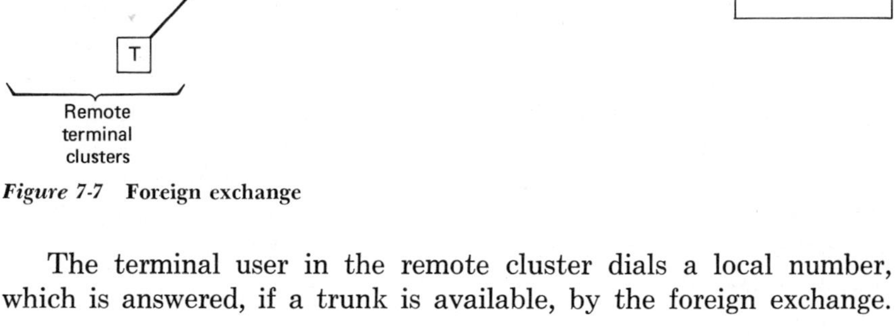

Figure 7-7 **Foreign exchange**

The terminal user in the remote cluster dials a local number, which is answered, if a trunk is available, by the foreign exchange.

From there, the information flow proceeds directly across the dedicated voice band trunk, through permanently switched connections in the local switching office of the common carrier, and into the information processing complex. The effect of the foreign exchange is to eliminate the long distance charges that would be incurred if the terminal user were to direct distance dial into the information processing complex.

Usually when the number of dedicated voice band trunks between the foreign exchange and the information processing complex exceed a relatively small number and if all the terminals are operating at 10 characters per second or so, some form of multiplexing (time or frequency division) will prove more economical than the foreign exchange. This is due to the use (in foreign exchange) of the dedicated voice band trunks capable of several hundred characters per second for a single terminal at a time operating at 10 characters per second. Another possibility that should be considered is the use of WATS lines, which are discussed next.

Wide Area Telephone Service (WATS). The WATS offering as provided by the Bell System is available in two forms: outbound or inbound. Outbound is used when a specific location has a requirement to place a relatively large number of outgoing calls to geographically distributed areas. Inbound provides the reverse capability, where the geographically distributed locations must call into the central or headquarters facility.

Calls on WATS are initiated in the same way as a normal DDD call, except that the charge for the service is a fixed flat monthly rate or a measured time-plus-overtime basis.

The WATS user is provided with a voice band trunk, called an access line, between his location and a Bell System central office. The user may place as many calls as desired on this trunk. Each WATS line is arranged to provide either outbound or inbound service but not both. The charge for the trunk is a function of the geographic area in which calls are placed, with the inbound and outbound rates being identical.

The geographic areas covered in each of the six WATS areas available range from the states bordering the user's state as area one to the other 47 continental states in the U.S. as area six. The user's home state is not included in the area six offering. Intrastate WATS is provided in most but not all states. WATS is not available in Alaska or Hawaii.

Public Switched Broadband Trunks

Public switched broadband facilities are fairly new and are not yet available at all locations within the U.S. Western Union has announced a service that is currently available for alternate voice and data communication in a full-duplex mode. Two bandwidths are currently available—2000 and 4000 cycles per second, which support 600 and 2400 bits per second, respectively. While these rates are within those that are attainable on public switched voice band, they are the initial offerings of the service that will eventually provide trunks operating at 48,000 cycles per second bandwidth, with a corresponding higher data or information flow rate.

The Bell System offers a public switched broadband capable of operation at 50,000 bits per second. In 1972, the service was available only between New York, Washington, D.C., Chicago, and Los Angeles.

CHAPTER 8

Switching

The definition of switching from Chapter 4 reads: *a means of physically establishing or altering the path of information flowing through a node in the network.* It is frequently desirable from a fail-soft or backup point of view, or as a result of economic optimization considerations, to interpose a switching function between network nodes such as terminals and network processor, network processors and information processors, or other combinations. Switching in this sense concerns the physical establishment or switching of the information flow through the node rather than logical "switching" as performed in an administrative message switcher or even in a remote concentrator. The network processors used in those forms are "active" devices capable of exerting some form of logical control over the information flowing through them. The switches discussed in this chapter are "passive" devices that are essentially transparent to the information flow.

For ease in understanding and applying the switching function to the specification of an optimum information network, the switching devices have been separated into two basic categories—line/trunk switches and reconfiguration switches. They are discussed separately in the following pages.

Figure 8-1 illustrates the position of switching within the tree structure, which is shown through Level V.

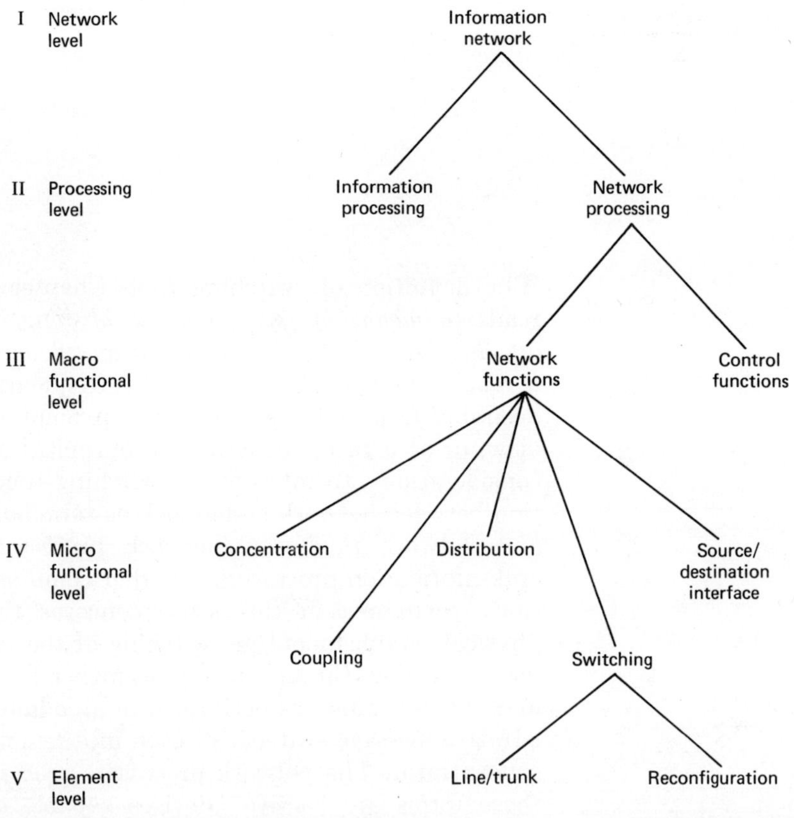

Figure 8-1 **Switching function**

8-1 LINE/TRUNK SWITCHING

Line/trunk switches are used to obtain a degree of optimization when it is necessary to provide a remote cluster of terminals with access to a network processor or information processing complex. They are of particular value when the cost of a single dedicated line from each terminal to the complex is prohibitive and, further, such a line is not required due to the low frequency and volume requirements.

Two types of switches are included in this category—automatic communications line switches and manual access switches.

Automatic Line Switching

These switches are placed in the middle of a cluster of terminals and are connected to the distant network processor by one or more trunks, as shown in Figure 8-2. Network analysis may indicate that,

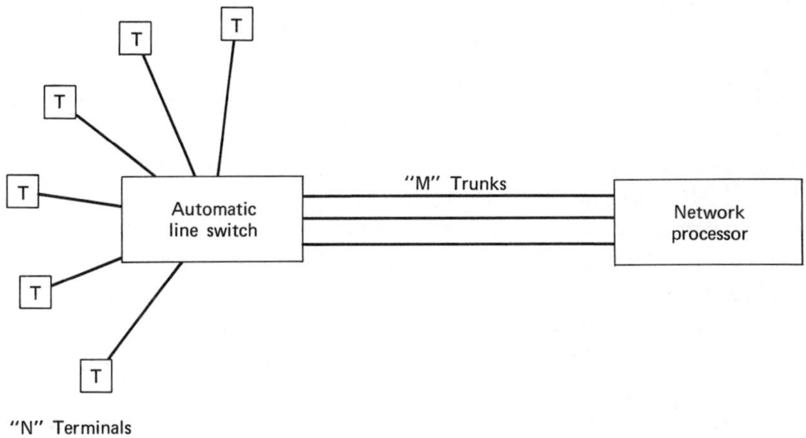

Figure 8-2 **Automatic line switching**

if "M" of the "N" terminals in the cluster can be active simultaneously, a satisfactory level of service is represented. The "N" terminals are connected to the switch by relatively short lines, and the switch is connected to the distant network processor by "M" dedicated trunks. The switch detects a request for access from a terminal, examines the trunks to determine if one is available, and switches the line to any available trunk found. This process is repeated until, at some point, all of the "M" trunks are busy. The "M+1" terminal that requests access is given an appropriate busy signal or similar indication, in which case the operator must try again later. When a terminal completes its interaction with the network and disconnects itself, the switch can reassign the trunk to another terminal that requests access.

In the simplest of these switches, the lines between the terminals and the switch and the trunk(s) to the network processor are all of the same type, operating at the same speed. More sophisticated versions permit a mixture of line types to connect the terminals, with dial-in and dedicated capabilities, varying speeds and disciplines, and a corresponding mix of appropriate trunk types to the network processor.

Automatic line switching can provide a degree of optimization within a cluster of terminals, usually at less cost than a programmable remote concentrator. Since the switch is a passive device, it is not capable of the active control or manipulation of the information flow that the programmable concentrator is. As a result of its transparency, all of the overhead associated with the terminals is moved to the controlling network processor. It should be noted that, while a line switch is a relay node and does resemble a centralized concentrator in function, it is, as defined in this book, not performing remote concentration. A remote concentrator uses a higher capacity trunk between itself and the distant network processor, while a line switch uses the same type of line on both sides.

Strictly speaking, the poll and select and contention forms of distributed multipoint concentration discussed in Chapter 5 are forms of line switching because the line used is capable of operating at the speed of the associated terminals and no faster. However, they are included there because the correlation to distributed multipoint concentration is greater than it is to line switching, which, as discussed in this chapter, is always centralized in form.

Contention (Manual Access) Switching

This type of line (Manual Access) switching is discussed in depth in Chapter 5, pg. 72, and is included here only to identify it as a form of line switching.

8-2 RECONFIGURATION SWITCHING

Reconfiguration switches are used not so much as a means of optimizing cost as for providing extended flexibility in an information processing complex. This flexibility provides a variety of functions, including switching lines from failed processors to the standby or backup, load leveling of information flow during peak periods, alternate routing at various times throughout the operating day, and other similar functions which require the ability to reconfigure the lines and trunks terminating in the information processing complex.

Reconfiguration switches are available in a variety of forms, but are grouped here into two major categories—those manually controlled and those program controlled.

Manual

In the simplest case, a reconfiguration switch is used to redirect the information flow from a failed network processor to a backup or standby processor so that service to the network is not interrupted for any longer than is necessary to accomplish the switch. This type of configuration is shown in Figure 8-3. All of the distribution net-

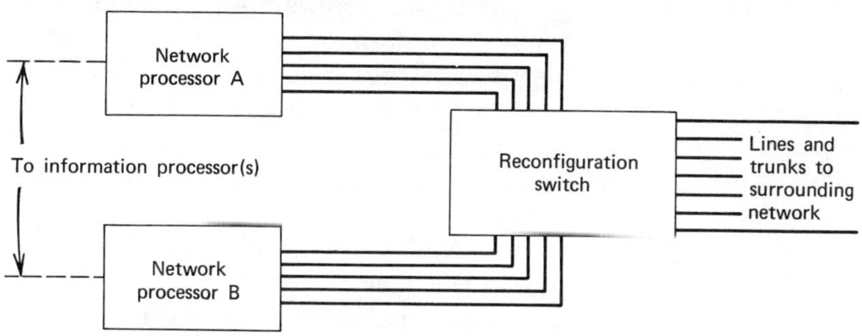

Figure 8-3 **Reconfiguration switching for backup**

work lines and trunks entering the complex are routed to both network processors through the reconfiguration switch. One of the network processors is designated as on-line and as such receives the incoming information flow and transmits the outgoing. The other is available and ready to take over in case of failure in the on-line processor.

When a failure occurs, network supervisory personnel must manually activate the reconfiguration switches to shift the lines and trunks to the standby. The standby processor may be in one of two modes prior to the failure—active or passive.

In the active standby mode, the backup processor copies or receives the information flowing through the switch at the same time as the one-line processor. It performs all of the same processing, queue management, and manipulation functions, with the exception that it does not transmit any outbound information. In this manner, an exact copy or mirror image of the files, queues, and network status tables is maintained in the standby processor. This obviously requires a completely redundant set of hardware, including mass storage devices, if configured on the active processor.

The biggest single advantage to be gained from an active standby processor is that it is ready to assume the load and initiate outbound transmission as soon as the reconfiguration switches are thrown by the supervisory personnel. The reconfiguration switch may be constructed in such a way that the active standby processor does transmit outbound information, but it goes to the switch and no further. In this case, throwing the switch simply enables the outbound information from the standby to reach the lines and trunks and disables the transmit side of the failed on-line processor.

In the passive standby mode, the backup processor is not copying the incoming information and is not maintaining mirrored files or queues. It may even be actively performing other functions such as software testing and debugging. In this case, it is necessary to load and start the standby processor with the appropriate software, throw the reconfiguration switches giving it access to the lines and trunks, and allow it to go through a restart and recovery procedure to get the network back into operation.

Obviously, in the passive standby mode, the time required to return to an operational status is longer due to the restart and recovery procedure required to change the passive processor's status to on-line. The queues and files of the failed processor are not available to it unless provision is made for switching the associated peripheral controllers, as well as the lines and trunks, to the standby processor. If, however, it is the mass storage subsystem of the on-line processor that has failed and the standby is passive, the restart and recovery must of necessity proceed without benefit of the files and queues.

It may be desirable in the active standby mode with fully redundant files and queues to provide the two processors with a handshaking capability that occurs periodically so the standby processor can detect a failure as soon as possible after it occurs and prepare to take over. It may even be the one to send a message to the supervisory control station indicating that the failure has occurred and the reconfiguration switch must be thrown.

The reconfiguration switch may be a single button that, when depressed, causes all lines and trunks to switch immediately, or it may consist of a separate switch for each line and trunk, each of which must be depressed individually. The switch, in either case, is multiple position so that the incoming lines and trunks can be connected to processor A or B or both. It may also include a separate switch position for the enabling or disabling of outbound information from A or B or both.

The multiple switch configuration, one for each line and trunk, has the advantage of allowing a portion of the lines and trunks to be switched to each machine. This may be the form of backup that is desired. Each processor can then perform all of the functions (receiving, processing, and transmitting) for the information flowing on the lines and trunks switched to it. In the event of failure of either processor, the other detects the failure through the lack of response to the periodic handshake, transmits an appropriate message to the supervisory control station, and, when the remaining lines and trunks are switched to it, proceeds with the necessary restart and recovery procedure.

While the single remaining processor may not be able to provide the same level of service to the terminals due to the number of lines it must now handle, it can at least maintain a somewhat degraded level, which may be sufficient until the failed processor can be repaired and placed back on-line. In this way, it is not necessary that the affected terminals be completely isolated and without service of any kind until repairs are completed.

The degree of interruption to the network and to the terminals that were active at the time of failure is a function of the type of backup that is provided. In general, the faster the recovery time, the more complex the hardware and software.

For a further discussion of redundancy, restart, and recovery, see Chapter 11.

A variation of the manual reconfiguration switch is shown in Figure 8-4. This manual reconfiguration switch is connected to several network processors, each of which may or may not be interfaced to an information processor. The switch can be used to direct the information flow between the lines and trunks of the network and any or all of the "N" network processors.

It may be desirable to switch certain types of lines to specific network processors dependent on the type of function that the lines and associated terminals or other source/destination devices are performing. An example might be the use of one of the network processors to perform the administrative message switching function while another is used to handle the time-sharing terminals in the network and still another is handling the remote job entry and inquiry/retrieval functions. Failure of a network processor in this configura-

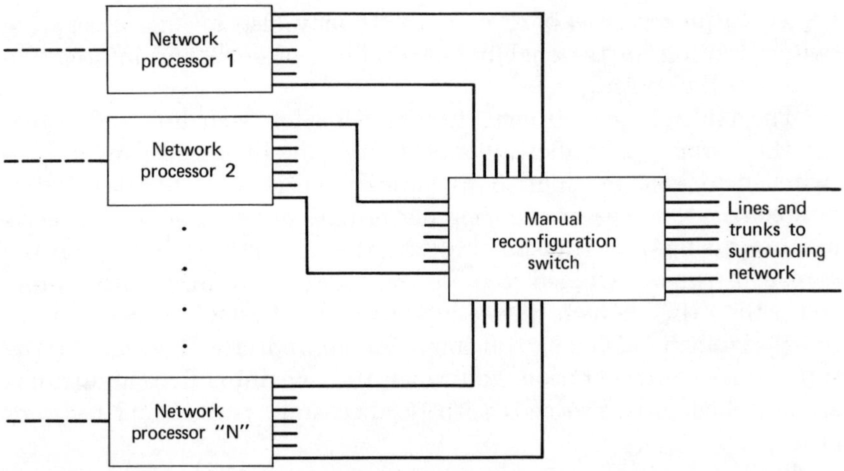

Figure 8-4 **Multiple processor reconfiguration switch**

tion results in its lines and trunks being switched to a designated alternate or standby where the load, perhaps at a degraded level, can be handled.

Another use of the switch configuration shown in Figure 8-4 is to provide a form of manual load leveling. The lines and trunks can be distributed among all of the network processors during the peak period of the operating day, perhaps the entire "prime" shift, and then reconfigured for the evening shift. This permits the use of an idle network processor and its associated information processor for other tasks or for scheduling preventative maintenance.

The lines and trunks terminating in the manual reconfiguration switch may include a variety of types, ranging from dedicated narrow band, dedicated and dial-in voice band, broadband, and combinations. Each network processor must be configured with the appropriate numbers and types of ports in order to accommodate the lines and trunks that are to be switched to it.

Program Controlled

Switches can be constructed to provide all the functions just discussed for manual reconfiguration switches, then placed under control of one or more of the network processors included in the configuration. Instead of being manually controlled or operated by the network supervisory control personnel, these switches are activated by the network processor.

This type of switch is desirable when it is essential that the reconfiguration be accomplished in the shortest possible time or if lines and trunks are to be reconfigured frequently during the operating day. Additional functions other than already discussed can be included in a program-controlled reconfiguration switch.

If it is not necessary that all the lines and trunks terminating on the outboard side of the switch be simultaneously active, a fewer number of ports may be configured in the network processor(s) to provide the desired grade or level of service. The network processor(s) can then accept incoming information selectively or on a first-come, first-served basis. It may be desirable to enable the network processor(s) to "busy-out" dial-in trunks on the switch. This permits a gradual, orderly shutdown of the complex by busying out the trunks as they go idle in preparation for the end-of-day procedure. This can also be used as a form of load leveling during peak periods of the operating day.

If dial-out capability through the switch is a requirement, the possibility of providing the switch with one or more dial channels that can be assigned to the desired trunk by the network processor should be explored. These dial channels can "float" across several trunks, remaining on a single one only long enough to accomplish the dialing function.

If a number of incoming trunks terminating at the switch are dial-in, it may be desirable to provide the switch with some form of holding capability. This allows the network processor to direct the switch to answer an incoming call and hold it until an appropriate port is available, at which time the line is connected to it. As soon as a previously assigned port disconnects, one of the trunks being held can be switched to it, thus speeding up the rate at which trunks can be assigned by overlapping the ringing and answering time.

Since a program-controlled reconfiguration switch is under direction of one or more network processors, provision should be made to prevent a failing or failed processor from locking up the switch and making it impossible for others to gain access to it for reconfiguration purposes.

Program-controlled reconfiguration switches are obviously more expensive than manual ones due to the greater complexity inherent in them. The fail soft or backup requirements of the network and the time allowed for restart and recovery procedures should be evaluated to determine which form of switch can be justified.

Some relatively small networks may require a single manual reconfiguration switch while other, larger networks will require the program controlled or perhaps a combination of both forms.

CHAPTER **9**

Source/Destination Interface

This chapter deals with the numerous characteristics, operating parameters, and disciplines that the great variety of terminals and other source/destination devices present to the designer of an information network. Some of these are logical considerations, while others are physical in nature. Rather than attempting to classify all of these devices in some tabular fashion, a functional discussion of the interface between the devices and the network is presented. This discussion is in the form of a list of considerations that a network designer should evaluate, as the particular combination of them inherent in the device being considered will have a definite impact on the hardware and/or software design of other elements in the network. The tree structure through Level V is given in Figure 9-1, showing the source/destination interface entry.

The topics discussed should be considered a guide which identifies the considerations important to the network designer.

CONTINUOUS/INTERMITTENT REAL-TIME

Some types of terminals are coupled directly to a single line that terminates in a network

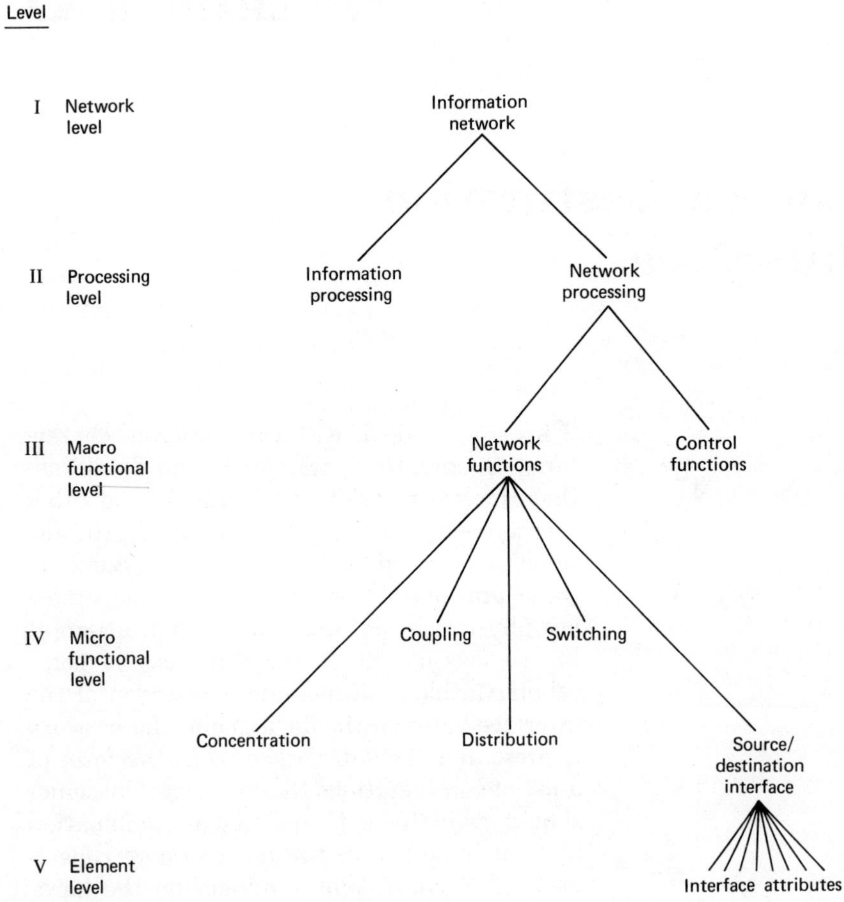

Figure 9-1 **Source destination interface function**

processor. An example of this is a teletypewriter in the same or an adjoining room, as the network processor it is connected to which is used as a supervisory network control station. It is the only terminal on the line and is capable of entering information directly without being polled by the network processor. Supervisory personnel simply type in the information at any time, and the network processor, therefore, must be ready to accept it at all times. The line discipline software in the network processor is slightly different for this line than for those lines interfaced to several terminals that must be polled and selected. Terminals interfaced in this manner can be considered as operating in continuous real-time.

Terminals operating in an intermittent real-time mode—poll and select, dial-in, dial-out—permit the network processor to exercise a greater degree of control over information flowing in the network. Under normal operating conditions—non-peak hours, no hardware malfunction or other condition causing a degraded level of service—the network processor moves information through the network as rapidly as possible, maintaining minimum queueing delays and response times. During peak hour conditions or in the event of a hardware malfunction that degrades the network's performance, it is frequently desirable to slow down or suspend some activities. The polling and selecting cycles can be slowed down, dial-in trunks can be placed in a busy status, dial-out activity can be suspended or slowed down, and other similar techniques can be used to relieve the network processor of a portion of its overhead momentarily until the peak period passes or the hardware problem is corrected. Terminals operating in the intermittent real-time mode lend themselves to this type of control more readily than those operating in continuous real-time.

Source/Destination

Some types of terminals are capable of acting as an information source and destination, while others are always a source or always a destination but not both. A teletypewriter used as a time-sharing terminal via the public switched voice band distribution network is an example of a terminal that operates in an intermittent real-time mode and is both an information source and destination. A Receive Only (RO) teletypewriter used as a network control logging device is an information destination only, as it cannot enter information into the network. Various types of factory feedback terminals containing card or badge readers at each work station are information sources only and are not capable of acting as destinations.

Evaluation of this consideration aids in identifying the software necessary to interface with the terminal—transmit, receive, or both—and also aids in the structuring of the numerous tables that must be maintained by the network processor. This table organization is important as many networks have combinations of all three possibilities—source only, destination only, and both—and the network processor must be able to determine if information has been entered to be sent to a device that is an information source only and is incapable of receiving.

Fixed/Mobile/Portable

All terminals and other source/destination and relay devices that can be addressed fall into one of these three categories.

A fixed device is one that is installed in a given location, coupled to a given trunk or line, and remains there for a relatively long time. The device's address can then be related, essentially permanently, to a specific line or trunk for use by the network processor in directing information flow to it. Thus, the device's location and line are always known, and information may be routed directly to it unless it has been placed on intercept or has an alternate destination designated to receive its traffic.

Mobile terminals present a significantly greater problem than the fixed variety. They may be teleprinters mounted in vehicles that are free to wander about the entire U.S. and still gain access to the network. Radio frequency couplers, distribution networks, and other facilities are provided in the cities or states where access is required, and it is only necessary that the vehicle be within range of any one of them to gain access.

In large nationwide networks which include this capability, it is necessary that the network processor(s) include the logic necessary to "keep track" of the terminals. This "keeping track" takes the form of maintaining and updating routing tables as the vehicle moves from one radio frequency relay node to another. For additional discussion of mobile terminals, see Chapter 10, pg. 141, Trunk Routing, Heuristic.

Portable terminals are those that are movable but still gain access to the network through a public switched or dedicated switched voice band distribution trunk. When these terminals dial in, they must be interrogated to establish their identity prior to being allowed access. Once a terminal is identified as valid, its input is accepted, and the network processor may also examine its files to determine if there is any information to be forwarded to the terminal while it is available.

In summary, fixed terminals do not move and can be reached at any time during the operating day as long as they are operational. Mobile terminals may request access from any number of locations and may, if so equipped, be reached through the use of a "Where Are You?" message sent to all relay nodes in the network by a network processor. Portable terminals cannot be reached until they initiate a request for access through a switched distribution network.

Coupling Technique

The various types of lines and trunks and the different kinds of terminals and other source/destination devices used determine what kinds of coupling devices are required. A network processor may have to interface with several types of coupling devices simultaneously, ranging from telegraph adapters on dedicated narrow band lines to several types of voice band—dedicated, switched, dial-out, serial/parallel—and on through one or more types of broadband.

Each type of coupler presents a different set of operating parameters and characteristics to the network processor. Several variations or options may exist within any given type of coupler, each requiring slightly different software. Each of the coupler types interfacing to a network processor should be evaluated along with its particular options to determine what software changes or alterations must be made.

Buffered/Unbuffered

Buffered and unbuffered terminals and other devices present the network processor with a variety of options when it is necessary to initiate a retransmission from one of them due to an error in the original transmission.

If the terminal is a teletypewriter with an operator at its keyboard, it is essentially unbuffered. When a character in error is received from it, possibly due to noise on the line or trunk, it is necessary that the network processor interrupt the terminal, then format and send a message to the operator asking for the retyping or retransmission of the last word, line, or block of information.

Most forms of cathode ray tube terminals utilize a controller that contains a buffer of some kind (delay line or other) in which the information is collected from the keyboard prior to transmission. At the end of a line, message, block, or other logical amount, a block check character is generated, appended to the block, and the whole block or buffer is transmitted to the network processor. Should an error occur during transmission and be detected by the network processor, a retransmission is required. This is initiated rather simply by the network processor, which sends a negative acknowledge and a request for retransmission back to the controller. The controller then responds by transmitting the buffer again. This procedure can be repeated until a valid transmission is achieved and does not involve the terminal operator.

Most of the newer terminal devices appearing today have buffering capability. This allows not only greater efficiency in utilizing the interconnecting line but will allow more terminals to be connected to a given line while maintaining the specified level of service to all.

Transmission of blocks of information between two networks processors is another form of buffered interface. Each processor generates the appropriate block check character or sequence for its outbound information and checks the incoming. Coded Acknowledge (ACK) or Negative Acknowledge (NACK) characters or sequences are exchanged between them to indicate successful or unsuccessful receipt of incoming information. Normally, a block of information is retained in the network processor's memory until an acknowledge response has been returned from the destination device.

Single/Multiple Speed

Network processors frequently encounter a single terminal or other source/destination device that is capable of multiple speeds. For example, some teletypewriters can operate at 10, 15, or 30 characters per second from the keyboard and 100 characters per second or more from the paper tape transmitter. It is necessary, then, that the network processor software be capable of associating the terminal's identification code with the appropriate ports that are required to interface at the various speeds.

Another example is a remote concentrator which uses a dedicated voice band trunk operating with a Bell System 201B subset (coupler) at 2400 bits per second as the information path to the central complex. When this fails, it can resort to a public switched voice band trunk using a 201A subset which operates at 2000 bits per second as a means of backup until repairs are made. The network processor at the central complex must include the dedicated 201B interface and the dial-in 201A interface as well as the supporting software to interface with the remote concentrator when operating in the backup mode.

Single/Multiple Code Set

Devices capable of more than a single code set are encountered in information networks. Remote concentrators accepting inbound information from a variety of terminal types may forward it to the central complex essentially as received. This results in the network processor at the complex being required to accept several code sets from the concentrator. It may translate them into a standard code prior to delivery to the information processor and similarly translate outbound information into the appropriate codes before sending it on to the concentrator.

A single device, the remote concentrator in the above example, appears to the network processor at the complex as a multiple code information source/destination. Appropriate software and/or hardware must be provided to handle the code sets occurring in the network.

It may be desirable, in the example, to move the code translation function out to the remote concentrator and configure the network such that the network processor at the complex always receives a single code. This would result in software and possibly hardware savings in the central network processor.

Error Detection/Correction

Relatively simple terminals such as Model 28 Teletypes provide no error correction or detection capability. More recent teletypewriters and other similar terminals generate and sometimes check a parity bit on each character. Still other terminals of the buffered type can produce block check or other "hash total" type characters for each outbound block and can check those appearing on inbound data. Newer developments include the use of forward error correction coding techniques that permit reconstruction of the invalid character(s) in the just received block, thus eliminating the need for retransmission.

Appropriate software and/or hardware is required in the network processors to utilize the variety of error correction/detection techniques that the terminals and other source/destination devices use.

Identification Technique

Terminals and other source/destination devices are provided with a variety of techniques for identifying themselves and/or the operator to the network. These range from answerback drums and discrete code generators to complex, multiple level interchanges between the operator and the network processor.

In networks where a high level of security is to be maintained to prevent unauthorized access, the identification technique chosen for implementation must be thoroughly evaluated and appropriate software specified.

Many teletypewriters are provided with an answerback drum that can be interrogated by a network processor. The drum is coded with twenty or more characters as specified by the user at installation time. When the network processor transmits the appropriate "Who Are You?" code to the terminal, the answerback drum is triggered and returns the information coded on it. The answerback is examined by the network processor to determine if it is valid. If it is, access is granted; if not, the terminal is disconnected. The answerback drum or other similar code generator identifies the terminal device only. It provides no indication that the operator using the terminal is cleared for access to the network.

Information and/or network processors that may be able to gain access to the network through the public switched distribution facilities are not equipped with answerback drums. They must be identified through the exchange of predetermined, coded character sequences which may be changed on a periodic basis. This requires appropriate software in the network processor(s) as well as tables of valid codes and a means of updating or changing the tables.

For a further discussion of identification, including operator validation, see Chapter 11, pg. 183.

Programmable/Operator Controlled

Since some types of terminals and source/destination devices are controlled by an operator and others are a form of processor under their own program control, the software required in the network processor(s) to maintain an effective interface varies considerably in complexity.

For operator controlled terminals, it is necessary to transmit a readable message in the appropriate language when asking for a retransmission, which is unnecessary from a remote concentrator. The former may require several words, while the latter may require just a few coded characters.

Considerably more complex control sequences can be exchanged between a network processor and a remote concentrator or other programmable device than between it and an operator controlled terminal. Generally, in the latter case, it is desirable to make the terminal operator's task as straightforward as possible to maximize speed and minimize errors. This usually presents a requirement for a fairly comprehensive set of error messages to be sent to the terminal operator at the appropriate time, spelling out in as much detail as possible the corrective action(s) to be taken.

SECTION IV

Control Functions–The Logical Network

This section, Chapters 10–15, provides an in-depth discussion of the control functions required to maintain the desired level of performance and optimization in the information network. While primarily concerned with the organization of software to provide the various control functions required, some degree of correlation with the network or hardware functions discussed in Section III is also necessary.

The control functions discussed in this section constitute the set of logical controls that are necessary to control the "physical" network discussed in Section III. These functions, when properly selected and implemented in the network processor(s), can be considered the "logical" network.

Many of the functions discussed are not so much "control" in nature as they are a technique or method to provide a capability within an information network. Examples of these are Chapter 12 on Journaling and Chapter 13 on Statistical Information Recording. They are included in this section in order to maintain the separation of function (hardware in Section III and software in Section IV) discussed in earlier chapters.

By using this section as a software roadmap, the network designer can select an appropriate set of software and control functions that, when interfaced with the hardware selected from Section III, will provide the desired set of capabilities within the resulting information network.

The software discussed in this section is entirely external to any information processor that may be configured in the information network. While functions similar to those described may be performed in information processors, the purpose here is to identify the "set" of network processor software and techniques available for use in optimizing the network processing functions of the information network.

A portion of the tree structure through Level IV is provided below in Figure 10-1 as a means of identifying the relative location of the control functions in the overall information network architecture.

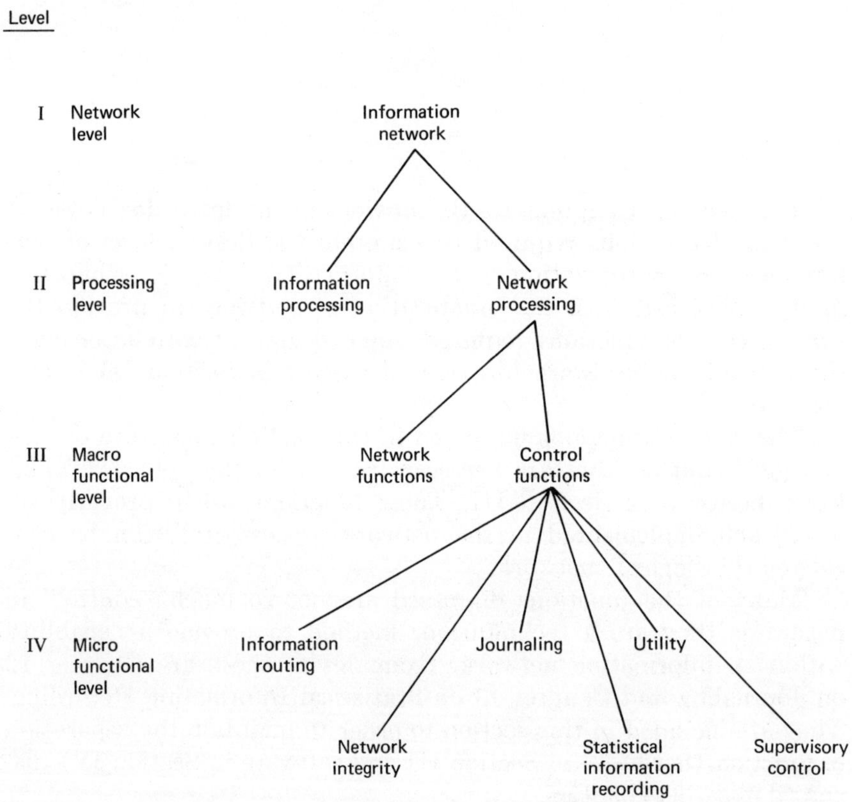

Figure 10-1 **Control functions**

CHAPTER 10

Information Routing

Information Routing includes those functions required to assure that information entered in the network is directed to the desired destination(s) within the specified priority sequence and time frame.

The tree structure through Level V is shown below in Figure 10-2 with a breakdown of Level IV Micro Function "Information Routing" into the six Level V elements.

10-1 ADDRESSING

Addressing is the way in which information is coded to indicate the destination(s) to which it is to be directed. Numerous techniques have evolved which provide considerable flexibility and also contribute to the ease of operation for terminal operators and users. Some of these techniques provide a means of optimizing the line and trunk usage of the network by avoiding the necessity of sending multiple copies of the same information when more than a single destination is indicated.

Every node in an information network that can be an information destination and/or source requires an identification code. The code may consist of a single character or a

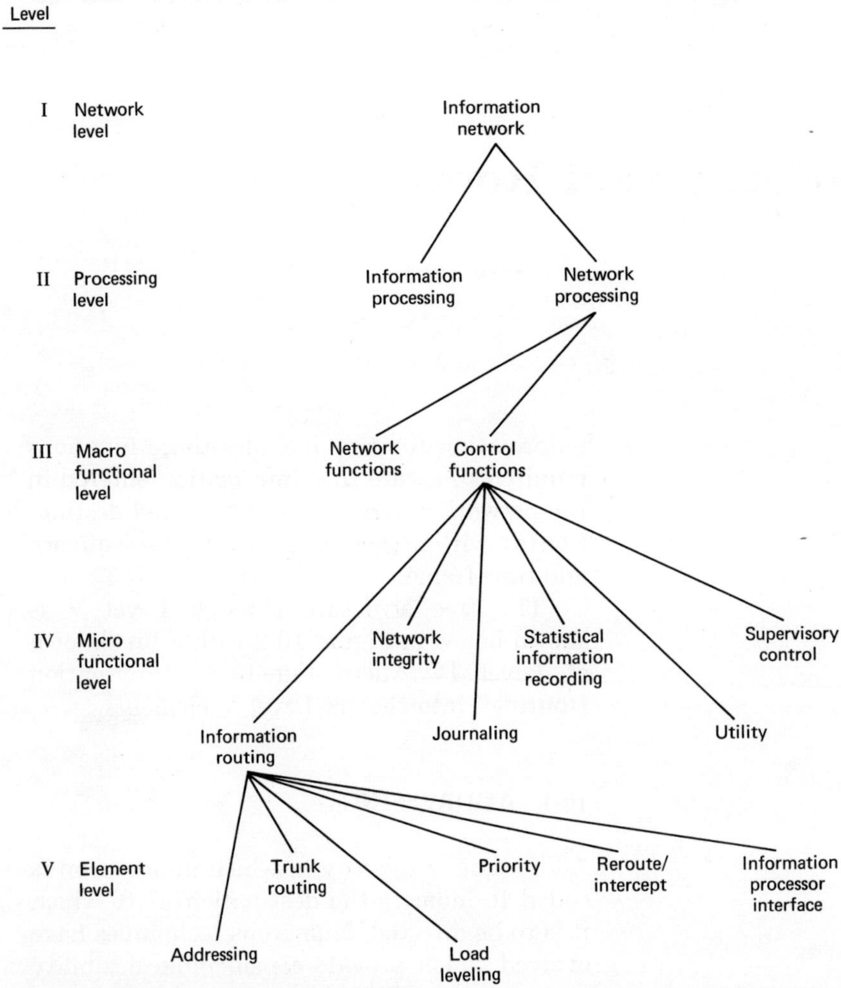

Figure 10-2 **Information routing function**

character sequence that uniquely identifies the node. The same code may be used to identify the node as the source of the information it enters and as a destination for information directed to it. In some cases, a different code is used for the source and destination designations.

There are five basic forms of addressing, which are the Level VI entries under the Level V heading "Addressing." They are shown below in Figure 10-3 and discussed further in following pages.

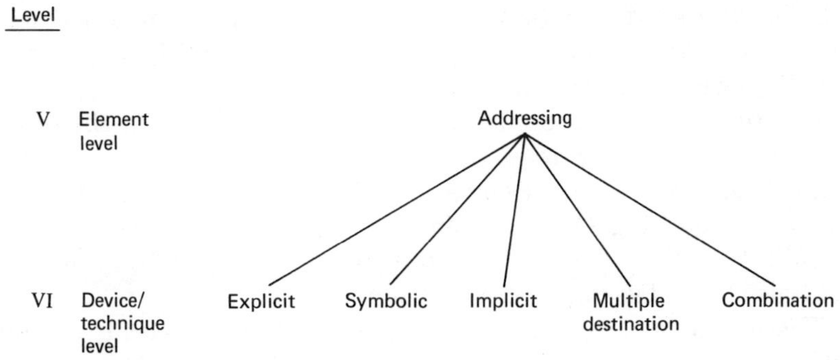

Figure 10-3 **Addressing function**

Explicit Addressing

In this form of addressing, the specific identification code of the intended destination(s) is/are included as a part of the information at the time it is entered into the network at its source. Only one terminal or other device in the network is assigned a given code.

Regardless of the form of the explicit destination code, it results in the information being directed to a specific destination device on a specific line or trunk. The code may be as simple as "1A," "1B," "1C" for destinations A, B, and C on Line 1, or it may be a higher level form. In networks where there is a single terminal or other device at each location or city, the code may be an abbreviation of the name of the location itself, such as "DET" for Detroit, "PHX" for Phoenix, or "LAX" for Los Angeles. In this case, the abbreviated destination code is converted to a specific device and line or trunk designation by the network processor.

It is desirable, if possible, to assign destination codes that are meaningful to operators using terminals in the network. The "1A," "1B," "1C" type of designation, while possibly simplifying the network processor software task, is much more difficult for an operator to associate with a desired destination than is the abbreviated location code. The pure abstract code will result in more misdirected or undelivered information because the terminal operator guesses rather than takes the time to look it up in the directory.

Symbolic Addressing

The "DET," "PHX," and "LAX" destination codes are a form of symbolic addressing. A meaningful symbol that is readily associated with the desired destination is not only learned and retained more rapidly by terminal operators but provides for considerably greater flexibility of information addressing.

In cities or areas where several terminals are located, the abbreviated symbolic codes may be expanded to include the city and terminal within the city designation—for example, "GAOPHX" for General Accounting Office Phoenix, "PAYPHX" for Payroll Office Phoenix, "WHSDET" for Warehouse Detroit, "DSODET" for District Sales Office Detroit, and many, many more.

These codes, like any others, are converted into a specific terminal and line or trunk designation by the network processor for delivery. Obviously, tables indicating the appropriate conversion must be maintained in the network processor(s) of the network. Provision should be made in the network processor software for the updating of these tables to reflect the addition or deletion of destination devices in the network.

It may be necessary, due to the volume of information directed to a specific destination, to provide more than one terminal at that location. The "WHSDET" symbolic destination code, for example, would then mean to deliver the information to any one of the several terminals located in the warehouse in Detroit. Groups of terminals in a given location, all having the same logical address, are known as rotary groups. Numerous other variations are possible with symbolic destination codes—for example, "IPRJE" means direct the information to any Information Processor in the network having Remote Job Entry capability.

In deciding to use extensive symbolic destination coding in a network, the designer should weigh the software required for code translation, the table maintenance and update problem, and other similar considerations against the benefits to be gained. If the adopted scheme is too involved and costly to maintain or is not used as extensively as anticipated, it becomes an unnecessary overhead or burden in the network.

In very large networks with perhaps tens of thousands of terminals, the table maintenance may become a different kind of problem, namely, fitting the necessary tables into the network processor to begin with. In this case, addressing and routing techniques that are not table driven must be explored. These techniques will use some form of logical destination code analysis to determine in which direction the message is to be directed. The first network processor to handle the message and each succeeding one will apply the same routing algorithm. The network processor that recognizes the destination code as belonging to a terminal that it controls will then direct the message to the specified destination.

Implicit Addressing

In implicit addressing, a specific or explicit destination code is not included in the information itself but is implied in one or more ways.

When a remote terminal is gaining access to the network through the public switched distribution network, for example, the information processor connected to the network processor that answers the incoming call may be the implied destination. This implication is a function of the number that was dialed from the terminal at the time access was initiated. One incoming number on the network processor may be assigned for this type of call, and another number may be assigned for other types. A network processor that is dialing out to a remote terminal is similarly using a form of implicit addressing. The destination is implicit in the number that is dialed. Obviously, after a dialed connection has been established, it is necessary that the initiating and responding terminals properly identify themselves.

Terminal devices that are permanently connected to the network via dedicated lines or trunks may also utilize implicit addressing. Information to be directed to the network's supervisory control station may not be explicitly coded as such; but by virtue of its format and/or content, it is identified as control information and directed accordingly.

The distinguishing feature of implicit addressing is that the destination code is not necessarily a specific or explicit code contained in the header of the information. It is implied by a switched network number or is implied by the type of format or content the information exhibits. The latter requires software in the network processor to evaluate or examine the information and deduce the appropriate destination.

Multiple Destination Addressing

It is frequently desirable to enter information once at a terminal and have it directed to several destinations rather than entering it once for each destination. Several forms of multiple destination addressing which provide this capability have evolved.

The first and simplest form requires that the code for each desired destination be included in the header of the information. These codes may be explicit, symbolic, or combinations thereof. It is the network processor's task to examine the multiple destination codes and convert them to specific line or trunk and terminal designations. Using this form, any terminal in the network is capable of entering information and specifying that a copy of it be sent to any possible combination of destinations. The translation tables maintained by the network processor should include an indication of the code set, ASCII, 4/8, etc., used by each terminal in order that the appropriate conversion can be identified and performed prior to the forwarding of the information to the destination. Additional destination device specific parameters maintained in the table include the line length, page size, form feed, and other similar control discipline indicators.

If the terminals or source/destination devices can be grouped logically by type, location, or some other characteristic, another more efficient form of multiple destination addressing can be used. Examples of such groupings are all district sales offices, all regional executive offices, the eastern region executive offices, the central region distribution centers, and others. A single code, sometimes called a group code, may be used to indicate each of these logical groups of destinations. The operator wishing to send a copy of the information to each destination in the group need only enter the single group destination code rather than the code for each individual destination.

If group destination code capability is included in the network, tables must be maintained indicating which terminals belong in each specified group and what their individual codes are. The information may be forwarded to the individual destinations with the group code destination designator so that the operator receiving the information is aware that it is a group message. When it is not desired that each destination be informed that it is receiving a group coded message, the group code may be changed to the individual destination codes so that the receiving operators are not aware that others have also received a copy of the information. This form of multiple destination addressing and delivery is sometimes referred to as "Book Addressing."

Multiple destination information codes may include one or more group codes and several individual explicit or symbolic codes when it is necessary to direct the information to larger numbers of destinations not covered by a single code. An extreme form of this is the inclusion of an "all stations" destination code to be used when every terminal in the network is to receive a copy of the information. A message sent to all stations of the network is also called a "broadcast" message.

It is the network processor's task to break the multiple destination coded information down and place a copy of it in the appropriate outbound queues. The network processor must also check for overlapping group codes so that a message will not be queued twice for the same terminal should it appear in two different groups. These queues may be maintained on a line basis or other similar organization. Some types of terminals can be equipped with a "stunt box" that recognizes one or more group select codes as well as the terminal's individual select code. With this capability, the network processor can select all of the desired terminals on a given line or trunk at once rather than sending a series of individual select nodes. In either case, it is desirable, from a line loading standpoint, to send a single copy of the information out on the line or trunk and have all the desired terminals receive it, as opposed to sending multiple copies on the line with just one terminal receiving it at a time.

Combination Addressing

Various levels of combination destination coding capability can be specified in an information network. For single station destination codes, a limit may be imposed which specifies the maximum number of codes that may be included in the information header. This limit may be a form of control to prevent the indiscriminant use of the multiple destination capability.

It may or may not be desirable to allow mixtures of single and multiple destination group codes in a single header. The single destination codes may be any of the acceptable explicit or symbolic codes. Due to the fact that the group codes may overlap—i.e., a single destination appearing in more than one group—care must be taken to recognize that such destinations may receive more than one copy of the information when multiple group codes are allowed in a single header.

The primary reason for permitting combinations of destination codes is to minimize the number of copies of the information that must flow in the network to reach all of the intended destinations. Ideally, the originating terminal is required to enter the information just once. There may be exceptions to this, however, due to the imposed maximum destination code limit, for example. If the originator wishes to send the information to 25 individual destinations that cannot be reached through the use of group codes but the network allows a maximum of 15 destination codes in the header, the information must be entered twice. The first header can contain the first 15 destination codes and the second the last 10. Both headers must be followed by a complete copy of the text or body of the information.

10-2 TRUNK ROUTING

Trunk routing concerns the selection or specification of an appropriate path through the lines and trunks of the network between the information source and destination(s). In smaller networks, the routing may be a fixed function of the line and trunk configuration with a single defined path existing between any information source and destination (see Figure 10-4).

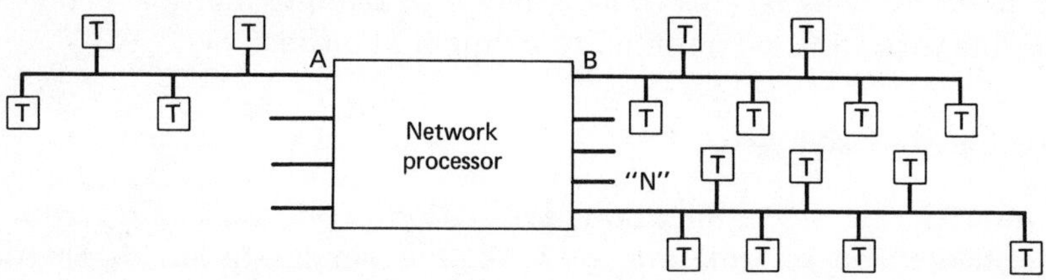

Figure 10-4 **Simple trunk routing**

In this illustration, information must flow from the terminal to the network processor and out on the appropriate trunk to the designated destination. If the trunk associated with the source or destination fails, there is no alternate routing possible. This illustration is typical of a small-scale administrative message switching network with several terminals on each trunk in a distributed multi-point fashion.

In larger networks, alternate trunk routing may be possible due to the trunk configuration. This capability may have been specified and implemented to provide a higher degree of network availability, as shown in Figure 10-5.

Figure 10-5 shows three network processors in different cities, each serving the cluster of terminals surrounding it and each connected to the other two by a suitable distribution trunk. At location C, an information processor is interfaced to the network via the network processor located there.

Information entering the network from a source in any of the three clusters can be routed to a destination in either of the others

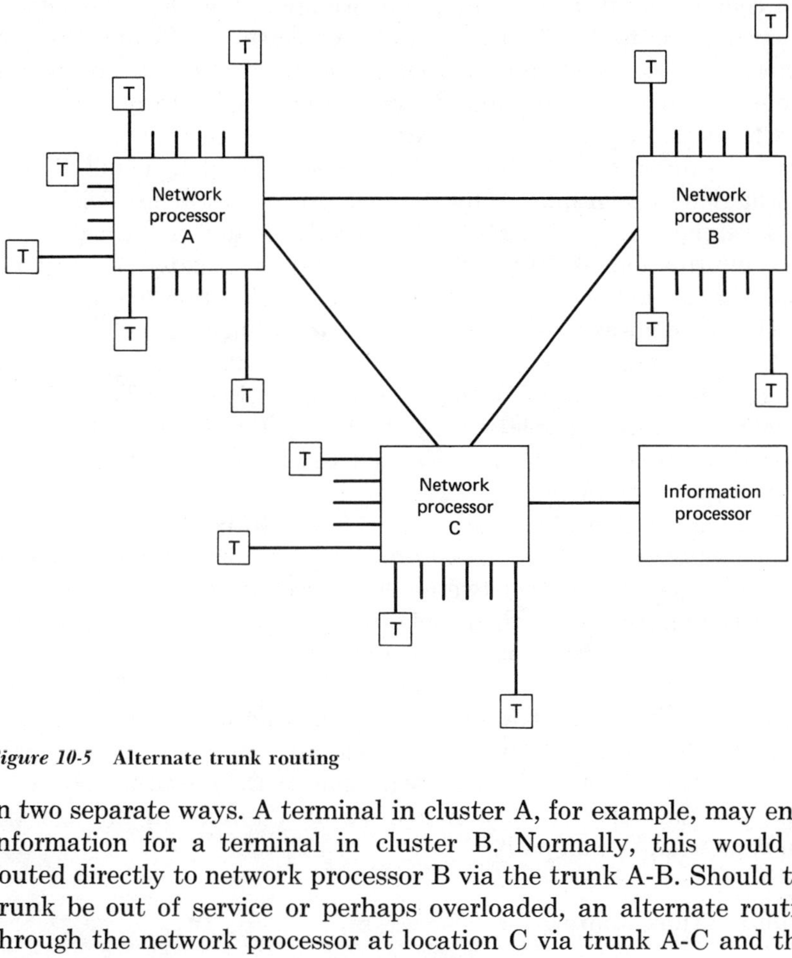

Figure 10-5 **Alternate trunk routing**

in two separate ways. A terminal in cluster A, for example, may enter information for a terminal in cluster B. Normally, this would be routed directly to network processor B via the trunk A-B. Should this trunk be out of service or perhaps overloaded, an alternate routing through the network processor at location C via trunk A-C and then on to location B via trunk C-B is possible.

In this configuration, any one of the three interconnecting trunks, A-B, A-C, and B-C, can be removed from service and communication still maintained between the three clusters. The time involved may be slightly longer due to the intermediate relay requirement, but service is maintained.

Several variations of trunk routing can be defined. A representative set of these is discussed in the following pages.

Explicit Trunk Routing

In explicit trunk routing, the trunk or line selected to deliver the information to its intended destination is determined by the destination code of the device. Assume, for example, that the terminals on the trunks connected to the network processor in Figure 10-4 are permanently coupled and will remain so until the configuration is changed. A terminal on trunk A enters information to be forwarded to a terminal on trunk B. The destination code is examined by the network processor and, through its tables, related to trunk B. The information is then queued by the network processor for delivery to the terminal when trunk B becomes available and/or all higher priority information on it has been delivered. The network processor maintains a complete table of all source/destination-to-trunk relationships and always directs information accordingly.

Each network processor in Figure 10-5 maintains a complete list of terminal-to-trunk relationships for those it services and a terminal-to-network processor relationship table for those terminals in the other clusters. Information is directed to its local terminals by the terminal-to-trunk tables.

For information originating in its cluster to be directed to a terminal in another, the terminal-to-processor table is examined to determine to which of the other two network processors it should be sent. The receiving processor then looks up the appropriate trunk designation and queues the information accordingly.

Normally, the network processor tables in Figure 10-5 are structured to minimize the trunk loads between network processors and minimize the routing delay times. When any one of the trunks fails, the two affected network processors change their routing tables to eliminate the failed trunk and redirect all information through the longer alternate trunk path.

Implicit Trunk Routing

In implicit trunk routing, the specific path to the destination is not designated or maintained in tables in the network processor but is an implied function of the destination code or type of information being transmitted. Dial-in and dial-out using a switched distribution network are examples of the former. The number that is dialed implies a specific destination. The actual route through the switched network to the destination is unknown and unimportant so long as the call is completed and the destination reached.

Some types of information can be recognized by a network processor through an examination of the format or content. Information entered at any source that is to be directed to the supervisory Network Control Station (NCS) is one example. The coding in the header indicates that the information is of a control type, which implies that the destination is NCS. The network processor that first examines the information routes it by the most expedient path to that destination. If only one such path exists, it will be used every time. When more than one path exists, the least busy one is utilized to assure the earliest possible arrival time at the destination.

The distinction between implicit and explicit trunk routing and the corresponding forms of addressing is not always clearly defined. Analysis of the coded header of the information by a network processor is required to identify the specific destination and possibly the trunk routing to be used. In networks containing numerous relay or concentration nodes that are cleared to different levels of security, for example, explicit routing may be specified and maintained to assure that information of the higher security classifications is not routed through a relay node of lower clearance.

Heuristic Trunk Routing

This form of trunk routing is required in those networks containing mobile or portable source/destination devices. These terminals gain access to the network from a variety of locations in such a way that the maintenance of fixed routing tables is impossible. Consider the network shown in Figure 10-6 as an example. The network is nationwide, with network processors at each of the five relay nodes shown. With the dedicated trunks shown connecting these nodes, information can be routed from any source to any destination by a variety of routes. Each relay node includes a radio frequency distribution network used to interface with mobile terminals mounted in vehicles. These mobile terminals may stay within a specific city and always interface with the same radio frequency distribution network, or they may travel between two or more of the cities. Information entered from a mobile terminal to be directed to a fixed destination (teletypewriter, information processor, or other) is routed in an explicit or implicit manner using appropriate tables in the network processors. Information entered to be directed to a mobile terminal requires a different approach.

If the mobile destination is known to be always in the vicinity of a specific relay node and its associated radio frequency transmitter, the information is routed directly to that node where it is queued. The next time the terminal requests access at that node, the information is delivered.

If the terminal is known to travel between two or more nodes,

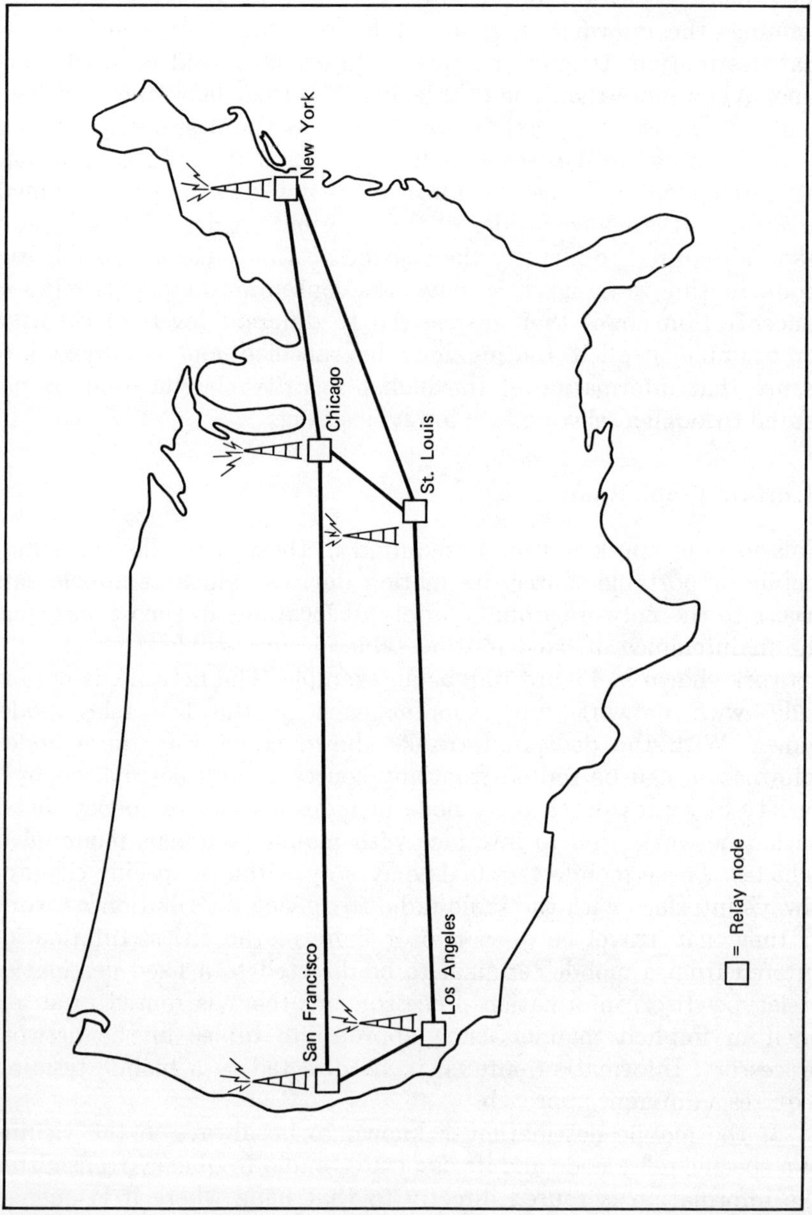

Figure 10-6 **Network supporting mobile terminals**

that node which accepts the incoming information may queue it there and send a message to the two or more possible nodes indicating that it has information for the specified terminal. When the destination terminal gains access through one of these nodes, a message is sent to the node holding the information in queue, indicating that the terminal has been contacted. The information is then directed to the appropriate node for delivery to the terminal through the radio frequency transmitter.

If it is possible for any mobile terminal to gain access through any relay node, the above technique must be expanded accordingly. It is usually more efficient for the node which accepts the incoming information to queue it and send a short message to the others indicating that it has information for a specific terminal than to send copies of the complete information to all of them. This reduces the amount of information transmitted between nodes and queued at all of them and provides a corresponding reduction in mass storage requirement for the queues.

When the desired terminal has been located and the information forwarded to the appropriate relay nodes for delivery, the other node must be notified of the action and instructed to cancel the terminal locator request.

It is possible to equip the vehicles containing the mobile terminals with a device which aids in locating them. When it is necessary to get high priority information directed to the terminal, a message is sent to all possible nodes requesting them to locate the terminal. Each node, through its associated radio frequency transmitter, broadcasts a specific signal that, if the vehicle is in range, results in the return of an answerback to the node, thus locating the vehicle and terminal.

The use of portable terminals in the network, illustrated in Figure 10-6, presents a similar problem. These terminals access the network by dialing in to one or more of the relay nodes through a switched distribution network. Information is entered and, if the destination is not a fixed terminal, queued at the node until the destination is located. The network processor accepting the incoming information sends the appropriate request for location to the other nodes and awaits a reply. Portable terminals must initiate a request for access before they can be located, since they use a switched distribution network.

Portable terminals may range from acoustically coupled teletypewriters as used for time-sharing to small acoustically or inductively coupled, battery-powered devices. The latter may be used by traveling salesmen to enter the preceding day's order information. Information directed to these terminals may be in the form of audio or voice answerback words since they may not include hard copy capability. In this case, each of the nodes in the network must include the appropriate voice generator or voice response equipment if it is to be used with these types of terminals.

The network processors in networks that include mobile and/or portable terminals must be provided with appropriate software logic and queueing capability to manage the information flow between the source and destination terminals efficiently. Sufficient mass storage must be included to queue the incoming information until the destination has been located. Software logic to generate, execute, and cancel location requests is required. Alternate routing paths between relay nodes for backup capability may be a requirement. The network processors are required heuristically, or in a self-teaching manner, to maintain the appropriate routing tables and change or update them as terminals move from one relay node to another.

10-3 LOAD LEVELING

Many forms of load leveling can be implemented in an information network to reduce the delay times that may occur due to peak periods of activity or the failure of some element in the network. Load leveling may be manually initiated by network supervisory personnel at peak periods or when the overload is recognized, or the network itself may initiate it when a predetermined overload threshold is reached. Similarly, when the overload condition passes, the supervisor may enter a coded message to restore the network to its normal state, or the previously overloaded network processor may restore itself automatically.

The network shown in Figure 10-6 can be used as an example for a discussion of load leveling. Assume, in addition to the mobile and portable terminals discussed earlier, that each relay node services a number of fixed terminals on dedicated lines and trunks. Several varieties of load leveling are possible.

If a particular relay node reaches an overload condition and is servicing a number of distributed multipoint trunks in a poll and select manner, the polling cycle can be lengthened—i.e., longer time delay between successive polls—or suspended completely for a brief period of time. This permits the network processor at the node to apply a greater portion of its processing time to the already in-route information in order to clear it out so that normal polling can be resumed.

If the portable terminals are gaining access to the network through switched trunks, the answering rate of incoming calls can similarly be slowed down. If equipped with the appropriate coupler or switch, incoming trunks can be "busied out" so that calling terminals receive a busy signal instead of a no-answer, the latter of which causes them to wonder if the network is up and running at all.

If multiple network processors are provided at each relay node for backup purposes and the backup is idle or passive, it may be brought to the active state and assume a portion of the load. This requires an appropriate line/trunk switch between the network processors and the terminated lines and trunks.

Heavy volumes of information flowing between New York and San Francisco through the Chicago relay node in the example may result in an overload. The Chicago relay node may request that a portion of the information flowing in each direction be routed through the St. Louis node until the overload period is over. Thus, information would then flow from San Francisco to Los Angeles through St. Louis to New York, bypassing the overloaded Chicago relay node. While the time required may be somewhat longer than normal, it is less than that required to go through Chicago during the overload period.

In networks with multiple levels of priority assigned to the information flow, delivery of lower level information may be slowed down or delayed and only higher level service maintained until the overload period ends.

A load leveling requirement may exist in an information network for one or both of two basic reasons—either the information flow in the network itself has overloaded one or more relay nodes, or the load at a specific source/destination node has grown beyond a predetermined threshold.

The load leveling discussed so far has concerned information flowing from a source terminal to a destination terminal in the network. If two or more of the destination devices in the network are information processors interfaced to it through the network processors at the relay nodes, additional load leveling possibilities may exist.

If the information processors are providing a multidimensional capability such as remote job entry, time-sharing, and local job entry and the network relay node that feeds one of them becomes overloaded, it may be possible to divert a portion of the information flow to one of the others. Remote job entry tasks that do not require access to a specific data base or file in a specific information processor can be executed by any information processor capable of the function. The movement of files between information processors is possible but may simply add to the overload condition due to the volume of information involved.

Time-sharing programs entered into the network to be compiled and executed but, having no specific file requirement, may similarly be directed to any less heavily loaded information processor complex and/or relay node.

The load leveling philosophy adopted for the information processor(s) in a network is a complex problem by itself and is beyond the scope of this book. However, to the extent that it influences the associated network processor(s), the problem cannot be considered independently. While the network processor(s) may contribute to the handling of overloads within an information processor, the converse is not always possible.

If a manual form of load leveling is chosen, the means for detecting the overload and informing the supervisory personnel must be included in the network so that appropriate action can be taken. This may include the specification of volume and/or maximum delay time parameters that the network processor(s) monitor and take action on when these are exceeded. Supervisory messages are then entered, indicating the appropriate action to be taken. Similar indication is given when the overload condition passes and a return to normal operation is desired.

If the automatic or dynamic form is chosen, the network processor(s) must include, in addition to the detection capability, the logic necessary to implement the appropriate leveling function, inform the supervisory personnel of the action, and return the network to normal operation when possible.

10-4 PRIORITY

Many classes of information networks require only a single level of priority for information flowing in them. If information volumes are low enough and response or delay time tolerances high enough, then information routing in a strict first-in first-out manner is satisfactory. In these networks, there is no information so urgent that the maximum delay time anticipated for its delivery is unacceptable.

In other networks, due to the extreme urgency or rapid response time requirements of certain types of information, the normal delays encountered may be intolerable. For them, two or more levels of priority may be required.

In these multiple priority networks, several levels of consideration exist. Once the necessary number of priority levels has been determined, it must be decided if all terminals and source/destination devices in the network will be permitted to use all levels. It may be desirable to limit certain types or classes of terminals to a lower portion of the priority groups, limiting the use of higher, more urgent levels to specified terminals such as the network control supervisory station(s).

If the use of priority levels is restricted in some such manner, provision must be made to handle incoming information which has a priority level outside those designated for the originating terminal. The message, or a portion of it, may be returned to the originator with instructions to restate the intended priority level, or the message may be accepted and forwarded at the highest level that the originator is allowed to use.

The tendency in multiple priority level networks for users and operators to enter information at higher levels than actually necessary frequently becomes a problem. Eventually, in a two-level system, the "rush" queue becomes the "normal" queue, while the "normal" queue is essentially unused and empty. This can be overcome to some extent by performing a context analysis on the information header and identifying certain types of messages that, by definition, need not be above a certain priority level. The network processor can then allow these kinds of messages to be forwarded at any level of priority up to, but not above, the defined maximum, regardless of the priority designation included in the header.

The degree of urgency for higher levels of priority must also be decided on. Normally, for all but the highest priority level, any message transmission that was initiated prior to the appearance of a higher priority level message in the queue is completed before the higher priority message is started outbound. It may be a requirement that, as soon as information of the one or two highest priority levels appears in a line or terminal queue, any in-progress outbound messages of lower priority are interrupted prior to completion. The higher priority information is then started outbound immediately.

This interrupt level can also be specified in a number of ways. The current line of information may be completed so that, when the message is restarted, it begins with a new line, or only the current word or even character may be completed before the interruption. In extremely high urgency stations, usually in government or military networks, the current character is interrupted if possible so that the high priority information can be started almost instantly.

The network processor must be capable of capturing and retaining the position and status of the line or trunk prior to the interruption, so that the interrupted message can be resumed after the higher level information has been delivered. It may be necessary, depending on the urgency of the interruption, to back up and retransmit a portion of the message that was interrupted. This would require an appropriate flag or indicator inserted in the message, warning of possible duplication.

Some types of terminals operated in a poll/select mode can indicate that a normal or high priority message is waiting to be sent. The network processor then polls the higher priority indicators first and accepts any incoming messages before the lower or normal priority messages are accepted.

Another problem occurring in multiple priority networks involves lower level information that remains in queue for excessively long periods due to the volume of higher priority information ahead of it. Limits can be defined for each priority level indicating the maximum time that information is to remain undelivered in the queue for that level. When information has "aged" in a specific queue for the specified time and is still undelivered, it is automatically moved a level or more higher in priority and requeued. Depending on network conditions and the number of priority levels involved, information may "age" through several priority-level queues before actually being delivered. A statistical record of this aging should be maintained by the network processor for use in analysis and possible redefinition of the parameters.

The aging times should be carefully studied and specified to avoid the situation that can occur during the network's busy or peak information flow period. If the aging parameters are too short, then, as queueing delays increase during the peak period, more and more information is aged through higher priority level queues, which by definition will be delivered first, until all information winds up in the highest priority queue. Separate aging parameters may be necessary for the normal and for the peak volume periods. The network may detect the transition between peak and normal periods and switch parameters automatically, or the supervisory personnel may enter the appropriate control message to initiate the change.

10-5 REROUTE/INTERCEPT

It is frequently necessary to interrupt or inhibit the normal flow of information through a network. Terminals, lines, trunks, and other hardware elements may fail or become temporarily inoperative. Networks covering several time zones will have portions of the source/destination devices shut down for the evening on the east coast, while those on the west coast remain in operation for several hours. The use of a reroute and/or intercept capability greatly facilitates the management of information in the network during these periods.

Reroute

Rerouting involves either the alteration of the normal path of the information between its source and intended destination or the designation of an alternate destination that it is to be delivered to. The illustration in Figure 10-6 can again be used as an example.

Assume that a terminal in a cluster serviced by the Los Angeles relay node enters information to be routed to a destination serviced by St. Louis. Normally, the information would flow directly between the two relay nodes, which represents the most expedient routing. Should the connecting trunk between the two become inoperative or the load on it become excessive, rerouting can be used to forward the information to its destination within a reasonable time frame. The reroute would consist of delivering the information first to San Francisco, where it would be forwarded to Chicago and then to St. Louis, thus preserving a grade of service, even if somewhat less than desired.

The reroute may occur automatically if the network processors include the logic necessary to recognize the need and implement the function, or it may be manually initiated by network supervisory personnel.

Another form of reroute involves the designation of an alternate destination. Assume that, at some location in the network, several terminals are located within the same room, floor, or building. If one of the terminals is inoperative for an extended period, it is usually necessary to provide some means of retrieving the information in queues waiting to be delivered to it. If an appropriate terminal is in close proximity to the inoperative one, the information can be rerouted to it and hand carried to the designated destination.

Rerouting to an alternate destination may be used at the end of an operating day for a group of terminals in a building. All but one of the terminals may designate the remaining one as an alternate when they shut down for the evening. The remaining terminal is kept operational for the remainder of the network's operating day, or possibly continuously, and receives any information still in queue to be delivered to the shut-down terminals. In this way, the information is available the next morning, the terminals do not have to request the undelivered information when they start up, and it is not necessary to keep all of the terminals operational all night.

This form of reroute can also be accomplished automatically provided the network processor(s) have the list of alternate destinations available, or the designated alternate can be manually entered by supervisory personnel.

Intercept

For those instances when the normal information routing must be interrupted and it is not practical or desirable to designate an alternate destination, some form of intercept capability must be included. Intercept implies that the information is not delivered to a destination device but is retained in a suitable intercept queue someplace in the network for delivery at a later time.

Terminals that must be removed from service for a brief period so, for example, the paper, preprinted form, or ribbon can be changed, can enter a control message requesting that information to be delivered to them be held until the change is completed. The network processor maintaining the queue for that terminal effectively places its information in an intercept queue. When the terminal completes its change and is ready to accept information, a second message is entered requesting that it be removed from intercept and the information be delivered.

Another use of the intercept function is to retain information to be delivered to a terminal which has shut down for the day. At the end of the day, the terminal enters a control message indicating it is shutting down and that any undelivered information or information that appears later is to be held in intercept. When the terminal starts up the following morning, it enters a message indicating that it is ready and will accept any information in the intercept queue.

The intercept function may be applied for reasons other than holding information to be delivered to unavailable terminals. Intercept queues may be maintained for the storage of incomplete information or information that must be corrected by the originator before it can be delivered. This may be more efficient than discarding a lengthy message due to an error and requiring the originator to reenter it in its entirety after it is corrected.

Information entered at a security level above that for which the designated destination is cleared to receive may also be placed in an intercept queue. An appropriate message must then be generated informing the network supervisory personnel of the action and asking for disposition instructions.

10-6 INFORMATION PROCESSOR INTERFACE

The interface between an information processor or processors and the surrounding network is critical to the overall efficiency and success of the information network. This interface is frequently a source of severe problems due, among other things, to the manner in which the requirement evolved, as discussed in Chapter 2.

Two basic modes have evolved and are currently employed to interface information processors to their surrounding networks—single or multiple line controllers and front-end network processors. To the extent that information processors with single and/or multiple line controllers attached must act as their own network processor, much of the following discussion applies to them as well as to the front-end network processor.

The following discussion provides a functional description of the more commonly used information-to-network processor interface techniques. The relatively simple one-to-one configuration is described first and is then followed by numerous extensions and variations.

The tendency to consider the information processor/front-end network processor interface as a master/slave relationship can lead to the design of less than optimum configurations. While early systems were frequently configured this way (both in hardware and in software), more recent developments and techniques suggest that the two should be treated as equals.

The information processor should be free to go about its tasks with a minimum of interruption and interference from the front-end network processor. The passage of information into it, whether directly to core memory or through a shared disk subsystem, should proceed at a rate controlled by its own operating system. Certain types of highly interactive programs, requiring rapid response or turn-around times, may demand that a high level of attention be scheduled.

This level of freedom can result if most of the terminal-specific software procedures are removed from the information processor and performed in the appropriate network processor, either front-end or remote.

The front-end network processor should be similarly allowed to direct its own activities concerning information flow from the surrounding network. The interaction with the information processor for the passage of information and control sequences should occur within the priority levels established. Information going directly to core memory within the information processor may require an access request that will be granted when the memory area is available. Information passed through a shared disk file can usually be written to the file without such a request and simply appended to the queue being constructed.

The normal flow of information between an information processor and front-end network processor is usually sufficient to confirm their mutual operational status. During periods of relative inactivity, it may be desirable to pass periodic "Hello" sequences across the interface to maintain a status check. Failure of either processor to respond to this check serves as notice to the other that a failure has occurred. At this point, the appropriate restart/recovery procedure can be initiated.

Additional discussion of the various combinations of information and network processors is contained in Chapter 5, Centralized Concentration, which deals with the front-end network processor as a form of centralized concentrator, while the current chapter is concerned with its function of interface between the information processor(s) and the surrounding network of information source/destination devices. The diagrams are repeated here to stress the two different functions being performed by the network processors—a form of centralized concentration and an interface between the information processor(s) and the surrounding network.

Single Information Processor

The interface between a single Information Processor (IP) and its single front-end network processor is illustrated in Figure 10-7.

The two processors are usually directly connected by a cable and

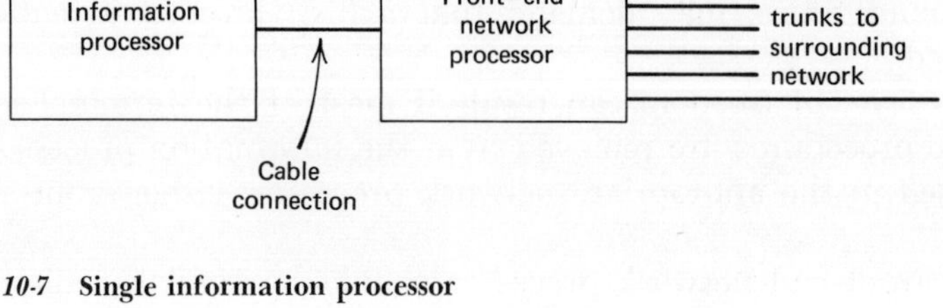

Figure 10-7 **Single information processor**

are not normally more than 50–100 feet apart. Information flows between the two over the cable at rates sometimes approaching the core memory speed of one or the other. The incoming (to the IP) information may be placed directly in core memory or may be routed through an input/output channel similar to those used for peripheral devices like magnetic tapes or disk storage subsystems. This configuration is the "I" example discussed in Chapter 5.

It is the network processor's responsibility to provide the information processor with an efficient and flexible interface to the surrounding network. Proper evaluation of the required functions will determine which processor can more optimally perform them. The separation of function philosophy developed in Chapter 3 must be applied if any reasonable degree of optimization is to be achieved. The information processor should perform those functions that it was designed for; the network processor should do the same.

As its sole link to the outside world (the surrounding network), the network processor can provide the information processor with a number of capabilities that can contribute greatly to its overall throughput and performance characteristics.

The network processor acts as a buffer between the information processor, capable of handling thousands of characters a second, and the terminals, operating at tens or hundreds of characters per second. By collecting logical blocks of information and forwarding them to the IP at much higher speeds, the network processor reduces the overhead involved in collecting incoming information.

The network processor can assume all of the various line, trunk, and terminal interface disciplines involved, convert the information to a single unified form, and with appropriate identification information included, present it to the information processor. Incoming code sets may be converted to that used by the information processor, with preliminary editing, terminal identification, and verification completed and a host of other essentially overhead functions performed. Ideally, the network processor can cause the variety of terminals in the network to appear as a single type or style.

An advantage of the front-end network processor over the multiple line controller is its ability to continue functioning and maintain an interface to the connected terminals even though the information processor has failed or is no longer operational. This simplifies the restart procedure from the terminal operator's point of view by eliminating the need to retransmit information in progress when the information processor fails and its associated multiline controller suddenly stops functioning due to lack of control.

In general terms, the front-end network processor performs three basic functions: the direct interface to the surrounding network and terminal environment; the buffering of inbound and outbound information between the information processor and the network; and the management of the information flow between itself and the information processor.

Since the single cable is the only connection between the two processors, the information routing is fixed and varies only in the direction it moves. The information processor appears as a single information source/destination node to the network processor and presents its associated interface parameters to it as do the lines, trunks, and terminals on the other side.

Multiple Information Processors

A single network processor may provide a complex of several adjacent information processors with an interface to the surrounding network, as shown in Figure 10-8. This is the "radial" configuration mentioned in Chapter 5. In this configuration, a cable connection exists between the single front-end network processor and each of the "N" information processors. Numerous possibilities exist for the divi-

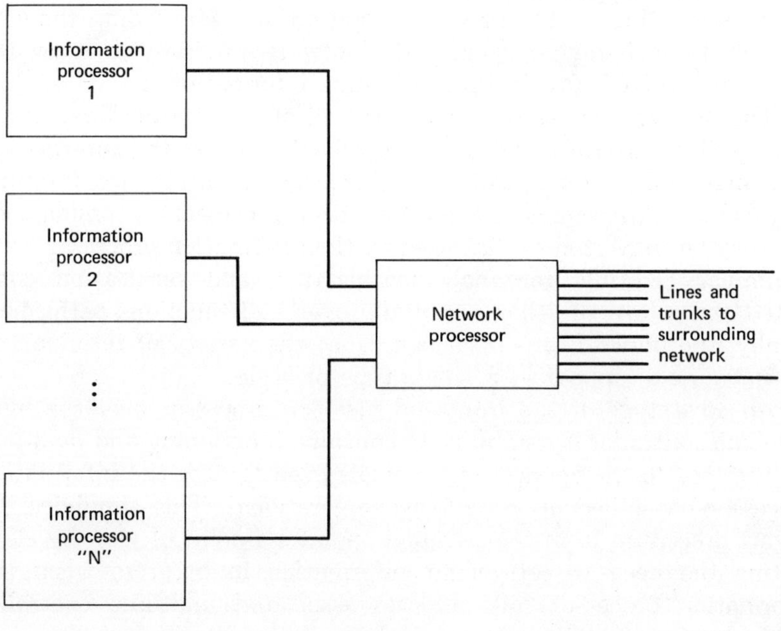

Figure 10-8 **Multiple information processors**

sion of functions and tasks between the information processors. The network processor is supplied with the logic to identify and maintain the appropriate interfaces between the information processors on the one side and the network on the other.

When the load and network interface requirements of the individual information processors in the complex are not sufficient to justify a separate front-end network processor for each and it is desirable to provide for an interchange of information between them, this "radial" configuration may be an optimum choice. The separate software and overhead problems associated with the use of multiple line controllers on the information processors is avoided, and performance of the complex as a whole is improved.

The information processors on the one side of the network processor appear as "N" information source/destination nodes with their associated parameters, and as such, the information routing to them may be either fixed or variable. In fixed routing, certain types of incoming information or the information flow from specific types of lines, trunks, and terminals are routed to specific information processors and the associated paths do not change. In variable routing, incoming information is routed to the information processor with the lightest load, perhaps as a form of dynamic load leveling, or may be routed on some other changing basis.

It is possible to use a single network processor as the front-end for several information processors produced by different manufacturers. Currently, this usually requires specially designed hardware in either the information or network processor or both. Since the network processor is frequently the more flexible of the two, consideration should be given to placing the special interface hardware in it. This simplifies the interface from the information processors' side by permitting them to retain a standard hardware and possibly software position. Frequently, the network processor with its special interface hardware and software can be made to appear as an already recognizable interface or device, such as magnetic tape or disk storage subsystem, to the information processor.

"Y" Configuration

As a means of improving the interface between an information processor and its front-end network processor, a mass storage subsystem can be included as shown in Figure 10-9. The mass storage subsystems most frequently used are rotating disks or drums capable of storing from several thousand to several tens of millions of charac-

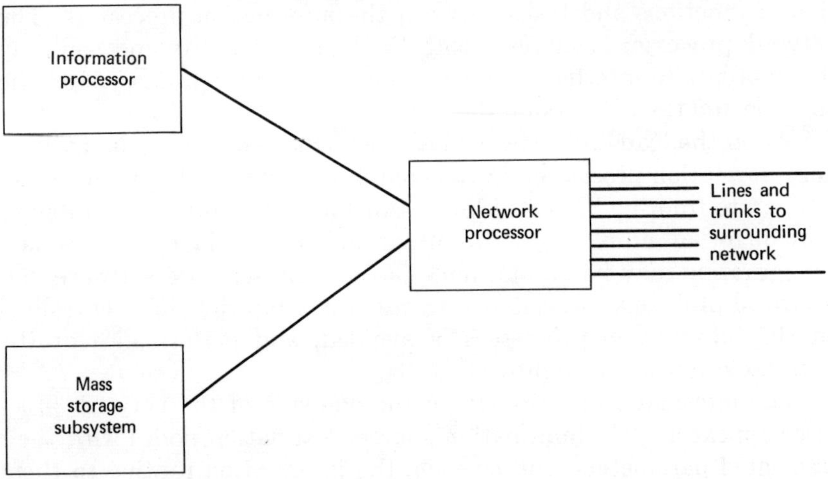

Figure 10-9 **"Y" configuration**

ters. These are connected to the network processor as a peripheral subsystem through an appropriate interface.

In addition to the software necessary to control the network on one side and the interface to the information processor on the other, the network processor must include the logic necessary to maintain the various inbound and outbound queues in the mass storage subsystem. Additional discussion of the "Y" configuration is contained in Chapter 5-1, Centralized Concentration.

"Delta" Configuration

In the "Delta" configuration, the interface to the network processor and the network is more deeply integrated into the information processor than in the other configurations. Access to the mass storage subsystem by both processors, as shown in Figure 10-10, while requiring additional software in the information processor, greatly facilitates the queue management problem by further reducing the associated overhead. Inbound and outbound information need only be handled once, as compared to twice in the "Y" configuration.

The bulk of the information passed through the two processors goes through the mass storage subsystem rather than through the cable connection. The cable connection is used primarily for relatively short control type information that indicates the status of queues in the file—complete and ready for processing, complete and ready for

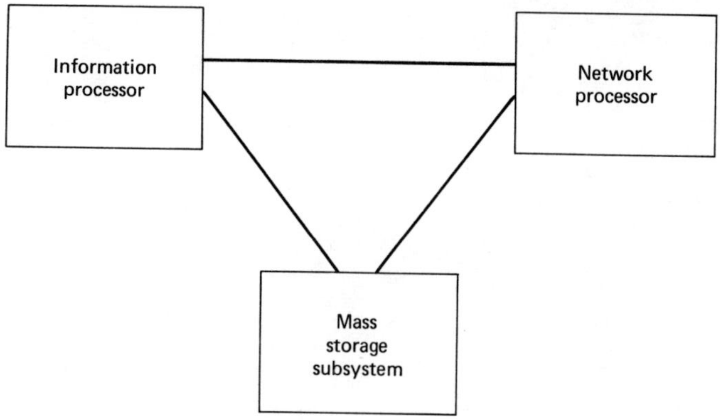

Figure 10-10 **"Delta" configuration**

delivery to the destination, incomplete, and others—which greatly reduces the queue maintenance overhead in both processors.

Additional discussion of the Delta configuration is contained in Chapter 5-1, Centralized Concentration.

CHAPTER 11

Network Integrity

Network integrity includes those functions necessary to insure that the information in the network is delivered accurately without distortion or errors introduced during distribution, that the failure of one or more hardware elements can be adequately detected and an appropriate restart/recovery procedure initiated, and that only authorized terminals or source/destination devices and operators are granted access to the various levels of the network.

The tree structure through Level V is shown in Figure 11-1, with a breakdown of the Level IV Micro Function into the three Level V elements.

11-1 INFORMATION INTEGRITY

Information integrity is concerned primarily with the accuracy and validity of information flowing between information sources and destinations in the network. This includes a number of Level VI functions, which are listed in Figure 11-2 and described in the following pages.

Error Detection/Correction

Many techniques, both hardware and soft-

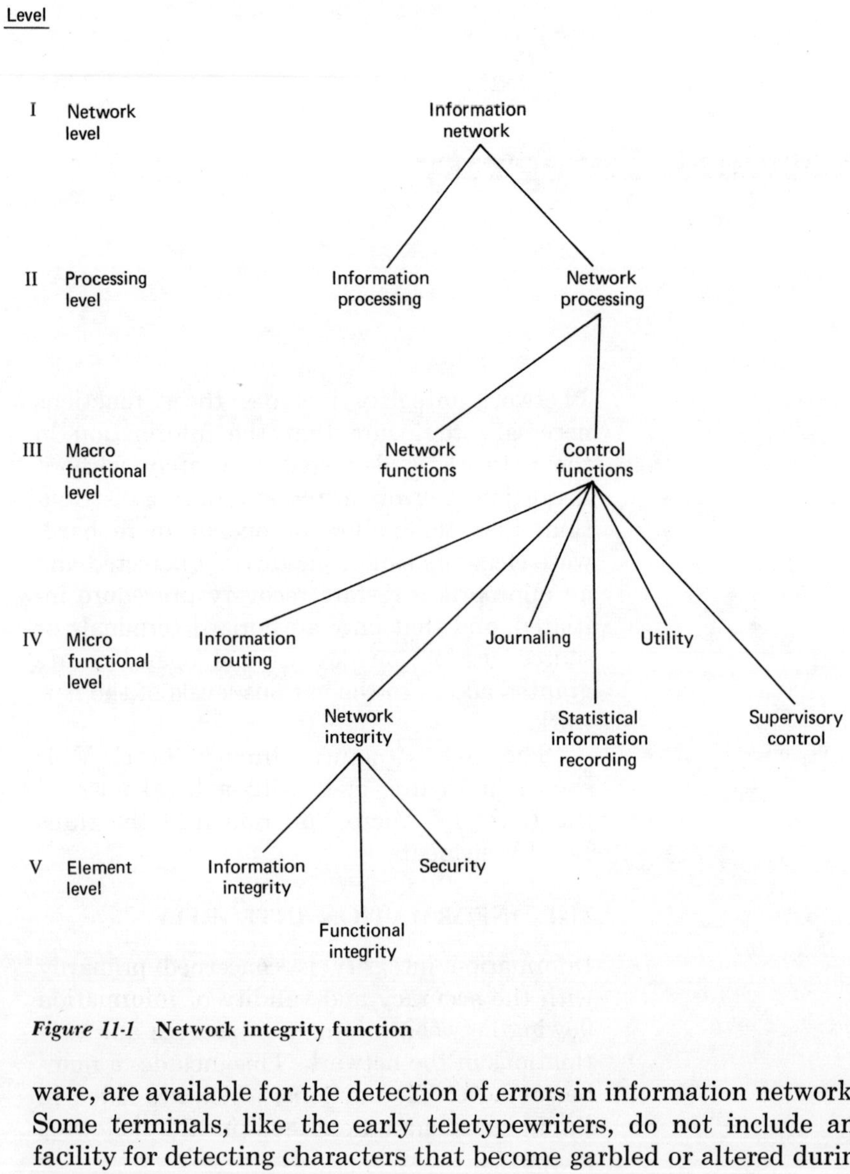

Figure 11-1 **Network integrity function**

ware, are available for the detection of errors in information networks. Some terminals, like the early teletypewriters, do not include any facility for detecting characters that become garbled or altered during transmission unless the resulting altered bit configuration is one not currently being used. It is frequently left up to the terminal operators to examine received information and, if a character or set of characters appears faulty or out of context, request a retransmission.

Later developments have produced terminals and other source/

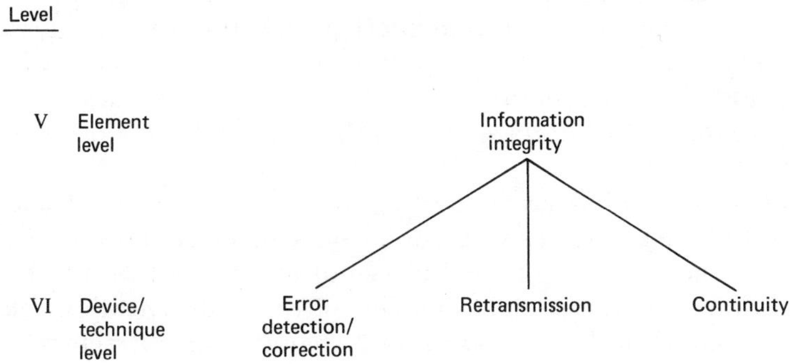

Figure 11-2 **Information integrity function**

destination devices capable of producing a parity bit included as a part of each character transmitted. The parity of the character is either even or odd. In even parity, if the information bits of the character had an even number of one bits, the parity bit is set to a zero; for information bits with an odd number of one bits,, the parity bit is set to a one also, thus maintaining the even parity. The total number of one bits, including the parity bit in an even parity character, is always an even number. For odd parity schemes, the reverse is true, with the total number of one bits, including the parity bit, always an odd number.

Source devices then generate characters of even or odd parity. Destination devices, when receiving the information, check each incoming character for the appropriate parity condition. If the destination device is receiving an odd parity character set and one character appears with even parity, an appropriate signal is produced, indicating that an error has occurred somewhere between the information source and destination.

Some source/destination devices maintain a single parity, even or odd, for all information and control characters in the set. Others use one parity for information characters and the other for control characters. In this way, the receiving device is given a signal that a character of the alternate parity has been received; and before being discarded or treated as a faulty information character, it is checked to determine if it is a control character.

Depending on the type of source/destination device, the parity generation/detection function may be performed entirely by the hardware or by the software or by a combination of both. Terminals such as teletypewriters usually rely on hardware parity generation and detection, while programmable devices such as network processors may use pure software or a combination of hardware and software. For complete flexibility, network processors should be capable of generating and detecting both even and odd parity, as they are frequently required to interface with both types of source/destination devices.

More sophisticated source/destination devices capable of operating in a buffered mode can be equipped with error detection techniques that handle whole logical blocks of information rather than a single character at a time. The simplest of these involves the generation of a "block check" or "hash total" character or characters to be appended to the transmitted block of information. These block check characters are derived through an appropriate algorithm that is applied to the information block.

The destination terminal similarly generates a block check character, using the same algorithm, as it receives the information. If the block check character it generates matches the one appended to the block by the source device, the information was probably received correctly. If they do not match, an error occurred somewhere between the source and destination devices.

It is possible to implement both character parity and block check error detection techniques in a source/destination device. The block check sequence assures that the block was transmitted properly. If it is in error, the individual characters can be examined to determine which one is in error.

Newer devices are being produced that include a "forward error correction" code capability. This technique involves the use of an algorithm on the block of the information to be transmitted, resulting in a forward error correction code that is transmitted with the information. The receiving device, through analysis of the received information block and code, can reconstruct or correct the error, thus eliminating the need for retransmission. Block check and forward error correction codes will not detect excessive multiple or compensating errors in information streams.

Retransmission

When an error is detected by a receiving device and forward error correction capability is not included, it is necessary to go back to one or more preceding sources or transmitters and request a retransmission. Depending on the type(s) of source and possible intermediate relay devices, the retransmission request can assume many forms.

If the source device is a keyboard operated teletypewriter with character parity and the information is being typed in by an operator, it may be necessary to generate and send a request for the retyping of the word or line of information containing the incorrect character. The software complexities of identifying the specific word containing the incorrect character to the operator are usually such that the identification of the line it occurred in is accepted as satisfactory.

If the information is being entered from a paper tape transmitter on a teletypewriter and an error is detected, the tape must be stopped and a message generated and sent to the operator. This message requests that the tape be examined and, if found satisfactory, backed up to some appropriate starting point and reentered.

Numerous other types of errors can occur on devices using a paper tape transmitter. Usually, the tape is prepared off-line and mounted in the transmitter when complete. When the device is polled, or when the operator initiates the transmission on gaining access to the network, the tape is allowed to enter and the operator may leave that terminal to attend to others during the transmission. Occasionally, as the tape passes through the reader or transmitter, it sticks in such a manner that the character under the read station is transmitted over and over. The receiving network processor must recognize this problem, interrupt the transmission, and format and send a message to the terminal operator requesting that the tape be fixed and reentered.

Another similar malfunction occurs when the end of the tape containing the designated end-of-message code is either torn off accidentally prior to transmission or was never included. The network processor must recognize the incorrectly terminated message and initiate the appropriate retransmission request.

Incorrect information received from a buffered source device requires a different retransmission technique. Usually, with buffered devices, an Acknowledgement (ACK) is returned if the information was received correctly, and a Negative Acknowledgement (NACK) is returned if received incorrectly. The ACK may be interpreted as the signal to send the next block, while the NACK is a request to send the current block again. This interchange between source and destination devices is usually an automatic hardware function and does not require the generation of lengthy messages sent to the operator requesting manual intervention.

Following a predetermined number of retransmission attempts from a source device, if all remain incorrect, the network processor generates an appropriate error message and forwards it to the network supervisory terminal informing the operator of the condition and location of the malfunctioning terminal.

Continuity

To guard against lost or misdirected information in the network, some form of message continuity check is required. This check frequently takes the form of a sequence numbering technique for incoming and outgoing messages.

All source devices in the network may be required to include a sequentially assigned number in the header of all information entered. The network processor maintains a table of incoming sequence numbers by source device and does not accept the information unless it contains the expected number. If the terminal operator attempts to skip a number, a message is returned indicating what the expected number is. The operator must then check to determine if the attempted sequence number is in error or if the message containing that number was prepared but never entered.

Similar tables of sequence numbers can be maintained for outbound information. Each message delivered to a destination contains a sequential number that should be one greater than the last message received. Terminal operators can verify the sequence number and, if one is found missing, can enter a request for the message containing the missing number to be retransmitted.

It may be necessary to maintain several levels of inbound and outbound sequence numbers. For example, several different groups of users using a common terminal may wish to keep separate inbound sequence number charts to avoid confusion. Separate inbound sequence numbers for each of the priority levels may also be advantageous.

Outbound sequence numbering by priority level for each terminal may be required as well as separate numbering of single and multiple destination messages. If outbound information to a specific terminal contains a sequence number for each priority level, these numbers very quickly become different, as the percentage of information directed to the terminal at each level varies. When the terminal receives information as one of several destinations on the same line or trunk—group code select, for example—a separate sequence number is required if continuity to all destinations is to be guaranteed.

11-2 FUNCTIONAL INTEGRITY

The functional integrity of the network involves those steps required to detect the failure of hardware elements and initiate an appropriate action. Depending on the desired availability of the network, various levels of hardware redundancy may be specified and included in the design. The Level VI entries in the tree structure under the Level V entry Functional Integrity are shown in Figure 11-3.

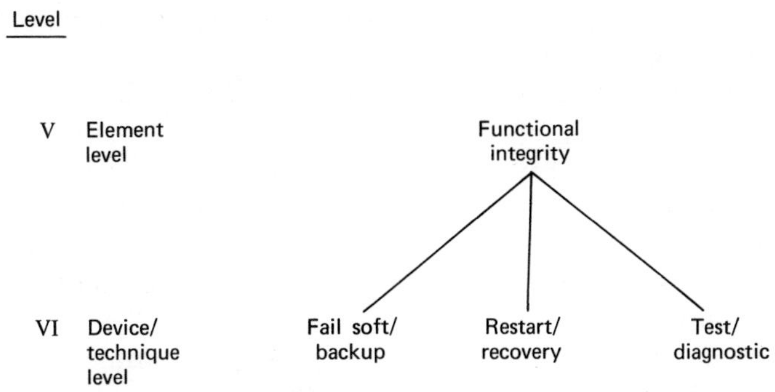

Figure 11-3 **Functional integrity function**

Fail Soft/Backup

In networks with a high availability requirement, it may be necessary to include significant fail soft and/or backup capabilities. These may range from the ability to reconfigure the network using the remaining operational hardware such that a reduced or degraded level of service is maintained to a completely backed up or redundant configuration capable of fully maintaining the original specified level of service.

The level of availability required influences the hardware selection at all levels, ranging from the source/destination devices and their associated couplers, to the distribution network (the relay or concentration nodes, multiplexors, and network processors), to the various types of switches, and on to the information processors.

If a given location must have an operational terminal available at all times, it may be necessary to provide a second or redundant device. This device may be fully operational and on-line at all times or may be idle and ready to be put into service when required. The greater the number of on-line devices at a given location, the higher the probability that at least one of them will always be operational. Software is required in the network processor(s) to accept and implement the alternate destination routing that is necessary when one of the terminals fails.

The method of coupling the devices to the distribution network also influences the selection of a backup capability. Mobile terminals that must be backed up require a second device capable of interfacing to the same, or possibly an alternate, subchannel in the radio frequence distribution trunk. Portable terminals coupled acoustically or inductively to a switched distribution network, while not requiring much in the way of additional hardware, do require the appropriate alternate destination routing software.

Fixed terminals coupled directly to a switched distribution network via a subset and, as such, having an assigned destination code or phone number, require either a second fully duplicated device on a separate phone number or a separate device that replaces the inoperative device on its number. The time required to make the switch in the latter case may be a limiting factor in the decision to use that form of backup.

Backup of the distribution network presents a similar set of considerations. Dedicated narrow and broadband lines and trunks must usually be duplicated if full backup is required. It is possible in some instances to use a form of switched distribution network as backup for dedicated lines and trunks. Some networks such as ARPA provide inherent backup through the use of the alternate routing capability. If a terminal normally operates on a dedicated voice band line or trunk which fails, it can be switched to a dedicated or public switched facility provided that the network processor(s) also have access to the switched distribution facility. Software must be provided in the network processor to accept the incoming information from the source device on the switched network instead of the dedicated line or trunk it previously occupied.

For the various forms of in-plant distribution networks, it is usually easier to duplicate the line or trunk in the original form than to attempt the use of a different form for backup. The great variety of in-plant distribution networks and combinations possible preclude an in-depth discussion of their backup possibilities.

Backup of the various forms of concentration or relay nodes in the network must also be considered. Normally, with high availability requirements, alternate routing capability must be included in the network to provide a way to keep much of the network operational should a relay node fail. If the relay node is servicing a cluster of local terminals in addition to acting as relay for other distant clusters and backup for the local cluster is required, duplication of the relay node device may be required.

For centralized time and frequency division multiplexors, standby units can be provided and used to replace the failed device. This replacement may be manual, with the lines and trunks being physically moved to the standby unit and operation resumed. If the normal mean time to replace the unit physically is unacceptable, it may be necessary to provide a form of reconfiguration switch as described in Chapter 8, Reconfiguration Switching. With such a switch in place, it is only necessary to depress or throw the appropriate switches to effect the replacement.

The backup of the various network processors in the network is another key element in assuring high availability. If the time to move the lines and trunks to the backup processor physically is unacceptable, reconfiguration switches, either manual or automatic, are required. Reference to the diagrams and text in Chapter 5, Centralized Concentration, and Chapter 8, Reconfiguration Switching, will provide the reader with an insight into the relative magnitude of the backup and switching problems to be evaluated in specifying a high level of availability. Due to the large number of ways in which network processors and/or network/information processor complexes can be configured, an in-depth discussion of all of them is not provided here.

In general, any level of backup in a network requires the inclusion of an appropriate set of software in various network processors. This software ranges from the ability to detect a given terminal accessing the network through an alternate line, trunk, or relay node to adjusting the routing tables accordingly. At the other extreme is the logic required in an active standby network processor to detect failure of the on-line processor and initiate the reconfiguration through a program controlled switch.

Network Reliability. A consideration that will greatly influence the selection and configuration of backup or redundant network elements is that of reliability. While this consideration is more appropriate to the design of information networks than the definition presented here, it is of value and will be covered briefly.

Every element of an information network will have an associated statistical number which is a guideline to its reliability. This number is called the Mean-Time-Between-Failure, or usually just MTBF. The MTBF is typically expressed in hours or some other unit of time.

The MTBF of an element is a statistically derived guideline expressing the number of hours the element can be expected to function before it fails. The confidence level associated with such statistically derived MTBF's is increased with the passage of time. Statistics collected through the observations of installed, operating elements are compared with the predicted MTBF. Significant deviation from the predicted MTBF is usually cause to reexamine the design of the element to determine which components are contributing to the early failures.

The confidence level of the MTBF for relatively new elements is lower, then, due to the lack of sufficient observational data with which to confirm the prediction. Older, more established elements with tens or hundreds of thousands of hours of operation will exhibit MTBF's with very high confidence levels. Newer technologies and production techniques are being incorporated by manufacturers in their designs, one desired result being a higher MTBF.

Since network elements are made up of smaller subassemblies, which in turn are made up of individual parts, the MTBF for the element as a whole is a rather complex number to derive. This derivation is beyond the scope of this book and will therefore not be discussed.

Associated with the MTBF for an element is a second number called the Mean-Time-To-Repair, or simply MTTR. This number provides a guide-line concerning the period of time required to repair the failed element.

The network designer armed with ranges of MTBF and MTTR figures on an element by element basis is now in a position to examine the backup requirements of the network and identify the various levels involved.

For those elements of the network with extremely high availability requirements (areas where failure cannot be tolerated at all), the obvious solution is to provide full redundancy. The designer is then in the position of having to derive a new statistic—the probability that both elements will fail or be down at the same time.

Terminal devices for clusters should be selected (as far as reliability is concerned) on the basis of the MTBF and MTTR statistics. The higher the MTBF (the longer between failures), the higher the price will usually be. Balancing these figures against the effect of the terminal's failure on the people who use it will lead to an acceptable selection. In some cases, standby terminals may be less expensive than a single terminal with a satisfactory MTBF.

For those terminals that will not be duplicated or backed up, a high MTBF should not be the sole reliability selection criteria. The MTTR now becomes a factor. How easily and conveniently can the terminal be repaired? If field repair personnel are available in the area and can repair the terminal on-site, that is one MTTR guideline. If the terminal must be repaired off the user's premises or even returned to the manufacturer, quite another MTTR figure presents itself. On-site repairs accomplished in a few minutes or hours may be quite acceptable, while off-site repairs requiring days or weeks may be totally unacceptable.

Relay node devices present a similar reliability problem. Failure of a relay node device, isolating an entire terminal cluster, is a somewhat more visible problem than the failure of a single terminal. The MTBF and MTTR figures for relay node devices should be considered at two levels. The first level concerns the MTBF figure for the individual channels or subchannels of the device. Failure of one of these channels may not affect the operation of any other channel, and only a single terminal will be denied access. The second level concerns the MTBF for the unit as a whole. What are the MTBF figures for failures that will cause the entire element to go down, taking all the terminals in the cluster with it?

The same MTBF/MTTR evaluation relative to the desired availability criteria apply to relay node devices as well as to terminals.

Active relay node devices such as network processors involve more complex MTBF/MTTR considerations. The individual channels of the network processor will have one set of MTBF figures. The memory, processor, and control logic modules will each have their own figures. The channels to peripheral subsystems, such as disks, and the peripheral subsystems themselves will have still others. In general, that module of a network processor having the shortest MTBF and causing the entire node to go down should it fail can be considered the weakest link. The MTBF and MTTR figures for this module should provide adequate guidelines for the selection of the network processor and its level of redundancy.

Similar evaluations can be made in the selection of other network elements such as couplers, switches, lines, and trunks. The design of larger networks involving tens of thousands of terminals, dozens of network processors, and thousands of miles of interconnecting lines and trunks will be facilitated through the use of appropriate models and simulators capable of utilizing element MTBF and MTTR figures as parameters. These models will identify key areas where a failure would significantly degrade the performance of the network as a whole. These areas can then be examined in more detail concerning the level of redundancy that is to be selected.

Restart/Recovery

When a hardware failure occurs in some element or device in the network, some level of restart and/or recovery is required to resume normal, or possibly degraded, operation. These levels vary from that required when a single terminal fails to the major task of recovering from the failure of a network or information processor.

In addition to maintaining or restoring normal operation following a failure, the restart/recovery procedure is responsible for the integrity of the information flowing in the network at the time of failure. Various levels of logic are required to assure that information is not altered or lost and that possible duplicate information generated as part of the recovery procedure is identified as such.

Failure of a terminal that is off-line or is not actively sending or receiving information is relatively straightforward. A message is entered indicating that the terminal is out of service and information to be delivered to it is to be held in queue or delivered to a designated alternate destination. When the terminal is returned to service, an appropriate message is entered requesting the in-queue information to be delivered or the alternate destination designation to be canceled.

Terminals that are receiving and/or transmitting information when the failure occurs present a slightly more complex restart/recovery problem. If incoming information from the terminal is interrupted due to failure of the terminal, several possibilities exist. If none of the information has been processed and queued for output, the entire message may be discarded and the incoming sequence number indicator for the source adjusted accordingly. If processing and outbound queueing of the partial message have occurred, it may be desirable to remove the information from the queue or leave it in the queue for delivery. The latter choice requires that the information be appended with a trailer indicating that it is incomplete due to failure at the source. This must also be done in those networks that start information outbound to the destination before receiving the end of message indication from the source.

It is a requirement in some networks that messages queued for a specific destination that is inoperative be examined to determine if any of them are above a specified priority level. Any information in this category is then forwarded automatically to a designated alternate destination or rerouted to a network supervisory terminal.

When the destination device fails during the receipt of information, the network processor must restore the queue tables and pointers to indicate that the in-progress information has not been delivered and to initiate the possible indicated alternate destination or rerouting.

Failure of a relay node presents a somewhat different problem depending on the type of device being used at the node—frequency or time division multiplexor or network processor—and whether or not any backup hardware is included in the network to cover the situation.

Passive multiplexors, such as time and frequency division, when failing, generally appear to be the simultaneous failure of all the terminals or source/destination devices they are servicing. Recognition of this event by the controlling network processor results in the initiation of recovery routines similar to those already described for individual terminal failures. Indication that the relay node device itself has failed is noted, and an appropriate indication is sent to the network supervisory control terminal for action.

If backup hardware is included in the configuration, it is manually switched in or, if on-line and ready, it is automatically cut over under control of the network processor. Since these kinds of passive devices do not contain information queues of any length other than the information passing through them at the time of failure, the treatment of them as so many individual terminals failing simultaneously is facilitated.

Failure of a network processor at any of the various nodes in a network usually presents the network designer with the greatest problem concerning restart and recovery.

If a network processor acting as a remote concentrator at a relay node in the network fails and backup or alternate routing capability is not included, the terminals being serviced by it are unable to regain access. Information flowing in both directions at the time of failure is interrupted and will have to be retransmitted later.

It cannot be guaranteed that information in the remote concentrator's memory can be saved, and this must usually be considered lost. Under this condition, it must be assumed that not only the information in progress at the time of failure must be retransmitted. Also, preceding outbound information in the remote concentrator but not yet delivered to the terminals or inbound but not yet forwarded to the information processing complex must be retransmitted as well.

In this case, when the backup device is started or the malfunctioning one repaired, messages must be sent to all source devices requesting retransmission of all inbound traffic starting from a point in time far enough back to assure that the information lost in the concentrator's memory at the failure time is reentered. This reentered information should be tagged either by the terminal operator or in the concentrator as such so that the ultimate destinations are alerted to look for possible duplication.

A similar restart procedure is necessary between the remote concentrator and the network processor at the other end of its higher capacity trunk. Outbound information queues to the remote concentrators must be backed up and retransmitted as well as tagged to alert the ultimate destinations for possible duplication.

The continuity of inbound or outbound sequence numbers must be maintained during the restart process to assure that no information has been lost.

Remote concentrators or network processors that do not include any mass storage capability can be reloaded and started in a number of ways. If a peripheral device such as a card reader or paper tape reader is available and the processor is located at an attended site, the programs can be loaded using either one of them as the input device. If a suitable input device is not available or the concentrator is located at an unattended site, the programs must be forwarded to it from a node where a network processor with suitable mass storage capability is located.

This remote loading capability requires some form of "reboot" or restart logic in the processor that is to be loaded. This logic is used to receive the incoming program information, place it in memory, determine if it was received correctly, and initiate normal operation when ready.

Some network processors are equipped with a small built-in paper tape reader on which a tape in the form of a continuous loop containing the restart logic is mounted. When repairs are complete and the processor is again operational, this tape is read into core memory and executed, initiating the request for delivery of the operating program.

Other network processors maintain this restart logic in the form of an optional or plug-in read-only memory with a capacity of a couple of hundred or more instructions. This memory can be coded with the appropriate restart logic to be read into main memory and executed, much the same way as the paper tape, when the restart sequence is initiated.

Network processors with mass storage subsystems included in the configuration add another element for consideration in restart and recovery. If the configuration is a single network processor with a single disk or drum attached and no backup included, failure of the mass storage subsystem itself does not necessarily take the network processor down.

Up to the limits of core memory available, the network processor can complete the transmission of in-core outbound information and accept as much as possible of the in-progress inbound. The outbound information should be tagged or appended with an indication that it may be incomplete due to the failure, while the incoming may have to be interrupted and terminated due to lack of space. In this case, the terminal or other source device must be requested to reenter the information at a later time or, if possible, obtain alternate access to the network through another relay node.

In any event, the network processor can continue to respond to requests for access and provide service for those activities not requiring the mass storage subsystem. A message is returned to all others indicating that the failure has occurred and requesting that they try again later.

When the mass storage subsystem has been repaired and returned to operational status, some level of restart/recovery is required. Attempts may be made to reestablish interface with the source devices that were interrupted and either resume activity at the cutoff point or initiate a complete retransmission. Information in outbound queues can now be delivered when the destination devices are reached. Numerous tables, pointers, and indicators must be updated and/or reinitialized to reflect the operational status of the relay node.

Some period of time ranging from minutes to hours is usually required before normal operation is achieved. This is a function of many things, including the length of time the mass storage subsystem was out of service, the number of active source/destination devices at the time of the failure, the amount of information queued for delivery, whether or not the failure occurred during a peak period, and other similar considerations.

If the mass storage subsystem is backed up on the single network processor due, perhaps, to a significantly shorter mean-time between failure, several possibilities exist for covering the failure of the on-line unit. If the standby unit is not interfaced with the network processor and must be manually connected or switched to it, a restart similar to that described for the nonredundant case is required. This may be necessary if the network processor is unable to interface with more than one mass storage subsystem at a time.

Whenever possible, both mass storage subsystems should be connected and running at all times. The network processor can then maintain a completely duplicated set of files, one in each subsystem. One subsystem can be designated on-line or active and the other standby. All information written to the active subsystem is also written to the standby. All "reads" from the file are from the active subsystem only.

In the event of failure of the active subsystem, the network processor ceases reading and writing to it and switches to the standby. A minimum of interruption of service is encountered due to the fully duplicated files. Generally, the only recovery action necessary is to reinitiate the read that was in progress on the active file at the time of failure and switch to the standby file for all subsequent reads.

Obviously it is impossible to maintain duplicate files while one is down for repair. When the repairs are complete and the unit is available again, it may be necessary to copy or reproduce all, or a portion, of the files from the now active one to the repaired one, thus restoring the completely duplicated state.

In the single network processor/single mass storage subsystem configuration, failure of the processor obviously brings the network, or a portion of it, down. The restart and recovery procedure to be initiated when repairs are complete can be greatly facilitated if certain precautionary measures are included in the software design.

It must be assumed that all in-core information will be lost when the network processor fails, even though this may not always be the case. All tables, pointers, and status indicators kept in core memory are then unavailable to the restart/recovery routine when it is initiated.

To aid the restart/recovery logic in establishing a point of known reference or status, the critical or key tables and other in-core information should be periodically written out to the mass storage subsystem. The period between such "snapshots" can vary from fractions of a second to seconds or minutes, depending on many parameters, including the number and speed of the source/destination devices, the mass storage subsystem characteristics, the size of in-core buffer blocks used for incoming and outgoing information, and others.

The restart/recovery procedure can retrieve the snapshot from the mass storage subsystem and reconstruct the core memory tables as they existed just prior to the failure. This aids in the identification of the active source/destination devices at the time of failure and whether they were transmitting and/or receiving. Appropriate action can then be taken to reestablish the interfaces and initiate the required retransmissions.

When both the network processor and the mass storage subsystems are duplicated, a somewhat more complex problem exists. This configuration is illustrated in Figure 11-4. In this fully redundant configuration, one network processor and mass storage subsystem are active while the others are running in a standby mode ready for an immediate switch to active in the event of a failure. Both network processors may be receiving the incoming information from the net-

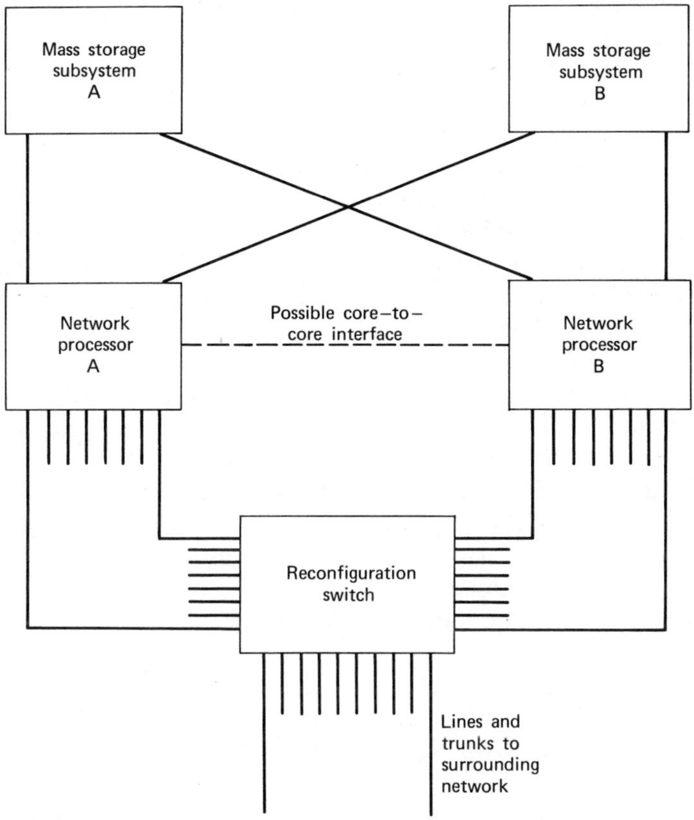

Figure 11-4 **Duplicated configuration**

work's lines and trunks through the reconfiguration switch. Through a hardware and/or software convention, only one of them is actively transmitting information outbound through the switch.

The files are fully duplicated and maintained by the network processors. Each network processor is capable of accessing both mass storage subsystems; and in some network processors, a high-speed core-to-core interface capability is possible as indicated by the dotted lines in Figure 11-4.

Failure of either the standby processor and/or mass storage subsystem is the simplest and will be discussed first.

If the standby network processor is maintaining the duplicate file in the mass storage subsystem and is the element that fails, two possibilities exist. The duplicate file function may be suspended until the processor is repaired. This approach requires a recovery routine to restore file status when the processor is repaired, which is not as simple and straightforward as may appear at first glance. This also involves a somewhat greater risk of serious interruption should the active file subsystem fail prior to completion of repairs.

A more desirable alternative involves the shifting of the duplicate file function to the active processor when the standby processor fails. While adding some overhead, an up-to-date duplicate file is maintained to cover the failure of the active mass storage subsystem.

Failure of the standby mass storage subsystem leaves no alternative but to abandon the duplicate file until the hardware is repaired and then initiate the indicated recovery procedure to restore it to its up-to-date status. This restoration can be executed in either of two ways.

If it is necessary to restore the duplicate file as rapidly as possible, the appropriate software must be included in both processors to pass the required files and control information from the active file to the standby. This is complicated by the continuing activity in the active subsystem. This complication may be alleviated somewhat by interrupting the active subsystem long enough to bring the standby up to date and then restoring normal operation.

An alternative to the immediate on-line restoration of the standby mass storage subsystem involves waiting for a period of minimal network activity on the active subsystem and then interrupting it long enough to restore the standby or possibly even delaying until the network is shutting down for the day and restoring the standby as part of the off-line end-of-day procedure.

Failure of the active mass storage subsystem results in the active processor switching to the standby files. A slight delay may be required to assure that the standby processor completes all in-progress writes to its file and is exactly up to date. This delay, of a few seconds at most, is a result of slight variations that exist in access and/or latency times between the mass storage subsystems.

Following repair of the faulty mass storage susbsystem, a recovery procedure similar to that described for restoring the standby file is required.

Failure of the active network processor initiates a takeover by the standby, which can be accomplished in any of several ways.

The standby processor, either by program control or external manual action, initiates transmission of outbound information through the reconfiguration switch. It may use its own backup file or the active file copy. Regardless of which choice is implemented, it is desirable that the backup processor maintain both files to provide added protection in the event of a mass storage subsystem failure.

It must be assumed that all information, tables, and pointers in the failed processor's memory are lost. If the standby processor was closely matching the active, little interruption occurs on the outbound information. The amount of interruption depends on the time required to perform the reconfiguration switching function. It is usually necessary to include the capability to retransmit a portion of the in-progress outbound information and append it with appropriate indicators warning of possible duplication. This is a firm requirement in those standby network processors that are not "actively" processing the incoming information but relay on periodic "snapshots" of the active processor's in-core tables and pointers.

Failure of the information processor that the network processor(s) is/are interfacing with need not result in the cessation of all activity at that network node. All information flowing through the node but not directed to the information processor can continue uninterrupted. Information to be delivered to the IP may be queued by the network processor for delivery later if sufficient mass storage capability is included in the configuration. For those network processors not including mass storage, the information must be discarded or returned to the source for reentry later.

Return of the information processor to operational status requires a restart/recovery procedure capable of restoring normal operation and maintaining the integrity of information flowing between it and the network processor at the time of failure.

Most of the preceding discussion centers around the failure of one or more components or elements in the configuration. Various combinations of these failures will not necessarily cause the network, or that portion of it, to go down. In these instances, the appropriate restart/recovery procedures are initiated as described.

A different type of failure—power—will take every element in the affected area down unless standby or auxiliary power is available. The restart/recovery from this type of failure may vary considerably, depending on the configuration, the elements involved, the proximity to supervisory personnel, and other similar considerations.

Those elements covered by standby or auxiliary power supplies may experience a momentary interruption while switching to the alternate supply. While not removing the element from service, the interruption may be noticed (depending on its status at the time of interrruption—sending, receiving, etc.) and the appropriate recovery procedure initiated.

Those elements not covered by backup power will cease operation entirely. The restart/recovery procedure initiated when power is restored will more closely resemble the start of day procedure.

Terminal devices will have to enter the equivalent of a good-morning message to verify operational status to the network processor. Sequence number or other control information parameters can be exchanged to restart traffic in process at the time of the failure.

Network processors restarting will also approximate the start-of-day procedure, with added functions necessary to reestablish incoming and outgoing messages interrupted by the failure. Prior to this, the network processor must reload its programs (from either a local or remote source) and go through the recovery procedures necessary to establish, as nearly as possible, the various table and queue states at the time of failure. As is the case with most other types of network processor failures, the in-core information (programs and other information) must be considered lost.

Test/Diagnostic

If high availability and strict information integrity are specified design goals, it may be necessary to include some level of on-line test and diagnostic capability in the network. This capability may range from relatively simple test messages entered periodically to the use of built-in test and diagnostic hardware included in various network elements.

The function of test and diagnostic procedures, whether executed on-line or during specified preventative maintenance periods, is to detect existing or potential malfunctions during the test period, rather than during the transmission of live information which may be distorted or altered and possibly remain undetected.

Terminals can add a measure of assurance to their accuracy by periodically entering a specified format test message. The test message is identified to the network as such and is formatted in such a way as to exercise most, if not all, of the terminal's capabilities and/or options. One test message may be able to exercise all options, or several messages may be required for simplicity of preparation. All characters in the code set, both information and control, should be included in the test message, as well as any format control that the terminal can execute.

These inbound test messages are examined by the receiving network processor and compared to a known copy for accuracy. Conformance with the known indicates that the terminal is still accurate and an appropriate acknowledgement is returned. Any deviation results in the return of a negative acknowledgement, which usually calls for the test message to be reentered. Since the detected error may have originated in the distribution network and not the terminal, two or more attempts may be necessary to complete the test satisfactorily. Failure of the terminal to complete a satisfactory test indicates that it probably has experienced a failure of some type, and a message must be sent to the indicated supervisory control personnel informing them of it.

The distribution network should not be excluded as a possible source of the error. If the terminal has dialed in through a switched network, it should be instructed to disconnect and dial in again, if possible, to determine if this action clears the error.

Terminals indicating a hard or continuous failure should not be allowed to enter information into the network until corrections have been made and the tests rerun for verification. If a terminal is incapable of entering correct information, its ability to receive correctly becomes suspect also. Test messages can be sent to the terminal to determine its ability to receive, provided that the already detected failure does not prevent it from properly responding with the appropriate ACK or NACK.

As in the inbound test message, errors in the outbound may have been introduced in the distribution network. A number of retries should be executed before deciding that the terminal is in error.

Any question concerning a terminal's ability to receive correctly should result in its being placed in a nonoperational category, and all information to be delivered to it should be placed in an intercept queue or rerouted to a designated alternate destination.

Periodic outbound test messages, in addition to determining the terminal's status, can be used as an indication of the network processor's ability to deliver information correctly. Test messages received by terminal operators should be examined for error and, when any is found, the exchange of additional test messages in either or both directions should be initiated. Through this exchange, it may be possible to narrow down or pinpoint the location of the malfunctioning element.

Similar test and diagnostic messages may be exchanged between network nodes that do not involve interaction with a terminal operator. Remote concentrator or network processor to front-end network processor and front-end network processor to information processor are two examples.

Information blocks of a predetermined size and content, with known lateral redundancy or other block check characters, can be exchanged periodically and checked for accuracy. Frequently, when the interconnecting trunk is idle for any length of time, the test message is sent even though the specified period between tests has not elapsed. As before, the error may have been introduced in the distribution network, not the source or destination device, and an appropriate number of retries should be executed before indicating a permanent error.

Failure of the test message to arrive within the specified time frame when the trunk is idle may indicate that the source device or trunk is no longer operational. If attempts to reestablish the interface fail, an error message should be directed to the specified supervisory terminal and a recovery procedure initiated.

In large multiple node networks with several network processors involved, test messages may be originated in them periodically for explicit routing through the others and return to the originator. A failure to receive an exact copy of the test message is an indication that an error was introduced somewhere in the network, and further step-by-step tests are then required to locate its source.

Network processors with random access mass storage subsystems attached should periodically exercise them by writing data to disk and reading it back to a different core location for a character-by-character comparison. Existing or potential failures can thus be detected as early as possible and backup procedures initiated. While it is perhaps not practical to test every track or sector in this manner, an effort should be made to test each surface and each physical drive or handler if possible. In multiple surface or multiple disk drives, a spare is often designated to be used when a failure occurs.

An increasing number of devices are appearing that have an integrated or built-in test and diagnostic capability. Frequently, this includes the ability to "loop back" the transmitting and receiving sides of the device.

Network processors can be configured with the loop back capability on each line or trunk termination. Under program control, the transmit side is looped directly to the receive side and a known test character sequence is sent out. If any deviation occurs, an error exists within the network processor, and further testing is required to identify the exact location.

If the test sequence is received correctly, the loop back can be moved out to the coupler and the procedure repeated. Now the test sequence flows through the transmit side of the network processor channel or port and the transmit side of the coupler and is then looped back to the coupler's receive side and into the network processor.

Following successful completion of the loop back within the local coupler, the distant or remote coupler can be instructed to loop back, and the test can be repeated. This technique or capability is available in some terminals and provides still another level that the loop back function can be extended to.

Figure 11-5 illustrates the several levels of loop back just de-

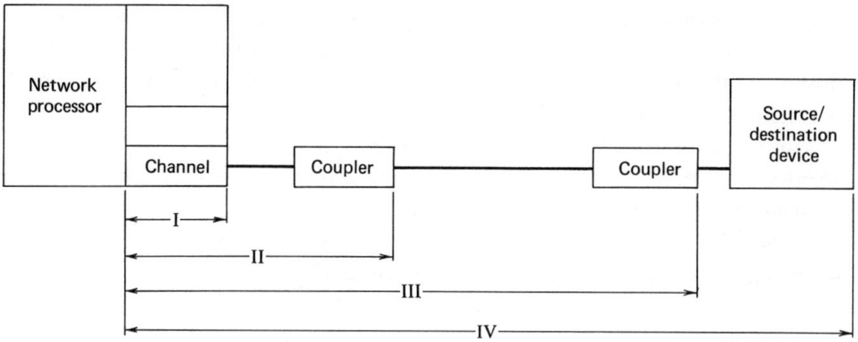

Figure 11-5 **Diagnostic loop back**

scribed. This multiplicity enables the network processor to isolate rapidly and determine the relative location of the error source, which provides significant time savings for its repair. An error message can be generated and delivered to the appropriate network supervisory control terminal locating the error and indicating the type of repairs needed.

The loop back function in the various elements shown in Figure 11-5 may be under either manual or program control. Manual control requires that a switch be thrown or a button depressed, which does not lend itself readily to on-line testing and diagnosis. The program controlled version, while probably more expensive, requires only a coded character or character sequence to initiate and terminate the loop back and therefore is ideally suited for on-line testing.

Depending on the specified frequency of testing, the required network processor software may be permanently core resident (in core at all times and ready for execution) or stored in the mass storage subsystem and called in as an overlay when needed.

Some network processors include the necessary logic to detect various types of environmental errors or extremes, in addition to the normal "system" errors such as parity failure, loop back, and others. Sensors are included in the hardware configuration to monitor such things as temperature in the cabinets and relative humidity. When maximum and/or minimum thresholds are reached, the processor is notified of the condition and can prepare for an orderly shutdown, if necessary, to protect itself from damage. Error messages can be generated and delivered to the network supervisory control terminal indicating the status and action taken.

Other sensors may monitor the incoming electrical power supply to determine if it remains within specified limits or tolerances concerning voltage and frequency. Any out-of-bound condition is detected immediately, which usually results in a rapid but orderly shutdown. Sufficient time to send an error message to network control is not usually available.

Optional battery power supplies are sometimes used if loss of service due to a power outage is unacceptable. The batteries are kept charged by the primary power supply as long as it is available. When it fails, the processor switches immediately to the battery supply with no interruption of service, then sends a message to network control indicating its status and the possibility of shutdown if power is not restored before the batteries are exhausted.

Some newer systems will accomplish the switch to the backup batteries so smoothly that the network processor does not even detect it. It is desirable in this case to notify the network processor through an appropriate status indicator so that an indication of the possible shutdown can be generated and sent to supervisory control.

If primary power is restored prior to the batteries being drained to a specified minimum capacity, the processor reverts to it and starts charging the batteries again. Battery supplies capable of maintaining the processor and its associated couplers for periods of an hour or more are readily available.

Companies with very high availability requirements are frequently going to complete standby emergency power systems. These systems are capable of supplying sufficient power to drive not only the network processor, modems, auxiliary storage subsystems, and terminals but the lights and air conditioning of the facility as well. Facilities so equipped are capable of operating independent of the local power supply essentially indefinitely at full network availability.

Motor generator sets may be implemented if full standby power is not required but sufficient power for an orderly shutdown is. These sets consist of an electric motor powered by the primary electrical supply which drives a generator and a large heavy flywheel. The inertial energy of the spinning flywheel is sufficient to drive the generator within specified voltage and frequency long enough to permit an orderly shutdown of the processor when primary power fails.

Depending on the size and mass of the flywheel and the power requirements, this period may extend from fractions of a second to a second or more. This is adequate to allow the processor to store volatile registers and indicators in memory prior to power loss. The stability of the power supplied through these motor generator sets also provides a good form of protection from power transients or surges which, in many processors, will trigger a restart procedure.

A desirable feature in a network processor is the ability to initiate an orderly shutdown procedure when power fails and also automatically commence the start-up when power is restored. When power fails and a halt is imminent, due either to lack of battery backup or failure to restore primary power before exhausting the batteries, the processor should shut down and wait. When power is restored to normal tolerances, the processor should be capable of detecting this, automatically initiating the start-up cycle, and, when operational, commencing the restart/recovery procedure. In many cases, disk subsystems that have cycled down due to power outages must be restarted manually. This factor may influence the choice of remote network processor/disk storage subsystem combinations.

This capability is particularly valuable in remote concentrators or network processors situated in unattended locations that would entail several hours delay for supervisory personnel to reach them and initiate the restart sequence manually.

11-3 SECURITY

Information network security is an increasingly important concern of network designers. Large state- or nation-wide networks present a variety of problems involved with the prevention of unauthorized access to the network and its information. Security precautions or measures must be implemented at various levels and involve numerous hardware and/or software techniques.

The Level VI entries in the tree structure under the Level V entry Security are shown in Figure 11-6.

The following pages present a discussion of those aspects of security that deal with the communications side of the network. Different security measures are required in the information processors of the network and are beyond the scope of this book. (See *Functional Analysis of Information Processing* by Grayce M. Booth, Wiley, 1973.)

Terminal Identification

Each source/destination device in the network should include some means of identifying itself to the network. This not only aids in identifying it as an information source and/or destination but provides a level of security as well.

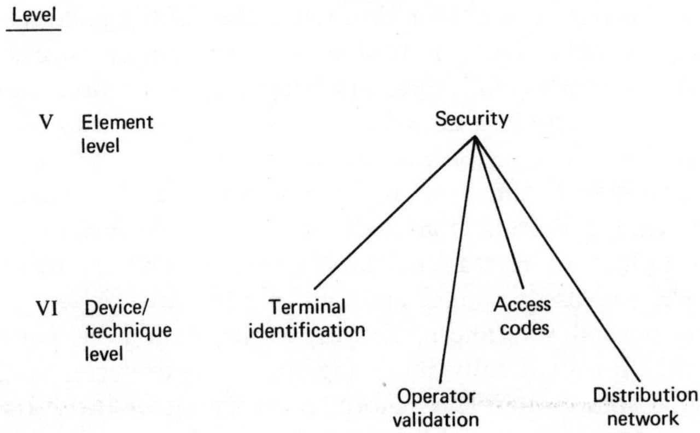

Figure 11-6 **Security function**

Fixed devices on dedicated lines or trunks do not generally include a specific hardware identification technique. Since they are not often moved but remain on the same line or trunk, their identification is implied. Such devices may, however, respond positively to the poll/select sequences as a means of indicating operational status and the ability to accept or enter information.

Teletypewriters or other devices coupled permanently to a switched distribution network with an associated number can be equipped with an answerback device of some type that, when interrogated, enters the identification information coded on it. This code may be several characters, usually 20 or so, and its content can be specified at installation time. It may provide a simple device identification such as the symbolic destination code or may include additional information such as location, type of device, security clearance, or other similar information.

While providing some measure of security, these answerback devices are not foolproof. It is a relatively simple task to remove the coded drum in devices so equipped and substitute another drum containing the altered code necessary to foil the security check logic of the network. A more desirable technique involves the use of a small microcoded or read-only memory device that contains the coded information electronically, rather than mechanically, as is the case with the drum. While not impossible to foil, the coding and implementation technique of these devices can make unauthorized access extremely difficult. In those networks where physical security is not maintained, however, the line or trunk may be tapped and the answerback recorded and played whenever access is desired.

Another approach to establishing the validity and/or location of a terminal requesting access through a switched distribution network involves dial-back. Any terminal dialing in must present its own phone number to the network along with its identification information, and then it must hang up or disconnect. Following validation of the received information, the responding network processor dials back to the terminal and initiates the identification sequence again. Passage of this test assures that the terminal is in a known, acceptable location and is not an unauthorized terminal with a phony answerback device calling in from an invalid phone number or location. Obviously this technique is not entirely foolproof either, unless strict maintenance or security of the entire switched network, including all lines, trunks, and switching centers, can be guaranteed.

Mobile and portable terminals present a more significant problem. Since mobile devices usually interface with the network through some radio frequency technique, anyone with a similar terminal and knowledge of the allocated radio frequencies can gain access. Electronically coded identification devices, similar to those described for dial-in terminals, can provide some measure of security. Encrypting devices may also be included in the associated transmitters and receivers to add still another level of assurance. The scrambling and/or identification codes can be changed either periodically or randomly, with the new codes known only to the network security personnel.

Portable terminals dialing in from any location within the public or dedicated switched network and acoustically or inductively coupled can also be equipped with coded identification devices and scramblers. This guarantees only that the terminal itself is valid and not necessarily calling in from a security location, unless the dial-back capability can be included with the acoustic or inductive coupler.

Establishing the identity of programmable source/destination devices such as network and information processor can be done via software or programmed exchanges of information that can be as complicated as required. The validity of these interchanges may be established either through the evaluation of their content and/or the timing intervals between the interrogation and the response. The processing capability inherent in programmable devices makes it possible to vary the identification procedure dynamically on a periodic basis, even as much as several times during an operating period or day, if required.

Hardware identification devices similar to those described for nonprogrammable terminals can also be incorporated in network or information processors. Electronically coded or microcoded read-only memory options with identification information known only to the network security personnel could be included in the hardware design. If the options are in the form of a plug-in card or module, individuals with various clearance or security levels may be given separate cards coded with their appropriate identification and security clearance information. This plug-in security feature could be used in other types of terminals as well to permit several different people of varying clearance to use the same terminal and avoid the need for a separate terminal for each security level required.

Tables of source/destination device identification codes and sequences may be kept in a secure location within the network. They may be kept in core memory of the network processor(s) if they are small enough. For larger, more complex tables, it may be necessary to maintain them in a mass storage subsystem and call the needed portion in as an overlay when necessary.

Operator Validation

The security discussion to this point has concentrated on establishing the identity and validity of the source/destination devices. Having determined that a terminal requesting access is valid, it is also necessary to verify that the operator at the device is authorized to interface with the network.

Operators can be assigned codes that, when entered, identify the specific individual involved. Tables of acceptable operators must obviously be kept in addition to the source/destination device validation tables. It may be necessary to cross-reference the device and operator identification tables such that certain operators are authorized for access only through specified devices. This prevents a valid operator, cleared to a specific clearance level, from accessing the network through a device cleared to a higher or lower level.

Like the source/destination device codes, operator codes may be changed frequently to maintain higher security and cope with the problems of operators leaving the organization or losing their security clearance at a specific level. With multiple security levels specified for terminals and operators, control procedures must be included to assure that any alternate destination and/or operator functions do not violate the established security.

Access Codes

Following validation of the source/destination device and the operator, access to the various files and data bases must be considered.

It may be desired, due to their nature, to grant access to specific files on a "need-to-know" basis only. For example, perhaps only certain authorized finance personnel should have access to the financial files such as payroll, cost accounting, accounts payable/receivable, and other related types of information.

This controlled access can be achieved through the use of one or more levels of access code. The operator indicates which file access is being requested and is asked to submit the required password or access code. This first level may be all that is necessary for access to any portion of the designated file to be granted.

Additional levels may be required to limit access to certain critical or sensitive areas within the file, in which case additional passwords are required. Accounting clerks may be granted access to name and address portions of a file, for example, while only specified supervisory personnel can access overdue balance or credit limit information.

Access codes may also be used to limit the ability to enter changes in the file to those authorized to do so. This prevents both the inadvertent alteration of a file by inexperienced operators not familiar with the procedures and the deliberate entry or falsification of information within the file.

Access codes and their related software may become quite complex in large scale networks which have many separate or distributed data bases or files. This problem is compounded in those networks that may be providing the service for numerous individual and possibly competitive corporations.

Software procedures must be carefully designed and implemented to assure that proper clearance to information in the network is possible and that such clearance can be extended to geographically separated files when necessary without becoming so complicated as to be unworkable. Controls should be included to assure that it is not possible to manipulate the network into granting erroneous clearance to a terminal operator attempting to gain unauthorized access.

Distribution Network

Having established procedures that provide the required degree of terminal, operator, and data base security, one major area of concern remains for the network designer—security of the distribution network.

The great variety of distribution network possibilities create a problem for the designer who is attempting to achieve a relatively high level of security. Assuming that physical security measures at all terminal and processor locations can be maintained, the lines, trunks, and relay nodes between them must also be protected.

In-plant distribution networks present the greatest possibility for control due to their physical location and accessibility. Since all the lines, trunks, and relay nodes are within the user's property, a high degree of physical security can be maintained to assure that unauthorized access to the network via some electronic means is not possible.

If the size of the in-plant site makes continuous physical surveillance impossible, additional security measures must be provided. Hardwire lines and trunks may be strung entirely within an armored or shielded conduit from the point they leave the terminal until they arrive at a relay node or network processor. The difficulty involved in opening the conduit is a deterrent which provides some level of security. However, those determined enough to open the conduit may then tap the lines and gain access to the network as long as their physical presence is undetected.

The next level of security for hardwire lines and trunks in conduits is available by either evacuating or pressurizing the conduits and installing sensitive pressure change detectors. Opening of such a sealed conduit results in an immediate change in pressure, which is sensed by the detector so that an appropriate alarm is sounded. In addition to sounding the alarm, the detectors may automatically open the lines and trunks by tripping relays to cause all information flow to cease. Once tripped, the relays must be manually reset, thus making it difficult to override their function by some electronic means.

Beyond the physical means of securing the lines and trunks in the conduits, electronic devices may be included that monitor them continuously to detect any unauthorized tap or connection. Detection of such action can also be used to trigger alarms and/or disconnects.

Since any hardwire conductor carrying coded information emits energy in the form of electromagnetic radiation, it is possible to detect and copy this radiation, thus gaining access to the network without requiring a physical tap or connection. This can be prevented to a large degree by including sufficient metallic shielding in the conduit to assure that the radiated energy is contained within it.

Depending on the information flow rate and type of couplers used, various electronic scrambling techniques can be employed to make deciphering extremely difficult, if not impossible, even if undetected access is gained. Obviously, the information flow between nodes can also be encoded by the network processors and source/destination devices and/or operators, which adds still another measure of security.

Other forms of in-plant distribution networks such as radio frequency or optical trunks require different types of security measures. Anyone with a suitable transmitter/receiver within range of the radio frequency tower or antenna grid can receive and/or enter information in the network. Electronic devices are available which make determination of the specific frequencies being used fairly simple. Elaborate transmission/reception techniques plus processor-coded information and scrambling devices can be used to make information acquired from the network unintelligible.

Optical trunks operating in a line-of-sight mode in the infrared or visible spectrum present a security problem very similar to that encountered with radio frequency. Anyone with an optical receiver within range of the transmitters can receive and record the information flow. Depending on the distance between nodes, the simplest form of security involves physical shielding at each device such that the radiated optical energy is extremely directional and confined to as narrow a path as possible. This then requires that anyone attempting to interrupt and copy the information flow must be physically located at some point along the very narrow line-of-sight path. For fairly short distances, it may be possible to maintain physical surveillance between the nodes, either manually or electronically, and control access to the surrounding area.

Sensors can be included in each receiving device to detect a loss in intensity of the optical trunk. Normal atmospheric interference can be calibrated and allowed for, while a physical interference, as would occur if an unauthorized receiver were interposed in the path, can trigger an alarm system and interrupt the information flow.

Distribution networks other than in-plant involve security problems that are not as easily controlled. Included in this category are all the dedicated and public switched facilities. Since these facilities are supplied by common carriers, the user has little if any control over the security of the network once it leaves his physical premises and enters the common carrier control.

The problem is further complicated by the fact that interface to such networks must conform to rigid, well-known specifications and may involve numerous common carrier supplied elements such as couplers and terminals.

Access to common carrier facilities such as lines, trunks, relay towers, and switching centers is well controlled, and therefore, for most normal commercial business needs, the security provided is adequate. The most vulnerable area is between the source/destination device and the first external common carrier interface.

In-plant switch rooms can be entered and lines tapped with relative ease. Lines and trunks leaving the premises and mounted on poles, or entering underground conduits located on the property, can be identified and accessed. In addition to maintaining physical surveillance of these areas, information coding and/or scrambling techniques can be employed to further increase the network security.

It is probably true that no information network security procedure and technique is foolproof. Anyone with the technical competence, necessary resources and equipment, and enough time can eventually overcome the security measures and gain access to the network.

In general, the costs involved in providing higher and higher levels of security rise more rapidly than the new relative level of security they provide. It is the network designer's responsibility to determine what level of security is required and, after weighing its cost, deciding if it is reasonably optimum or not.

CHAPTER 12

Journaling

There are several possible requirements for the journaling function in an information network. Journaling serves two basic functions: (1) the storage of copies of information that have been delivered for retrieval and retransmission within a specified time frame; and (2) a means of effecting a restart/recovery procedure from a known point in time following a failure. Journals may also be used as a base for the historical collection and evaluation of statistics concerning the network's operation and for billing purposes where the cost of the network is distributed based on usage.

The tree structure through Level V is shown in Figure 12-1, with a complete breakdown of the entires under the Level IV entry Journaling.

12-1 CENTRALIZED JOURNALING

Maintenance of a journal of information that has flowed in a relatively small- to medium-scale network can usually be accomplished with a single centralized journal. This is always the case when the network consists of a single network processor controlling the entire

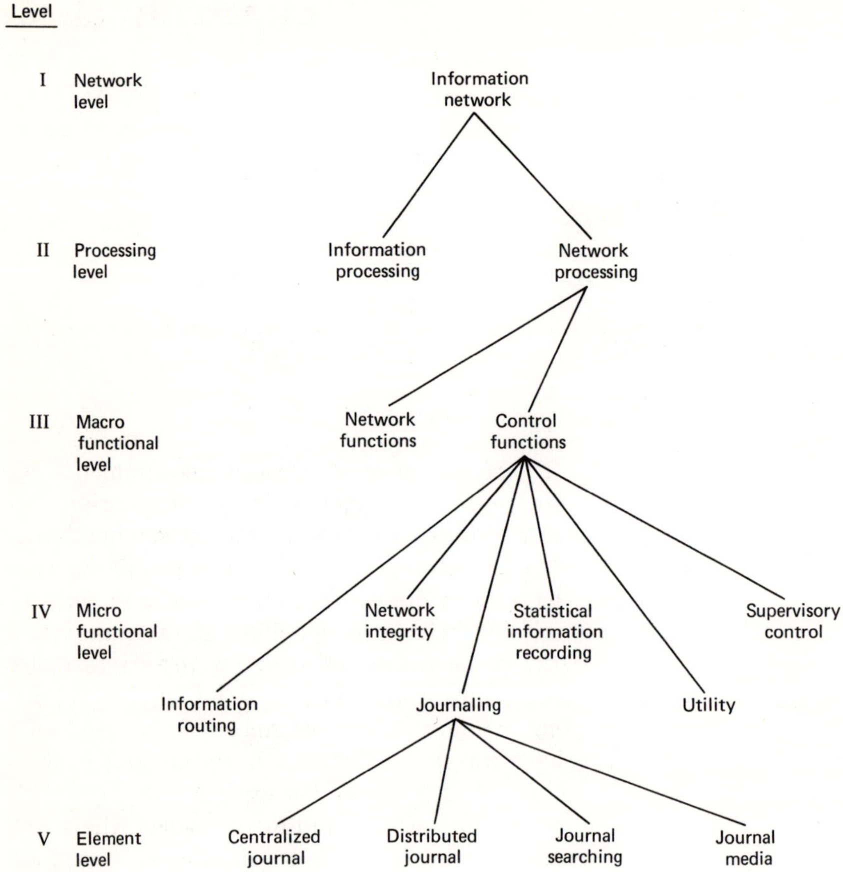

Figure 12-1 **Journaling function**

information flow between the source/destination devices.

The journal entry should contain all information entered by the source device, including its identification code, input sequence number, input time, priority code, message type code, output station or destination code(s), output sequence number, and time. This information is in addition to the text of the message itself. Some of the fields, such as incoming and outgoing time, will be added by the receiving network processor, while others will come from the source itself. Still other fields, such as the routing audit trail, may be added by other network processors through which the information passes on the way to the intended destination(s). Additional identifying destination(s) that could not be reached and any alternate destination or rerouting that occurred are also helpful.

Occasionally, while a hard copy terminal is receiving information, the paper will tear and jam the out-of-paper indicator so that the transmitting network processor is not notified of the condition and continues sending. The information is then all printed on the same line, or even on the platen or roller of the terminal. By the time the operator notices the condition, the network processor may have finished the delivery and terminated the interface. This necessitates a request for a retransmission of the information after the paper jam in the terminal has been cleared.

If outbound sequence numbers are maintained and included in the information, the operator can enter a request to have that specific sequence number message retransmitted. If the jam was not noticed for an extended period of time, several messages may have been delivered to the terminal, all of which were lost. In this case, the operator must request the retransmission of all messages following the sequence number of the last correctly received one. If outbound sequence numbers are not maintained, but time and date of delivery are, the request for retransmission must use these parameters. The time of delivery of the last correctly received information is entered, and a request for retransmission of all following messages is made.

Failure to maintain either outbound sequence numbers or time and date of delivery makes retransmission extremely difficult if not impossible. For this reason, inclusion of one or the other, and preferably both parameters, is highly recommended. Without them, retransmission requests and the associated journal searching must be performed using some sort of context analysis or comparison.

For example, if the source of the information is known or if several possible sources are suspected, the request may ask for retransmission of all information from the list of possible sources. If the content or type of message is known, the request may ask for the retransmission of all information of that type found in the journal. The software in the journal search routine is obviously much more complicated for this type of retransmission and results in inevitable duplication of information.

Information received correctly in hard copy or printed form, removed from the terminal, and later lost or misplaced also results in a desire for retransmission. As before, the use of outbound sequence number and/or time and date of delivery will greatly facilitate the retransmission procedure.

The journal maintained by the network processor is usually kept on some mass storage subsystem. The network designer must evaluate the journaling requirements to determine how much capacity is required to contain the volume of information to be maintained. He must also decide whether a random access form of journal—magnetic disk, drum, or card—is required or if a sequential form, such as magnetic tape, is satisfactory. The period for which the information is to be retained and available for retransmission is another important consideration.

If the network processor configuration already includes a form of random access mass storage subsystem for queue management and buffering, extension of this for the journaling function may be the logical choice. The period of time the information is to be retained and available for retransmission, typically one or two operating days, and the anticipated volume will indicate how much additional storage capacity is required.

If mass storage capability is not included in the configuration and journaling is a definite requirement, sequential access magnetic tape journals (usually less expensive than random access disks or drums) may be a better choice. The journal searching technique is obviously somewhat different in this case and usually results in a longer (depending on volume) retrieval time.

It may be a network requirement to maintain the current one or two days' information in an on-line journal available for retransmission in a relatively short time, up to five or ten minutes depending on current load in the network, and the preceding week or month's information in an off-line form. The on-line journal is then maintained in the configured mass storage subsystem—either random or sequential access—available for rapid retrieval. The off-line journal is kept on removable disk packs or reels of magnetic tape. At the end of each operating day, the oldest on-line journal information is moved to the off-line media and the resulting space made available for the next day's on-line journal.

12-2 DISTRIBUTED JOURNALING

In larger scale networks containing a multiplicity of distributed network processors and relay nodes, the journaling function must be considered in a somewhat different manner. Since all information flowing in the network does not necessarily flow through every network processor, maintenance of a centralized journal presents several added problems. Figure 12-2 illustrates such a network, and the following paragraphs discuss the journaling function as related to it.

The information network shown consists of two geographically separated information processing complexes, labeled locations A and

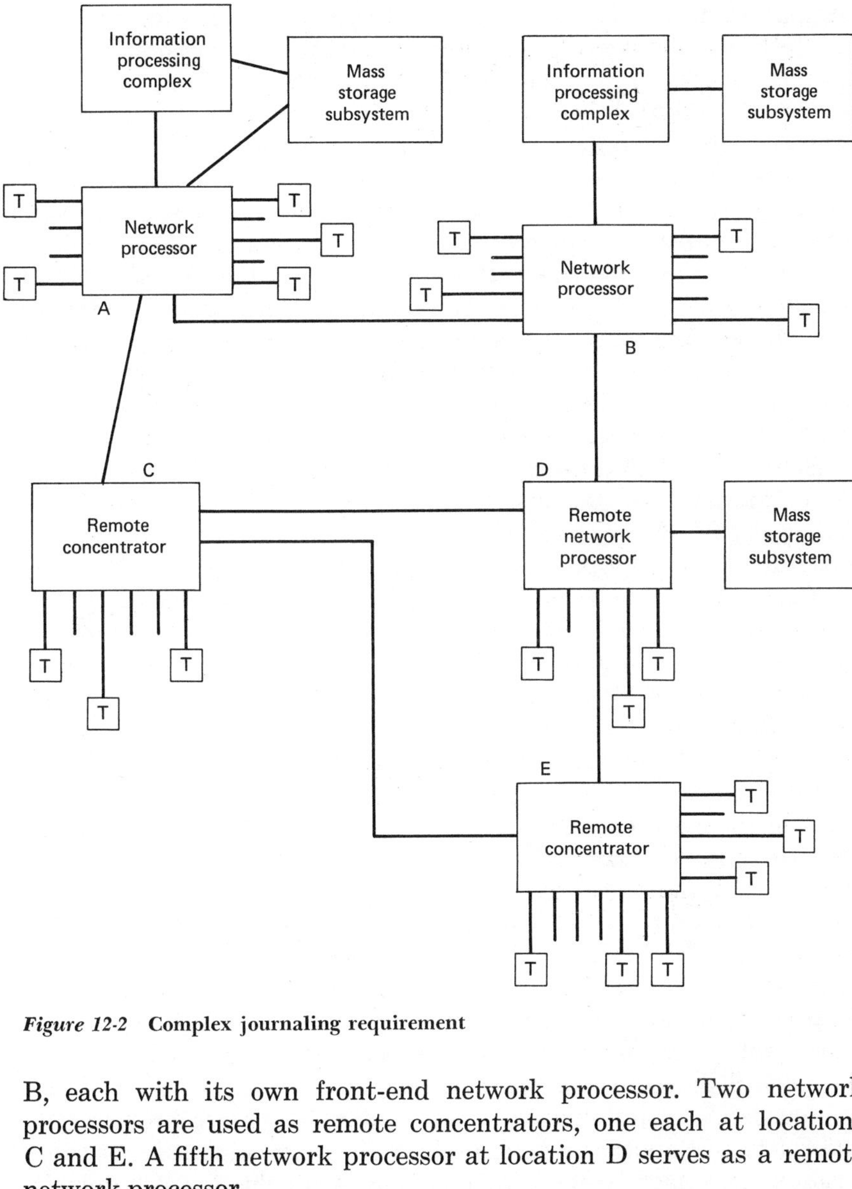

Figure 12-2 **Complex journaling requirement**

B, each with its own front-end network processor. Two network processors are used as remote concentrators, one each at locations C and E. A fifth network processor at location D serves as a remote network processor.

Mass storage subsystems accessible by the network processors and capable of providing journaling capability are indicated at locations A and D. A mass storage subsystem is included at location B but is not directly accessible by the network processor.

Each network processor services the terminals and other source/

destination devices surrounding it and provides them with an interface to the remainder of the network. Trunks are configured between network processors to provide a degree of alternate routing capability so that the failure of one of them, D, for example, does not prevent another, E, from maintaining access to the network.

All outbound information passing through network processor A can be journaled in the configured mass storage subsystem. This includes information delivered to network processors B, C, and D, as well as to the terminals in the cluster surrounding A. Information to be forwarded to the remote concentrator at E may also originate at location A. The outbound information passing through network processor A includes that generated by the information processing complex and that which is entered at other sources and is simply passing through the relay node.

Similarly, all information flowing through network processor D can be journaled in its mass storage subsystem. This includes information delivered to the terminals in its cluster and also information forwarded to network processors B, C, and E.

Duplication of journaled information is a possibility at this point. Information originating in complex A and sent to network processor C for forwarding to location D is journaled by network processor A. It is journaled again by network processor D when it is delivered to the destination device location in the cluster serviced by D. This problem is discussed further in Chapter 12-3, Journal Searching.

Information flowing through network processor B may be journaled in the mass storage subsystem associated with the information processor. Since the network processor cannot directly access the subsystem, it must pass the information to be journaled to the information processor. If the volume of information to be journaled exceeds certain thresholds, resulting in excessive overhead in the information processor, the possibility of changing the complex to a delta configuration should be explored. If the delta configuration is undesirable, a separate mass storage subsystem accessible only by the network processor is another alternative.

Journaling of information flowing through network processors C and E presents another type of problem. Network processors at these locations may each be servicing relatively small clusters of terminals, and a mass storage subsystem for journaling at each may not be economically justifiable. The journals for these network processors must be maintained at other locations having the required capability. Location C can forward a copy of all outbound information to network processor A to be journaled. Similarly, location E can utilize the journaling capability of network processor D.

The relative volumes of information passing through the five network processors must be evaluated by the designer to determine the optimum mass storage capability required for the journaling function and where it should be located. The distribution network overhead between locations E and D imposed by the journaling function, for example, must be considered to determine what type of trunk is required between them.

Security may present an additional problem in the configuration. If the security level or clearance at location D, for example, is below that of the other nodes and therefore information of higher security cannot be routed through it, the journaling function becomes more complicated. Location E is forced to maintain its higher security level, or possibly its entire journal, at A and route the information through location C.

The preceding discussion has assumed that all information flowing in the network is to be journaled. It may be acceptable or necessary to journal only selected portions or types of information. For example, control and supervisory information does not necessarily have to be journaled, as it is rarely necessary to retransmit it. Further, it is recorded on the network supervisory logging terminal, where it is available for reference if necessary.

In many networks, it is not normally necessary to journal information such as inbound remote job entry or the resulting output. This information is retained at a given node only long enough to determine that it has been properly received at the destination. For this and other types or classes of information that do not require journaling, software must be included to make the proper distinction and bypass the journaling routine.

12-3 JOURNAL SEARCHING

Having provided a form of journaling capability in the network, the designer must now include the software logic to identify and process a request for retransmission, initiating a search of the indicated journal and delivering a copy of the information to the requestor. Many factors must be considered in implementing journal searching capability to insure that other network parameters such as priority, information integrity, and security are not violated.

When an operator wishes to request a retransmission of information maintained in the journal, he must formulate and enter an appropriate message. Since such requests are in the category of service or control messages, they are recognizable as such and are handled differently than other types of information flowing in the network.

The first network processor to recognize the retransmission request must establish where the journal to be searched is located. If it is maintaining the required journal itself, it can initiate the search activity. If the journal is located at some other node in the network, the request is forwarded to that node.

Network processors maintaining journals include some form of mass storage subsystem. Since retransmission requests are not usually a high frequency activity, it is generally impractical, from an overhead point of view, to keep the journal search software in core memory on a permanently resident basis. A more desirable approach involves keeping the software in the mass storage subsystem and calling it in as an overlay as required.

The journal search software and other infrequently used utility type software routines are assembled and stored in the mass storage subsystem. When it is necessary to execute such software, it is retrieved, loaded (usually into specifically reserved memory locations), and scheduled for execution. Since many other software functions, such as line and trunk servicing, processing, and mass storage input/output activities, are of a higher internal priority, the search software may not enter execution for several seconds, until all higher priority activities have been satisfied.

Depending on the size of the network and relative frequency of journal search requests, it may be necessary to build a queue of requests in the mass storage subsystem rather than keep them in core memory. The journal search software then examines an in-core indicator to determine if additional requests are in the queue before relinquishing control following completion of the initial search.

Having located a request to be serviced, the search software must establish the status of the journaled information. It may be in the on-line journal if it is less than, say, 48 hours old. In this case, if the time of initial delivery is included in the request, it may be possible to narrow the area of the journal to be searched to a relatively small portion and avoid a search of the entire journal. This capability may provide for significant reduction in overhead and contribute to increased throughput of the network processor.

If the journal to be searched is off-line on magnetic tape or removable disks, the correct tape or disk pack must be identified and a request to mount it generated and delivered to the appropriate supervisory terminal. When the correct reel or pack is mounted and ready, the supervisory operator enters a message indicating that searching can be initiated.

Since the search routine is of relatively low priority and a continuous block of processor time long enough to complete the search cannot possibly be allocated, it is allowed to execute for some specified period of time, perhaps a few seconds, or until a higher priority routine is due to enter execution. At this time, the search is interrupted and control given to the higher priority routine. When all higher priority activities are complete, control is returned to the search for another period. This sequence is repeated many times, depending on the processor load at the time, the size of the journal being searched, and the relative location of the desired information in the journal, before search completion.

Depending on the memory space available and the number of overlay subroutines required in the configuration, it is possible that the search routine and its buffer areas and status at the interrupt time must be written out to the mass storage subsystem. When the higher priority routine terminates, the search is read back into memory and scheduled for execution again.

The searching software reads a portion of the journal into core memory and examines it, based on the submitted request parameters, to determine if it contains the information to be retransmitted. If a specific outbound sequence number has been requested, the search is relatively straightforward. If an approximate time-of-delivery is the only parameter, more than one message may have been delivered (depending on size and volume) around that time.

If specific parameters, such as sequence number and/or time of delivery, are not available, alternate search techniques must be employed. The request may include the first several words of the information text and indicate that a complete copy of the message matching those words be delivered. Variations of this include requests based on the content of one or more specified fields within the body of information delivered around an indicated time of day. Even though time of delivery may not be included in outbound information, it is usually included in the journal copy for this specific purpose.

When the requested information is located in the journal, it can be queued for delivery to the requesting terminal. Prior to delivery, however, it may be necessary to examine additional parameters and/or tables to determine if delivery is allowed.

In networks with multiple security conditions, it must be delivered if the requestor is cleared to the security level of the requested information. This clearance includes the requesting terminal operator and the terminal itself. It should not be possible to deliver information to a cleared operator at an uncleared terminal or, conversely, to an uncleared operator at a cleared terminal.

The priority of the requested information may be a factor in the priority of the retransmitted copy. The copy may be queued at the original priority level or at the priority of the request, depending on the designer's requirements. A third possibility is to provide a field within the request indicating at which priority to deliver the copy.

The information is now in queue for the appropriate line or trunk and will start on the way to the requestor when the line is free and all higher priority information has been delivered. The information may be delivered as is, with no indication that it is a retransmission. This results in a break in outbound sequence numbers, however, and it is more desirable to queue the requested information, header and all, as a completely new message with a new header that includes a correct sequence number and an indication that this is a retransmission.

If it is mandatory that all information in the network be journaled for legal or other reasons, then the retransmitted information must be journaled again with its new header. Other networks not requiring that retransmitted information be journaled again can simply log the event on the supervisory logging terminal so that a record of it exists.

The supervisory log entry of the retransmission request should include the following information or some appropriate subset of it: the requesting terminal and/or operator identification and time of request; the time of delivery of the copy; the security and priority parameters, and any other header or control information desired.

If the information is to be directed to a terminal serviced by the network processor performing the search, it is queued at the proper priority level and delivered. If it must be relayed through one or more intermediate network processors, the header may contain additional addressing and/or routing information.

If the network processor and mass storage subsystem maintaining the journal is not duplicated or backed up, the journal searching must be performed in the main system. If backup processor and storage subsystem are included and duplicate or mirrored files are being maintained, it is possible to perform the journal search in the backup. This relieves the on-line configuration of the associated overhead and provides a slight improvement in throughput characteristics.

Since the backup processor cannot normally transmit outbound on the lines and trunks, it must pass the information to the on-line complex for delivery. This can be accomplished through either a memory-to-memory interface or through the mass storage subsystem if dual access capability is included.

If journal searching and other utility type functions are being performed in the backup processor and the on-line processor fails, two choices are possible. The functions may be suspended until normal operation is restored, or they may remain in the backup processor as a part of the restart/recovery procedure.

12-4 JOURNAL MEDIA

The following is a summary of the various types of journaling hardware that may be applied to the function and includes a brief discussion of factors to be considered in producing the desired response times for journal search requests.

Tape Journals

If journaling is required at a node that does not include some form of random access mass storage for queue management and mass storage cannot be economically justified for the journaling function alone, sequential access magnetic tape may be the optimum choice. A controller with one or more suitable tape handlers, which need not be extremely fast or of high density, can be dedicated to the journaling function.

The network processor at the node writes a copy of all delivered or forwarded information to the journal after it receives confirmation of successful receipt by the destination device. In simpler networks, the complete message with its header, text, and trailer may form the complete journal entry, while in others a journal header may be added to the message for the more complicated search and control functions. The information may be written to the tape one message per block or, if memory size permits and message sizes are small enough, may be blocked in memory and written to tape as multiple entry blocks.

If journal searching is not performed at the node, a single tape handler may be sufficient. This assumes that supervisory personnel are available to change reels when the current one is filled, unless an entire day's journal can be contained on a single reel. If it is necessary to change reels during the operating period in a single handler configuration, this must be done fast enough to prevent memory from overflowing with information to be journaled.

Journal searching at a single handler node is difficult and may be impossible in some instances. While the tape is being rewound and/or searched, new information to be journaled cannot be written to it. If sufficient memory is not available to contain such information, journal searching is impossible and an alternate approach must be implemented.

The use of a pair, or more, of tape handlers provides several advantages. The network processor can alternate between handlers, filling one reel and switching to the other, which is mounted and ready. In this way, more time is available for an operator to remove the filled reel and replace it with a new one. The journal searching problem remains, however, as the processor essentially has access to just one reel at a time.

It is possible with a pair of tape handlers to overcome the searching problem, but more sophisticated software is required. At the start of the operating day or period, a new reel is mounted on each handler and made ready. The network processor then starts journaling on one of the reels. When a request for a journal search is received, the processor rewinds the reel containing the journal in preparation for the search and directs the following journal information to the alternate reel. When the journal search is complete, the overflow or alternate reel is rewound and moved back to the original reel, which is now used for journaling again. Due to memory size, information volume, and load considerations, it may not be possible to maintain a completely sequential journal.

An alternate approach involves leaving the overflow information on the alternate reel permanently instead of moving it back to the original at the completion of the search. While simpler from a software viewpoint, it presents two additional problems. Should both reels fill at approximately the same time, sufficient time may not be available to permit the operator to rewind a filled reel, demount it, mount a new reel, and make the latter ready for use before the remaining reel and available core space are filled. Secondly, unless comprehensive tables are maintained in memory indicating which reel contains which journaled information, both reels may have to be searched before the desired information is located.

In either case, information may have to be journaled while an alternate reel is being rewound to avoid a memory overflow, so it may be written on the original reel out of sequence before the alternate has rewound or before the transfer of information on the alternate has been completed.

Other problems associated with tape journals occur when a request appears for information that is on the alternate reel while the original is being searched for a preceding request. This and all following requests should simply be queued and serviced sequentially when the original reel has been restored.

Random Access Mass Storage Journals

A much more efficient and manageable journaling capability is provided by the use of some form of random access mass storage subsystem. Included in this category are disks, both fixed and removable, drums, and magnetic card devices. While frequently more expensive than magnetic tape, the increased efficiency and flexibility may be worth the added cost.

Information can be journaled in designated areas of the subsystem. This usually takes the form of queues organized on a line or terminal basis, or instead it may be written essentially randomly with linkage techniques used to establish the queues.

The biggest single advantage of random access journals is the ability to search the journal while at the same time continuing to fill it with copies of delivered information. It is not necessary to interrupt or delay either function to perform the other.

In nonremovable subsystems such as fixed disks or drums, a finite journal capacity is established. This limit may be determined by some minimum amount of on-line journal that is required, or it may simply be the space left over in the subsystem after all the other functions have been satisfied.

If it is a requirement that information be kept in an off-line journal for some additional period, it must be moved from the on-line subsystem to the off-line at scheduled intervals. For example, if two full operating days' information is to be maintained on-line while data for the preceding 20 working days is off-line, the preceding day's information must be moved to the off-line journal at the end of each current operating day. If the off-line journal is on magnetic tape, a part of the end-of-day routine consists of moving the information from the on-line journal to the magnetic tape, labeling it accordingly, and making the vacated space available for the following day's on-line journal.

If the mass storage subsystem is in the form of removable disk packs, with each pack holding several million characters, the on-line and off-line journals may be kept on these. This eliminates the need for magnetic tape controllers and handlers for the single purpose of maintaining off-line journals. If, however, the volume of information to be maintained off-line and the specified retention time are sufficiently high, the cost of the necessary disk packs may exceed the cost of magnetic tape equipment for the off-line journal function. The network designer must consider this and other related factors in selecting the off-line journal media or subsystem.

If removable disk packs are to be used, a daily (or other) function is required to move the oldest information onto a pack, label it, and indicate that it is to be removed, placed in storage, and a new pack mounted and made ready.

Random access magnetic drums are not usually removable, and on-line journal information requires some other form of subsystem—magnetic tape or removable disk—for the off-line journal function.

Response Time Requirements

Response time requirements involve the specified interval from the time the retransmission request is entered until the delivery of the desired information. The allowable latitudes in response time may affect the selection of the journaling subsystem. For example, if information volumes are high and the specified on-line response time is relatively short, it may be necessary to provide a random access mass storage subsystem instead of sequential magnetic tape.

Off-line journal response times may also affect the choice of a journaling subsystem. If relatively long response times are acceptable, magnetic tape may be the optimum choice. When the information is identified as residing in off-line journal storage, the appropriate reel or reels of tape is/are identified, mounted, and searched. Depending on the information volume, number of reels to be searched, and processor time available for searching, the response time may be on the order of 30 minutes or more.

If rapid response time is required even from off-line journals, magnetic tape may be unacceptable. Removable disk packs may be required in addition to a disk mapping technique that can narrow the area to be searched to a relatively small portion of the disk, thus avoiding the need to pass over all information ahead of the desired data, as is the case with sequential magnetic tapes. The mapping technique may provide pointers to areas in the disk based on original delivery times; line, trunk, or destination indicators; sequence numbers, or other similar parameters.

Response times to journal search requests may be further reduced by processing and initiating the search on a higher priority basis and transmitting the information out at as high a priority as possible. This applies to off-line as well as on-line journal search requests.

On-Line Journals

On-line journals are those in which the information to be searched for a retransmission request is still available to the searching network processor. It may exist in the form of sequential access magnetic tapes or as random access disk, drum, or card subsystems. It is not necessary to request any manual or supervisory intervention to locate the desired information.

Off-Line Journals

Off-line journals contain that information that has aged through the on-line interval and has been moved to an off-line form. This information is no longer directly available to the searching network processor. A request must be forwarded to the supervisory personnel asking that the appropriate tape reel or disk pack be located, mounted, and made ready before the search can be initiated. Off-line journals that must be available for searching are almost always in the form of magnetic tapes or removable disk packs.

CHAPTER **13**

Statistical Information Recording

The collection and evaluation of statistics concerning the flow of information in an operational network can provide the designer with valuable insight as to its performance at various times and under various loads. Properly selected and evaluated, this information can reveal the relative degree of optimization that has been achieved in the design and indicate further optimization that may be possible.

The desired statistics may be collected in one of two ways. The first involves the use of software routines that run in real-time and track the flow of information through the network processor. The second uses routines that are run in "spare" or relatively idle time frames and uses the journal file as its source of statistics.

For all but the smallest configurations, a combination of the two techniques will provide the most efficient results. Those time sensitive statistics (e.g., queue overflows) that require close tracking will be collected by the real-time routines, while the less sensitive ones used for hourly reports will be collected in spare time. Since the spare time task may execute considerably later than the actual event occurrences, the journal file must be used as the statistical source.

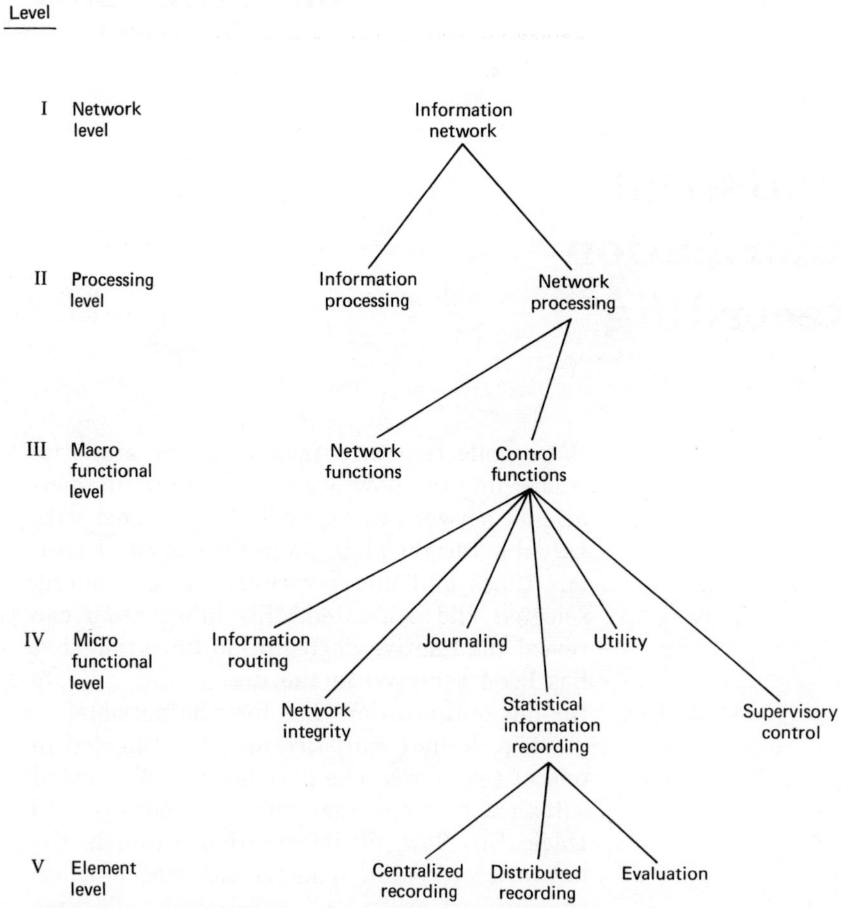

Figure 13-1 **Statistical information recording function**

The tree structure through Level V is shown in Figure 13-1, with a breakdown of the entries under the Level IV entry Statistical Information Recording.

13-1 CENTRALIZED RECORDING

Considerations similar to those used in selecting centralized journaling apply to the specification of centralized statistical information recording. For the relatively small- to medium-scale network with perhaps a single network processor, it becomes a logical choice to perform centralized recording.

All information flowing between the network's source/destination devices flows through the network processor and is handled by it at least once. At this time, numerous statistics to be evaluated are collected. Entries in the various tables maintained by the network processor on a line, trunk, or source/destination basis are made and/or updated with the statistical information.

For relatively small networks that do not make extensive use of the statistical information function, these tables may be maintained in core memory. Larger networks with a requirement for more comprehensive statistics may maintain the tables in the mass storage subsystem to conserve available memory space.

The degree to which statistical information is maintained is a function of several network characteristics and parameters. Those in the small to medium scale with relatively firm line, trunk, and terminal configurations may have minimal need for such statistical information. Since the configuration is stable and does not change rapidly and the load factors and volumes are known to produce acceptable performance characteristics, the use of elaborate statistical information reports may be of questionable value.

Larger networks consisting of several information processing complexes with numerous relay nodes and rapidly changing line, trunk, and source/destination configurations may require extensive statistical information reporting in order to maintain a specified degree of performance and optimization. As terminals are added to or removed from the network, the associated volume change must be evaluated to determine if a line or trunk change is also required. As line and trunk configurations change, the effect on the associated relay nodes —switches, multiplexors, and network processors—must be evaluated to determine if the extra load produces an unacceptable delay in the node.

The various parameters that may be used in producing a statistical report are discussed in a later section, in this chapter. In this, the centralized recording mode, the parameters are collected, evaluated, and delivered at the single centralized location. The reports may be generated automatically at the end of each hour, with a summary report at the end of each shift or operating day. Reports may also be requested by supervisory personnel at any time during the day. The hourly reports may include only a portion of the statistical information available, while the summary reports provide a complete, itemized breakdown of all parameters being monitored.

13-2 DISTRIBUTED RECORDING

In the larger, multiple relay node networks, the collection of all statistical information at a single, central location may be impractical due to time, volume, and economic considerations. In this event, some form of distributed recording is required to stay within specified performance parameters. The network used as an example in the section, Distributed Journaling in Chapter 12 is reproduced here in Figure 13-2 and is used as the base for the following discussion of distributed statistical recording.

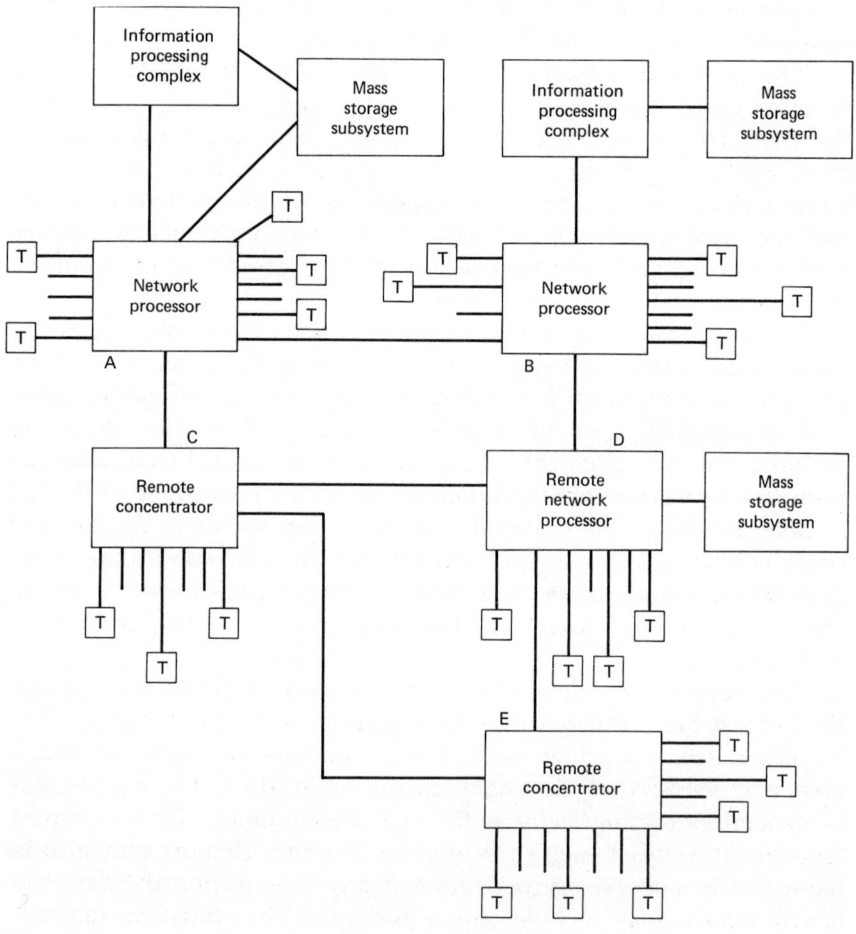

Figure 13-2 **Complex statistical recording requirement**

The network processor at location A can maintain statistical information files for all information flowing through it, including that delivered to the remote concentrator at location C. Depending on the volumes of information handled at C and the types of statistics being recorded, this function may either be divided between A and C or performed entirely at location A. For relatively low volumes and minimal statistical recording requirements, the network processor at location C may maintain its own tables and periodically send them to location A for processing. For large volumes and extensive recording requirements, the network processor at location A may maintain tables for both locations in the mass storage subsystem it shares with the information processing complex.

The network processor at location B may maintain its own statistical tables, either in core memory or in the mass storage subsystem associated with the information processing complex, depending on volume and table space requirements. In the latter case, the information must be periodically transferred to the information processor, which is then responsible for updating and maintaining the statistical records and for generating the specified reports.

The network processor at location D can maintain its records in the associated mass storage subsystem. It may also maintain those required for information passing through it to the remote concentrator at location E. It must be recognized, in this example, that the information passing through location D to location E is not necessarily all of the information reaching E due to E's interface with the remote concentrator at location C. The statistical records from all locations which forward information to location E must be collected and processed as a whole to determine the true performance of the network processor and terminal cluster located at E.

13-3 STATISTICAL INFORMATION EVALUATION

The following sections discuss some of the more commonly collected types of statistical information and the benefits gained from its evaluation. Not all types are found in each individual network. However, the types discussed should provide the network designer with a set to choose from in the specification of an optimum network.

Load and Volume Analysis

Volume analysis can be performed at several levels in an information network, ranging from terminals and other source/destination devices, through relay nodes (passive and active), to front-end network processors, and on to the information processing complex(es).

Volume statistics for terminal devices include counts of characters delivered to and received from each device by hour, shift, and operating day. In addition to character counts, message volumes in each direction may also be maintained. This information can be used to establish the relative percentage of inbound and outbound information at the terminal and can also be expressed as a percentage of the theoretical maximum capacity of the device.

If the device is the only one on a dedicated line, for example, and the statistical information report shows that it is operating continuously at or near its theoretical maximum capacity and, further, if the queues of information to be delivered to it tend to grow beyond acceptable limits, it may be necessary to replace the device with a faster, more capable one. Conversely, if the report shows that the device is never seriously loaded even during peak volume operating periods, it may be possible to provide the required grade of service with a slower, less expensive terminal.

When several terminals are interfaced to a single line or trunk, as in a poll and select environment, the relative volume statistics for the terminals and the trunk are useful in optimizing the configuration. If the trunk is operating at or near its theoretical maximum most of the time and the associated queue sizes are excessive, it may be necessary to move one or more of the terminals to another, less heavily loaded trunk. Similarly, two or more trunks that are relatively lightly loaded may be consolidated and the associated terminals placed on a single trunk. This assumes that the increased mileage on the single trunk does not exceed the mileage of the two individual trunks. Network analysis is required to make this determination.

If several terminals in a cluster are to be serviced by a concentration device, two possibilities exist—it may be necessary that all terminals in the cluster be simultaneously active or only that some number "M" out of the total "N" be simultaneously active. For the first case, the inbound and outbound volume analysis for each terminal in conjunction with the associated queueing delays determine if the grade of service to the cluster is satisfactory. If, due to varying loads and/or volumes between terminals, the queues for one or more terminals are shown to be backed up beyond acceptable limits in the network processor feeding the concentration device, perhaps a second trunk between the two is required.

For the "M" out of "N" case, network analysis must indicate what number of trunks of what capacity are required between the concentration device and the network processor to provide the desired capability. Periodic statistical evaluation of the load and volume levels and the queueing delays encountered will indicate whether or not the "M" out of "N" simultaneously active terminals are receiving an adequate level of service.

Trunks between network processors, such as those shown in Figure 13-2, should be monitored by the statistical information recording software. For example, since all of the information delivered to the terminals in cluster C is received from location A, the connecting trunk should be capable of handling the load necessary to provide the specified level of service. Examination of the relative load on the lines and trunks servicing the terminals and the trunk servicing the remote concentrator can determine if this is so. If the terminals are considerably less than fully loaded but the connecting trunk is continually loaded, the capacity of the trunk is insufficient and either a higher speed trunk of an additional trunk of the same speed is required. Conversely, if the terminals are heavily loaded and the trunk is never more than slightly loaded, even during peak periods, perhaps a slower, less expensive trunk could be used.

In the event that the terminals in the cluster and the interconnecting trunk are both heavily loaded, the queueing delay analysis in the statistical reports should be examined. If this shows that the information in queue at location A to be delivered to the remote concentrator at location C resides in queue considerably longer than information to be delivered to terminals serviced by network processor A, then the terminals at C and the interconnecting trunk may both be inadequate.

Analysis of this type is possible only if logic is included in the network processor software to log incoming traffic time of receipt and time of delivery of the information in the various queues. This time, although spread over several functions, can be considered as a gross queueing delay time.

Queueing delay times may be maintained on a terminal basis, reporting the minimum and maximum number of messages in queue for the preceding period and the minimum and maximum delay times in queue as well—and/or on a line or trunk basis, also. Further breakdown by priority or security level may also be included. If aging to higher priority levels is possible, a record of the number of messages aged between levels may be useful in establishing an optimum aging time.

Further analysis of the queue aging statistics will indicate if a single aging time can be applied to all priority levels or if, due to relative volumes and queue length, separate times are required. The frequency of upward aging during peak volume times relative to normal periods may indicate the need for separate aging times for the two conditions.

Network Processor Statistics

A variety of statistics concerning the performance of the network processor(s) may also prove useful in maintaining an optimum configuration.

The utilization of the disk queueing area as a function of volume per unit time will determine if adequate space has been allocated. The queue overflow threshold can also be expressed as a percent increase in volume before saturation or overflow occurs. The queue utilization may be determined on a priority level basis if such a technique is used.

Another limiting factor concerning the network processor's disk utilization is the maximum number of accesses made to the file per unit time. As this figure approaches the maximum possible, the need for additional and/or faster disk units will become apparent. This figure can also be expressed as a percent increase in volume per unit time to reach saturation.

The relative efficiency of the network processor itself can be measured by tracking the percent of time it spends in various software routines. While a more involved procedure that must be run in real-time, the results are of value in identifying which function will saturate first and at what volume of information.

The interference factor between intersecting software routines or between routines sharing one or more subroutines is also useful information. An example is the effect on in-core queues of a routine entering a common subroutine and temporarily inhibiting higher level interrupt routines from accessing the subroutine. Carried to an extreme, this inhibit function will cause a time-sensitive routine to overflow a queue, thus losing incoming information and overall integrity.

The use of various in-core buffer pools can also be tracked statistically. Frequently, the relative mix of line speeds will suggest the use of two or more strings of buffer blocks, each of different block size and string length. The utilization of the blocks within the strings relative to volume provides a measure of core efficiency and an indication that the string lengths and/or ratios should be changed.

Error and Status Analysis

In addition to the line loading and volume analysis, various reports indicating network status and error statistics may be required. A number of these are described in following pages to acquaint the network designer with the possibilities that exist.

Network processors normally maintain a set of tables reflecting the status of various components, including lines and trunks, of the configuration. If a mass storage subsystem is included, statistics concerning the remaining disk capacity in terms of characters or time to fill are helpful to supervisory personnel in considering some load leveling function that may be required. This information is generated automatically every hour or other period or is available on demand by the supervisory operator.

In addition to capacity, the network processor may be monitoring the mass storage subsystem for the incidence of errors that occur during read/write activities. The number of errors per unit time and the number of retries necessary to complete the action successfully are useful in determining when preventative and/or corrective maintenance is required. In most mass storage subsystems, some statistically determined number of errors is expected. The network processor logic must determine if the actual incidence of errors significantly exceeds this threshold and, if so, generate a message to supervisory personnel indicating the condition as a potential problem. In this way, corrective action may be possible before the unit actually fails and results in the disruption of normal network activity.

In some networks using disk subsystems, the error logging is maintained on a per disk or per surface basis. If the error rate on a surface exceeds the specified threshold or if the surface is suddenly unavailable, the network processor can switch to a spare disk or surface maintained for such events. Obviously, information on the now unavailable surface is lost and an appropriate recovery procedure is required.

Status of the various lines and trunks serviced by the network processor can also be maintained in addition to load and volume statistics. Indication that a line is active, inactive, or removed from service due to error or that the information is being rerouted to another line are examples.

If the line or trunk services several terminals or source/destination devices, additional types of information can be collected. Terminals on intercept or reroute, terminals down for maintenance or repairs, and other similar status information are just a few of these.

Statistics reflecting the terminal operator's accuracy can be helpful in determining if operator training is adequate and/or if the procedures are too complex. The number of messages invalidated due to incorrect header format or destination code, messages entered with invalid priority or security codes, attempted security violations, and other indicators are relatively easily monitored and included in the statistical reporting procedure.

The software to collect the various types of statistical information, while relatively straightforward logically, should be identified as early as possible in the design effort. For those networks with relatively light statistical report requirements, the software may all exist in the form of overlays which are called in and executed when desired. These routines accumulate information from in-memory tables and may pass over in-process queues to generate the desired report.

Larger networks with more comprehensive report requirements need correspondingly complex software. Portions of this software may be imbedded in the operating software of the network processor and execute in an on-line mode, generating or collecting the necessary statistics. Other portions may reside in the mass storage subsystem to be called in as overlays when a specified or requested report is to be produced.

Early identification of statistical information recording and reporting software will insure that it is properly integrated with the operating software and executes with a minimum of overhead and disturbance.

CHAPTER 14

Utility

This chapter discusses several functions that are frequently required in information networks and usually represent some form or degree of overhead. The list of functions is not necessarily all-encompassing but is representative of the types of functions that should be considered as utility. They should be evaluated to determine which is the logical or optimum place to perform them in the network and which hardware and/or software is required. In general, it is desirable to move as many of the functions as possible out into the network processor(s), thus relieving the information processor(s) of the associated overhead while increasing their throughput.

The tree structure through Level V is shown in Figure 14-1, with a listing of the entries under the Level IV heading Utility.

14-1 FORMAT CONTROL

In networks involving a variety of terminals and other source/destination devices, several different formats or interfaces may be encountered. Teletypewriter-like terminals exhibit varying line lengths and carriage control disciplines. Vertical form feed and horizontal

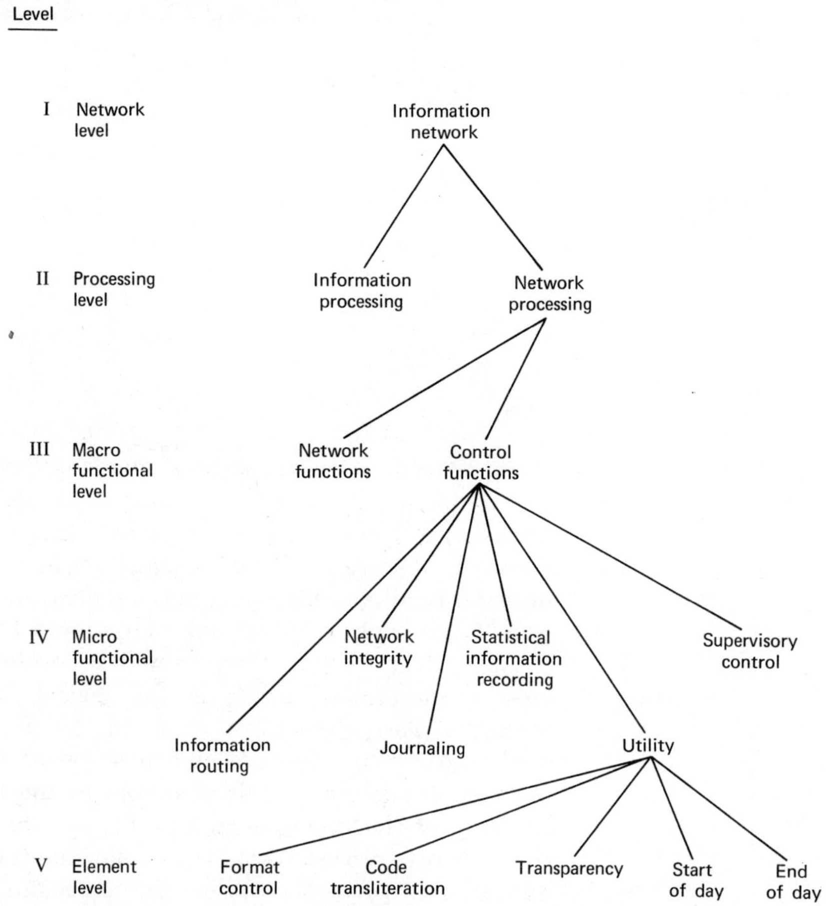

Figure 14-1 **Utility function**

tabbing features may be included or not, while upper and lower case character sets may be used. Such terminals also require that a carriage return and line-feed character be inserted at the end of each printed line so that the print mechanism is positioned for the following line.

Other similar format control functions include checking specific fields in incoming information to determine if they are all alphabetic or numeric as required and rejecting those found in error. Invalid information is thus detected in the network processor rather than an information processor, which results in a savings in the latter's overhead.

Blank suppression and the accompanying insertion of replacement codes represents another type of format control overhead that can be performed in a network processor more economically than in an information processor. The suppression technique involves sending a code indicating the number of blanks to be inserted at the receiving device rather than sending the actual required number of blanks. This results in a savings of time on the network lines and trunks, thus increasing their throughput potential. A similar suppression and insertion technique can be used when large volumes of numeric and/or alphanumeric information containing strings of consecutive zeros or other characters are encountered.

Other format validation controls include gross checking of field sequence, determining that the specified fields, in correct sequence (incoming sequence number, priority code, security code, destination code(s), end of message indicator, for example), have been input and the information is ready to be forwarded to the information processor.

14-2 CODE TRANSLITERATION

The current proliferation of terminals, processors, and other source/destination devices has resulted in the utilization of numerous code sets. Information network code set complexity ranges from the simplest, where the information and network processors and terminals all use the same code set, to the very complex, where, due to terminal and processor selection, many different code sets are encountered.

If terminals using one code set wish to send information to others using different code sets, the data must obviously pass through some device or processor capable of performing the indicated transliteration. It is not uncommon to find an information processor which uses one code set for internal processing but has a requirement to interface with a variety of terminals using several different code sets.

A logical place to perform the necessary code transliterations is in the network processor. Maintaining the required tables and algorithms there can provide a significant overhead reduction in the information processors of the network.

A partial list of code sets encountered in information networks today includes the following:

- ASCII
- EBCDIC
- 5-level Baudot
- 6-bit BCD
- 4 out of 8
- 2 out of 8
- 6-bit transcode

14-3 TRANSPARENCY

Another utility function that represents a degree of overhead is the handling of information in the transparent mode. In networks that include remote concentrators or network processors not equipped with mass storage or card input devices, it is necessary to send their operating programs to them from a suitably equipped location.

Since a program in executable form is essentially pure binary information, it does not conform to any specific code set. Depending on the number of types of nodes this binary information may pass through on the way to the remote processor, it may be necessary to enter a transparent mode. Transparent mode involves the sending of a code which informs intermediate nodes that the following block of information, of specified length, is to be treated transparently and simply passed on. This prevents the binary information from being interpreted as some other code set, which could cause any number of problems. When an 8-bit portion of it, for example, happens to be the same as an 8-bit control character in the other code set, it would be treated as that control character.

The network processor sending the transparent code blocks it in appropriate size blocks, adds the necessary control and block check characters, and initiates transmission. This is frequently done at the start of day when the remote processors are coming on-line and requesting their operating programs or when a failure has occurred and a restart/recovery procedure is required at the remote location.

Following successful receipt of the binary program information, the sending network processor terminates the transparent mode and returns to some other mode or code set used for normal operation.

14-4 START OF DAY

The network start-of-day procedure includes those functions necessary to prepare for the coming day's operation. It is required for networks that completely shut down at the end of the preceding day as well as for those that run continuously. The procedure is initiated by entry of an appropriate control message by supervisory personnel. The message contains the new day's date, current time of day, and other similar information used to initialize various fields and tables maintained by the network processor.

The start of day procedure may also attempt to establish an interface with the network's terminals to determine which of them are operational. It may also inform them that the network is operating and ready to accept incoming information. Any information left in the queues from the preceding day may also be delivered at this time.

The start-of-day software is usually maintained in the mass storage subsystem, then called in as an overlay and executed when the operating day begins.

If the network consists of several network processors acting as relay nodes, it is necessary to establish that they are all up and running before operation can begin. This requires individual start-of-day procedures at each node and may also involve the sending of operating programs to them from a location equipped with the necessary mass storage subsystem.

If the network spans several time zones, terminals will be entering their "good morning" messages at the appropriate time in their zone and requesting any information that may be in intercept queues.

In networks that operate continuously or around the clock, the start-of-day and end-of-day procedures are essentially one and the same, as both functions are performed at the same time.

14-5 END OF DAY

At the end of the operating day, several functions must be initiated to bring the network to an orderly shutdown. These functions may be initiated automatically based on the occurrence of a specified time of day, or they may be initiated as the result of a supervisory control message being entered.

Two basic types of end of day procedures exist—one for those networks that shut down completely for the night, and one for those that run continuously.

For those networks shutting down completely, it may be desirable to warn all connected terminals that shutdown is imminent and all activity should be terminated within, say, 20 minutes. No new incoming information is initiated or accepted, and polling ceases some time before actual shutdown. Dial-in lines are busied out or not answered. For message accountability purposes, the network processor may send each terminal closing down for the evening a message containing the last input and output sequence numbers. The operators can then check these against their own log to determine if any messages remain unaccounted for.

Obviously, shutdown at the precise moment specified may not

always be possible, as all incoming information initiated prior to the warning may not have terminated. Usually this information is allowed to proceed to normal termination, and then shutdown occurs.

In networks spanning several time zones, shutdown may occur in stages by zone. As terminals in the eastern time zone reach the end of the operating day, they terminate activity and enter a control or "good night" message to inform the network that they are shutting down for the evening. The network then places the terminals on an intercept basis and holds all traffic for delivery the next day. Similar activity occurs as shutdown time progresses to later time zones, until the last or western-most terminals have all entered their "good night" messages.

When all incoming information has terminated and all terminals and other source/destination devices have disconnected, the final end-of-day procedure can begin. All undelivered information remaining in the queues is repacked and readied for delivery the following day after the designated terminals enter their "good morning" messages, indicating that they are up, running, and ready to accept traffic.

The final hour's statistical report is generated along with a summary report for the entire operating day, and these are delivered to the appropriate supervisory terminal. If the network processor is one of several in the network, it may be necessary to deliver the end-of-day statistical reports to a designated central location for inclusion in a total network statistical report.

It may be necessary for a relay node network processor to remain active for a period of time after the terminals it services have shut down in order to provide the relay function for other nodes that have not yet shut down. In this case, its shutdown procedure includes two phases—one for its own terminals and the other when the relay function is no longer needed.

For networks that run continuously around the clock, the end-of-day procedure is somewhat different. At some appointed hour, usually midnight at the central or headquarters location, the end-of-day procedure is initiated. This is done either automatically or manually by supervisory personnel.

The date and time indicators are "rolled over" or updated, and other similar parameters are changed. The final hour's and the day's summary statistical reports are generated and delivered.

In this environment, the end-of-day software is usually an overlay that is brought in and executed concurrently with the continuing operational software. This presents a different programming problem compared with those networks that shut down completely and can run the end-of-day software in an essentially off-line mode.

Since portions of the terminals in the network may shut down for one or more shifts of the operating day, provision must be made to retain information to be delivered to them in either the normal or intercept queues. As the terminals going down for the evening enter their "good night" messages, they are placed on intercept until they return the following day.

Several additional functions may be necessary at network end of day. The current and/or preceding day's journal may be moved from on-line to some off-line media for historical storage. Tape files that may have been building during the operating day may require closing and rewind instructions. New disk packs mounted for the following day's journal may require initialization following physical mounting.

CHAPTER 15

Supervisory Control

The supervisory control function provides the network with an interface between the operating software and the supervisory personnel. Through the entry of coded messages, various forms of control can be exercised over the network's operation. This control may be in response to an abnormal or exceptional condition that has occurred and requires an external or manual decision to be made, or it may be a normal function, such as the addition of new terminals and trunks to the configuration.

Three broad functions are involved at supervisory control locations: entry of control messages by supervisory personnel with responses indicating execution; logging of all control activity; and delivery of periodic and summary statistical information reports.

The software required to execute the functions called for by various control messages may reside in core memory if room is available or may be maintained in a mass storage subsystem and called in for execution as an overlay. If possible, the latter case is more desirable as it frees more memory space for use by the operational software.

Since more than one control message requiring action may arrive at a given network processor at about the same time, it is necessary to queue them, either in memory or mass storage, and process them one at a time in the order received. The permanent core-resident executive software examines the next control message to be serviced, calls in the appropriate overlay routine, enters it into execution, and when that is terminated, repeats the procedure.

The tree structure through Level V is shown in Figure 15-1, with a list of the entries under the Level IV heading Supervisory Control.

15-1 CENTRALIZED SUPERVISORY CONTROL

A single, centrally located supervisory control location usually suffices for small- to medium-scale networks. It consists of one or more terminals capable of acting as a source and/or destination device.

Smaller networks may utilize a single device, which is used to enter all control messages and to which all responses or outbound control information are delivered. It may be a relatively simple keyboard input device or it may be equipped with a paper tape punch and reader. Cathode ray tube terminals are sometimes used, but they are generally more expensive and present the disadvantage of not producing a permanent hard copy of the information exchanged. This hard copy is frequently required as a permanent record of network control activity.

Larger centrally controlled networks may, due to the volume and frequency of control functions, require two or more terminals which as a group constitute the network control location. One terminal may be used for entering control messages while another, frequently a receive-only device, is used to maintain the log of the network's control activity.

The continuous form paper in the devices thus contains a chronological listing of the entered control messages and the control activity log, respectively. A third machine of the receive-only type may be included for the sole function of printing the hourly and daily summary statistical reports.

Consideration should be given to providing two or more control terminals, one of which is used as a standby or backup device in the event of failure of the on-line control terminal. The backup device may be used for the logging function under normal conditions but may also be doubled up to provide the control message input when failure of that device occurs.

Control messages are usually short coded messages containing the parameters necessary to initiate the desired function. Generally no more than one line in length, they include all or an appropriate sub-

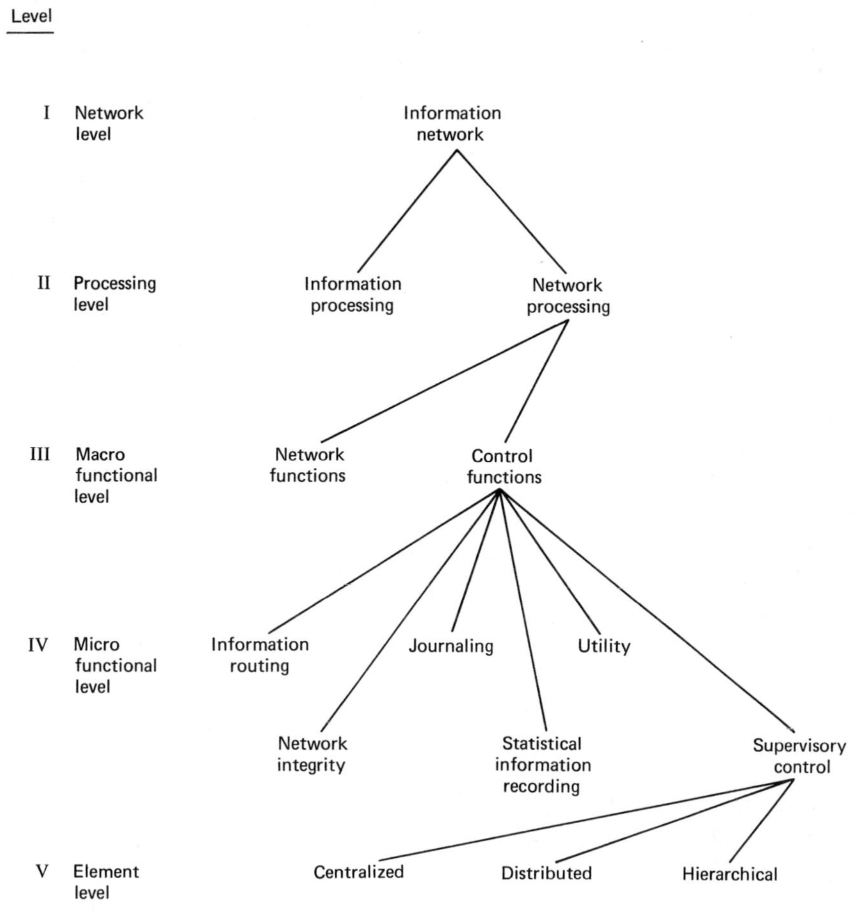

Figure 15-1 **Supervisory control function**

set of the following information: incoming sequence number, operator identification, terminal identification, control message type code, source and/or destination codes involved, security clearance code, plus information fields such as time of day, date, or other similar parameters.

Several of the more commonly used control messages are described in the following pages. They apply to all of the forms of supervisory control—centralized, distributed, and hierarchical.

Initiate Start of Day

For those networks that shut down completely at the close of an operating day, a start-of-day control message is required to initiate the following day's operation. For small- to medium-scale networks with all processors in a single location, the start-of-day procedure involves setting the time of day clock and date and preparing for the day's activity.

Larger networks with multiple information and/or network processors require multiple start-of-day procedures, including the sending of programs to those locations not capable of storing or loading their own and a means of affirming that all locations are operational.

Additional discussion concerning the start of day functions is contained in Chapter 14, Utility.

Initiate End of Day

For those networks shutting down completely, it is necessary to initiate the end-of-day procedure at the end of the operating day. This may be done automatically, based on a specified time of day, or by entry of a suitably coded control message.

The end-of-day procedure usually commences some time before actual shutdown, as discussed in Chapter 14, Utility.

Depending on the number of time zones spanned and processors involved, multiple end-of-day procedures may be required. Various locations may shut down manually or automatically at their own option, or all may wait for direction from the central or headquarters complex before initiating the end-of-day procedure.

Networks running continuously, either wholly or in part, are required to execute the end-of-day procedure concurrently with the operating software. This produces a somewhat different software design problem that must be evaluated to assure that the end-of-day software does not interfere with the operating software and that it is completed within a given time frame.

Place On Intercept

The request to place a specific destination on intercept may originate at the location itself—for paper or forms change, for example—or from a network control location because the destination device has failed or is being taken out of service. Source/destination devices may also be placed on intercept automatically as a result of their entering a terminal or station "good night" message.

All following information to be delivered to the destination is placed in the appropriate intercept queue, and the status indicators are updated to reflect the change.

Placing a terminal or destination device on intercept does not necessarily prohibit it from entering information into the network.

The device may still be perfectly capable of functioning as a source, even though it is unable to receive information.

A supervisory log entry is generated, indicating the time of the action and the destination device involved.

Remove From Intercept

When the destination device is again ready to accept information, a request to remove it from intercept status is entered, either from the device itself or from a supervisory control location. Any information accumulated in the intercept queue is delivered to the terminal at this time. A network log entry is generated, indicating the time the destination device was removed from intercept and who entered the request.

Add New Source/Destination Node

As a network grows and it becomes necessary to add new source/destination devices to the configuration, numerous hardware and software functions must be performed to implement these new devices. Ideally, the hardware and software changes can be made when the network is shut down for the evening or weekend, in which case the problems are greatly simplified.

Should it be necessary for the additions to be made while the network is operational, suitable control messages must be used to inform the operating software of the changes involved.

If a new terminal is added to an existing poll/select or contention trunk, it may be necessary to place the entire trunk on intercept and halt all incoming information. The trunk is then idle and the electrical interface can be accomplished. This idling can be produced with an appropriately coded control message.

A second control message is required to inform the software of the new device's identity—its polling/select codes, answer-back, security clearance, priority levels, polling sequence, and other similar parameters. This information is used by the operating software to update the various tables involved.

A third control message is required to remove the trunk from intercept and resume polling with the new terminal(s) now included.

The addition of a single source/destination device and a dedicated line or trunk that it alone will use can be handled in a similar fashion, with the exception that it is not necessary to place any line or trunk on intercept prior to the addition. The hardware connection is made, the identification parameters are entered, and the new line or trunk and terminal are activated.

Adding new devices to existing time and frequency division multiplexed trunks presents a similar problem. Depending on the hardware involved, it may or may not be necessary to interrupt the flow of information to the existing terminals while the hardware connection is made.

The addition of new dial-in devices is considerably simpler, in that a single control message identifying the device and its associated parameters is all that is necessary. As soon as the log entry appears indicating that the necessary tables have been updated, the new device is free to dial-in and gain access to the network.

Similar action is required to add new radio frequency coupled devices to a network. A control message is entered identifying the new terminal and its associated parameters.

In networks containing several network processors located at various nodes, information concerning the addition of new terminals must be forwarded to each of them so they can update their routing and/or queueing tables.

Delete Source/Destination Node

Continuation of network analysis or organizational changes within a corporation occasionally results in a terminal device being eliminated or moved. A series of control messages, essentially the reverse of those used to add a terminal, are required. Once the information flow to the terminal has ceased, a control message is entered instructing the network to remove it from its tables. It may be necessary in multiple processor networks to forward the delete instructions to the other network processors so that their tables can also be updated to reflect the change.

Information entered in a network for delivery to a terminal that has been deleted can be handled in a variety of ways. If no record exists in network software tables indicating that the terminal was removed, the destination code is simply interpreted as invalid, and the normal error procedure for that condition is initiated. If such a record does exist, an alternate destination may be specified to which the information is delivered, or it may be forwarded to a specified network control location for disposition.

Change Routing Table

Numerous conditions can occur which require the normal routing of information in the network to be altered. A specific terminal may be shutting down for the day while still expecting information to be delivered later in the evening. A control message is entered indicating that all following information is to be routed to a specified alternate destination which is known to remain operational for a longer period. The alternate destination may be in the same room or building, and the information delivered to it can be manually retrieved the following morning.

Alternate routing is also used when a hardware failure renders a terminal inoperable. Rather than retain information for the failed terminal in intercept queue, an alternate destination is specified and all information is routed to it. In this way, time sensitive information can be delivered with a minimum of delay until the hardware failure is corrected.

In larger networks with several relay nodes, alternate routing may be used to minimize delays encountered during peak activity periods. The configuration shown in Figure 15-2 is an example.

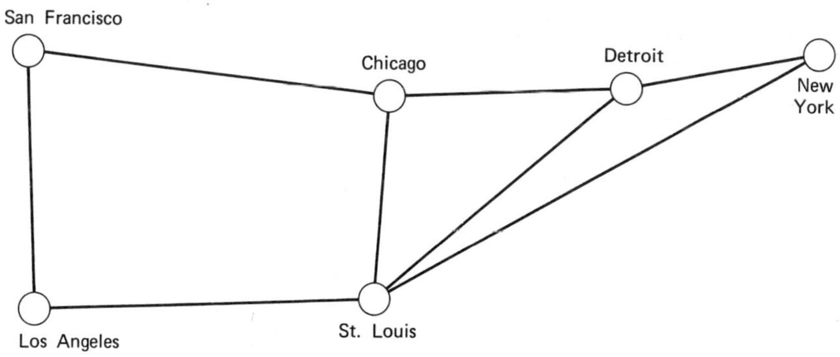

Figure 15-2 **Alternate routes**

In this example, sufficient trunks between the indicated cities have been included to assure that failure of any given trunk does not isolate a city from the network. In addition to this level of backup, the configuration can also provide a means of load leveling through the use of alternate routing techniques.

During normal periods, information flowing in the network between Detroit and San Francisco, for example, is routed through the relay node at Chicago, since this represents the most direct path. When the peak period of activity occurs at the Chicago location and the response and delay times encountered become excessive, an alternate routing technique can be initiated to reroute the information from Detroit through St. Louis and Los Angeles to San Francisco, bypassing Chicago. While the propagation or delivery time through this alternate route may be somewhat longer than the normal route, it may still be significantly shorter than that encountered during the peak period.

The alternate routing may be initiated manually through the entry of a supervisory control message, or it may occur automatically. In the latter case, each network processor at the various relay nodes examines its own volume and queueing delay statistics to determine if specified thresholds have been exceeded. When the thresholds have been exceeded, the appropriate alternate routing is initiated. This requires that messages be sent to the other nodes informing them of the peak load condition and the need for the alternate routing.

When the peak period has passed, the alternate routing is rescinded manually or automatically, and normal routing resumes.

If peak periods at the various relay nodes are predictable and occur at regular periods, the network processors at the relay nodes can be programmed to initiate the rerout function automatically when the specified time of day occurs. This is a somewhat simpler technique, as it eliminates the need to monitor various parameters to determine if the specified thresholds have been exceeded. It also eliminates the need to send control messages between nodes indicating the overload condition and requesting the alternate routing.

All Stations Broadcast

In many networks, the supervisory control station is the only one allowed to enter a message to be sent to all stations capable of receiving it. Such messages are frequently referred to as all stations broadcasts and are used for exceptional or emergency conditions when it is necessary to communicate with all network locations. The message is entered from the supervisory terminal and a copy of it is sent to all destination devices.

The network processor receiving the all stations message validates its origin and initiates the procedure to send a copy of it to all the local terminals it services as well as to all of the other network processors for delivery to the terminals they service. Depending on the priority structure of the network and the urgency associated with the all stations broadcast, it may be necessary to interrupt all current in-process outbound information and immediately initiate the all stations broadcast. If the urgency is not high, it may be simply queued in a lower level queue and delivered normally.

As is the case with other high priority or urgent information that requires the interruption of outbound information, software provisions must be made in the network processor(s) to resume transmission following the interruption. Depending on the level of urgency, the interruption may occur at the end of the current message, block, word, or character. In most business information networks, interruption at the message or block level is usually satisfactory. Government or military networks are usually the only types requiring instant interruption.

Add New Distribution Trunk/Line

Network growth and expansion frequently dictate the addition of new distribution lines or trunks. This requires a procedure similar to that for adding a new source/destination device to an existing line or trunk. Two basic functions are required to complete the addition.

The network processor that will control the line or trunk must have its tables and software updated to include the new facility. This will usually be done during an off-line period when access to the processor for the hardware modification is simplified. In addition to the changes necessary to reflect the new line or trunk, the source/destination devices to be serviced by it must be identified and the appropriate tables updated.

Other network and/or information processors in the network must also be informed of the identity of the new source/destination devices that may be included. While it is not generally necessary that they be aware of the specific line or trunk that was added, it is a requirement that the new terminals on the line or trunk be identified.

If the new line or trunk is being added to ease congestion or overload on existing facilities, the source/destination devices being serviced must then be moved and are not treated as new ones. In this case, it is not normally necessary to inform other information or network processors of the change as no new source/destination devices have been added.

Delete Distribution Trunk/Line

Removal of a distribution network line or trunk from a network processor involves one or more source/destination devices as well. If they are simply being moved to another line or trunk, as is the case when two or more lightly loaded trunks are combined, only the network processor servicing them is involved. Control messages indicating the new line or trunk and source/destination device configuration are necessary. Unless security clearance variations are involved, it is not normally necessary to inform other processors of the change.

If the deletion of the line or trunk also includes deletion of the source/destination devices, it then becomes necessary to inform other information and/or network processors of the change. Procedures described for deleting source/destination nodes can be implemented to handle information entered in the network to be delivered to a device that has been removed.

Request Journal Search

Control messages entered to request the searching of a journal for a second copy of information that has flowed within the network take a variety of forms and cause one of several actions to occur.

If the network journal is maintained at a single, centralized location, the request is sent there for disposition. If the requesting location is authorized to enter journal search messages, the responding network processor first determines if the desired information is still in the on-line journal or if, due to aging, it is in some form of off-line journal. This is established by analysis of the submitted parameters —sequence numbers, time and date of original delivery, etc.

If the desired information is still in an on-line journal, the request is queued for the journal search subroutine and processed accordingly. The search routine may be permanent core-resident or may be an overlay that must be called into memory before it can be executed.

Information in off-line journals requires that the appropriate magnetic tape or disk pack be mounted on a drive and possibly a message entered indicating that it is ready before the searching can begin.

A somewhat more complicated procedure is required for the searching of journals that are maintained on a distributed or decentralized basis. If the network processor that initially receives the search request is maintaining the appropriate journal, the search is initiated as previously described. Should the journal be maintained at some other location(s) in the network, the request must be analyzed to determine to which of the locations the request is to be sent. Depending on the search parameters submitted and the type of journaling implemented, it may be necessary to forward the request to all locations maintaining journals, one of which will respond.

In networks containing multiple relay nodes with network processors maintaining journals at several of them, information may be journaled in more than one location. The result is the possibility that two or more locations will respond to the search request since they all have the desired information in journal form. Two broad approaches exist to handle this situation.

In the first approach, the network processor initially receiving the search request polls the journal locations one at a time inquiring as to whether or not the information is available. Each polled location responds with either a negative reply, in which case the next location is polled, or a positive reply, indicating the information is available and will follow. In this approach, the software at each network processor location must maintain a list of all the other locations and the sequence in which they are to be queried. It must also have the ability to format the appropriate message containing the search parameters.

The second approach involves the sending of the search parameters to all journal locations asking only for either a positive or negative response. When these are received, one location, perhaps the closest responding positively, is asked to forward a copy of the desired information.

While the software to implement the second approach is somewhat simpler, the efficiency and overhead characteristics are not as desirable due to the line or trunk time required to forward the request to all locations.

Request Statistical Information Report

In addition to the normal statistical reports that are generated automatically every hour and delivered to the appropriate supervisory terminal, it may be desirable to allow manual request of various reports at any time of the operating day. If the available statistical reports are fixed in number and format, the control message simply indicates which one is desired and who is requesting it.

In more sophisticated networks, a list of the statistical parameters being maintained should be available and an appropriate language or generator provided to manipulate the parameters in numerous ways to produce reports tailored to specific needs.

Statistical information is collected on many levels, ranging from the number of characters sent to and received from a specific source/destination device during the preceding hour to complete hourly summaries of all activities at each network processor in the network and in the network as a whole.

Alter Poll/Select Sequence and/or Frequency

As load conditions vary on distributed multipoint lines that are operating in a poll and select environment, it is frequently desirable to alter the sequence of the polling and selecting to accommodate the shifting load and minimize both inbound and outbound queueing delays. This is usually done with a control message indicating either the new sequence to be used or designating a specific alternate sequence already in the network processor. Examination of the various hourly statistical information reports indicates at what period the load conditions occur that require poll/select sequence alteration. Obviously, following the peak period, it is necessary to restore the trunk to its original poll/select sequence.

In addition to varying the poll/select sequence, it may be necessary to alter the frequency as well. This is usually done as a means of slowing down the network or a portion of it when extreme load conditions occur that threaten collapse due to lack of memory space or processor time in a network processor. For example, adding one second to the interval between polling cycles on trunks that normally poll every two seconds can provide enough of a slowdown to avoid catastrophic collapse.

This form of safety valve can be implemented manually, in which case a control message is required each time the frequency is to be changed, or the network processor itself may monitor the memory and processor utilization parameters and initiate the slowdown automatically.

Initiate Reconfiguration

When it becomes necessary to alter the configuration of a network processor, due either to a hardware failure or to normal daily changes in the operating parameters, some form of control message is necessary to initiate the event.

Configuration changes range from enabling dial-in trunks or lines that have been busied-out or otherwise not available to moving (through use of a reconfiguration switch) lines and trunks from one network processor to another, either as a backup procedure or for load leveling, and to altering the flow of information from the network processor to one or more information processors.

In general, reconfiguration involves the alteration of known elements and should be distinguished from the addition of new elements (lines, trunks, source/destination devices, etc.) or permanent deletion of existing elements.

Reconfiguration capability may involve a variety of manual and/or program controlled line/trunk and/or peripheral switches. Depending on the particular configuration, one or more control messages may be required to effect the reconfiguration.

For manually actuated switches, one message is required to bring activity on a line, for example, to a halt and indicate what software reconfiguration is required, and then another control message is needed to indicate that the manual switching is completed and activity can resume. If the reconfiguration switch is under program control of a network processor, a single control message may suffice; the network processor brings the activities on the designated facilities to an orderly halt, initiates the switching function, and resumes operation on completion.

Initiate Restart/Recovery

Following failure of one or more hardware or software components that cause an interruption of service at a network processor location, it is necessary to initiate the appropriate restart/recovery procedure when the failure has been corrected. Depending on the complexity of the configuration and the functions being performed at the location where the failure occurred, this procedure may take a variety of forms.

In general, restart includes those functions necessary to establish connection with the devices that were active at the time of the failure, while recovery consists of the procedures required to reestablish the information flow with the degree of integrity specified.

Failure of a passive time or frequency division multiplexor servicing a cluster of source/destination devices, for example, requires that the restart/recovery procedure be initiated by the network processor servicing the multiplexor. A control message is entered, initiating the procedure, which involves reestablishing an interface with those terminals that were actively sending and/or receiving at the time of failure.

For outbound information, queues are rolled back to some logical restart point—line, block, message, etc.—and retransmitted. It may be necessary to add a trailer or flag to the retransmitted information indicating that it may be a duplicate, either wholly or in part, of information already received.

For inbound information, a message is sent to the affected terminals requesting that they retransmit their inputs starting at a similar logical point. Depending on the queueing and forwarding techniques employed in the network processor, the possibility of duplicated information exists here also, and an appropriate notice is required.

Failure of a network processor acting as a remote concentrator presents a similar restart/recovery situation. If it is capable of loading its own program from cards or paper tape, the restart may be initiated locally by supervisory personnel. If this is not possible, the programs must be sent over a trunk from the location where they are maintained.

The initial restart action in this situation is to reestablish the interface with the distant network processor servicing the remote concentrator. If no snapshot or checkpoint function is available, it must be assumed that the restart/recovery procedure has no way to reconstruct status at the time of failure. This necessitates a cold restart, resembling the start-of-day procedure, with the addition of the possible duplicate information flags mentioned earlier.

Network processors with mass storage subsystems included in the configuration make warm restarts possible if snapshot or checkpoints are defined so that critical in-core tables and indicators are periodically written out to the mass storage subsystem. The restart need only call in the latest snapshot and reconstruct from that point on.

In networks with high availability requirements that are configured with duplicate or redundant network processors, many restart/recovery possibilities exist. The duplicate processor may be in a cold, warm, or hot standby status and must be switched over accordingly.

In cold standby, the backup processor is generally running but is not loaded with the appropriate restart/recovery software and may even be in use for some other activity. Following the switchover of all lines, trunks, and peripherals, the restart/recovery software must be loaded and initiated. This form of backup requires the longest period of time to initiate.

Warm standby network processors are running with the restart/recovery software loaded and ready for initiation. The processor is usually cycling in an idle loop or may be running a continual test/diagnostic routine which is interrupted when the restart/recovery procedure is initiated. The T&D case provides a continual indication of the status of the standby processor and reduces the possibility of attempting a warm restart only to find that the backup processor has also failed and is unable to respond.

Hot standby involves a fully operational backup processor configured as an exact duplicate of the on-line processor. It is loaded and running with essentially the same software, copying all incoming information, maintaining the same in-core tables and mass storage files, if any, and doing everything except actually transmitting outbound information. Failure of the on-line network processor may result in a completely automatic switchover to the standby, in which case it immediately begins transmitting outbound with a minimum of interruption; or switchover may require that a control message be entered to initiate it.

With the current generation of available hardware, the costs involved in providing a hot standby network processor capable of initiating outbound transmission with no interruption place it beyond the reach of most commercial network users. It is, therefore, generally necessary to include in the hot restart software some level of backup or rollback to cover the possibility of duplicate information.

Restart/recovery procedures at levels lower than network processors and multiplexors are required in most networks as part of the standard operating software. Failure of a terminal device during transmission and/or receipt of information, for example, requires logic in the servicing network processor to detect the failure and take appropriate action. For outbound information, the queue pointers are updated to indicate that the information was not successfully delivered, and the terminals may be put on intercept automatically until the failure is corrected.

For incoming information, two or more possibilities exist. If the incoming information is still in the receiving network processor, either core or mass storage, it can be eliminated since it is incomplete, and the associated tables and pointers can be updated accordingly. If a portion of it has been passed on to another network node, it is necessary to generate and forward a control message to that node indicating that the transmitting terminal failed and the information from it is incomplete.

Add New Relay Node

Growth of a network, either through gradual expansion or acquisition, may result in the need for an additional relay node. Several control messages are required to make the addition and inform other network nodes of the resulting new configuration.

If network analysis indicates that a cluster can be adequately served by a passive time or frequency division multiplexor, the network processor servicing it will require hardware and software changes. The hardware changes involve the trunk to service the multiplexor, while the software changes include updating the various tables and pointers involved in interfacing to the trunk and servicing the source/destination devices connected to it. It is also necessary that other network processors in the network be informed of the identity and location of the new source/destination devices so their routing tables can be updated.

If the new relay node is to be a network processor, the software in it must be structured to interface with its complement of source/destination devices. As in the previous case, the rest of the network must be informed of their identity and location. In addition, the one or more trunks between the new and existing network processors must be configured and identified so that the appropriate routing tables can be updated. This new routing capability may affect backup or alternate routing schemes as well as normal routing.

Delete Relay Node

Deletion of a relay node is essentially the converse of its addition. Hardware changes are required to reconfigure the affected lines, trunks, and network processors. Software changes are necessary to reflect the loss of source/destination devices and/or routing capability.

If the deletion is part of a consolidation effort, and a portion or all of the involved source/destination devices will be changed to some other form of access to the network, then the appropriate line, trunk, and terminal addition messages are also required.

As is always the case when terminals are deleted, some procedure for handling information entered in the network to be delivered to them must be included in the affected network processors.

Enable/Disable Message Type

A form of supervisory control that can be imposed on a network and the terminal operators themselves is the ability to enable or disable a terminal or group of terminals relative to a specific message type. This control may be desired on either a scheduled or on a random basis.

Assume, for example, that a particular file is maintained on random access storage media by a host information processor that does not have concurrent update capability. This file is processed by a batch program on a daily or other periodic basis. During this processing, all transactions against the file are prohibited. A supervisory control message to the appropriate network processor(s) will cause all messages of that particular type to be rejected with an appropriate response to the terminal.

A second need for this form of control might involve a terminal manned by an operator not responsible for, or cleared for, entry of a specific message type or types. A supervisory control message to the appropriate network processor(s) will limit that terminal to only those message types allowed and will cause all others to be rejected.

It may be necessary in larger networks spanning broader corporate organizational structures to implement the enable/disable function on a terminal *and* operator basis. Some terminals may be enabled for a certain set of message types regardless of the operator's identity. Other terminals may be cleared for a similar set of message types, with a subset of these requiring specific operator identification procedures. In this way, certain sensitive message types can be restricted to specified terminals and specifically authorized operators.

Alter Send/Receive Limit

As a means of controlling the entry of excessive or unnecessary messages into the network, limits can be established and altered on a per station basis. These limits are in the form of maximum message counts that a given terminal may send or receive in a given time frame. The limits may vary as to the proportion of send and receive, and will also vary from terminal to terminal. Analysis of the various statistical reports produced by the network, coupled with reports from the terminal operators, will establish the guidelines for these limits.

The limits may be entered and/or changed by entering the appropriate supervisory control message. The limit may be per hour, per shift, or per day as necessary.

Another form of send/receive limit that is frequently necessary involves the maximum number of messages that may be received or sent during one "connect" period by the terminal. This form is most often used when several terminals share the same line or trunk in a distributed multipoint configuration. By limiting the maximum send/receive per connection, the time per connection is also limited. This insures that a single terminal will not utilize the line for inordinate time periods, depriving other terminals on the line of reasonable access rates. These limits may also vary as to send/receive proportion or as to time of day or other operating period.

Initiate Test/Diagnostic Procedure

The multitude of different hardware elements found in networks of even moderate size makes the tracking and identification of component failures difficult. The detection of a failure ranges from a manual procedure in smaller networks (a message was garbled on receipt or not received at all) to fairly sophisticated techniques employed in larger networks (error detection software has encountered a string of messages that fail the check character or sequence test). In any case, a failure has occurred and must be located and fixed before normal operation can be restored.

A series of test and diagnostic procedures can be initiated through entry of the appropriate supervisory message. The receiving network processor may start by causing the channel that interfaces to the digital subset on the suspected line to loop-back on itself. A test sequence is then sent out on the transmit side and examined on the receive side of the channel. If the sent and received messages agree, the channel is not at fault and the problem lies elsewhere.

If the subset is so equipped, the network processor can cause a similar loop-back to occur within it and repeat the test message. This now moves the test out into the network one more step. If the subset on the network processor is operating properly, the loop-back test can then be moved to the remote subset and repeated (if the subset includes the loop-back capability). Some terminal devices also include a similar loop-back test capability.

In this fashion, successive network elements between the network processor and the source/destination device experiencing difficulty can be tested. As soon as the test fails, the failed component has been identified, or at least the possible choices have been narrowed down to a manageable number. Since the components may be a great distance apart, considerable time can be saved in this manner, and that portion of the network can be returned to operational status as quickly as possible.

Other forms of failure can be identified through test and diagnostic procedures. A network processor suspected of failure can be tested by entering a message to be routed through it and returned to the test source or some other location. Message content, response time, adherence to priority levels, sequence number assignment, and other indicators can then be evaluated. Components of network processors, such as disk files and other storage media, can be similarly checked.

Larger networks will frequently include test and diagnostic subroutines in the network processors available for automatic execution. This execution may occur at regularly scheduled times or whenever an idle period occurs, and no higher priority activity will be delayed.

Clear Circuit

A circuit connecting a network processor to one or more terminals may fail for a variety of reasons, leaving one or more messages partially sent or received. If it is a hard (not intermittent) failure, a supervisory control message can be entered instructing the network processor to set the circuit (line or trunk) to idle. This activity may include backing the outbound queues of the network processor up to the start of the message(s) in process. This enables the complete message(s) to be retransmitted when the failure is corrected. Similarly, that portion of the incoming traffic that was received may be discarded. Sequence numbers maintained by the network processor may also require adjustment. When the failure has been corrected, a second supervisory message is entered, restoring the circuit to active status so that normal operation proceeds. It may be necessary to send a message to those terminals that were active at the time of failure, informing them of the problem.

It may be desirable to enter a "clear circuit" control message even though no failure has occurred. In this case, the network processor may allow all in-process messages to complete and will not accept any more incoming messages or initiate any more outgoing messages. The circuit will then reach a clear or idle state and can be used for the desired purpose, perhaps sending an all stations broadcast, initiating a test and diagnostic procedure, shutting down for the day, or other similar function.

Change Error Threshold

Numerous error thresholds may be established concerning the operation of various network elements. These thresholds should be flexible enough to meet the variations in error frequency that can and do occur. Examples include the number of NACK's accepted from a receiving device before a hard failure is assumed, the number of times a "no response" to a polling or selecting sequence is accepted before the terminal is declared out of service, and others.

These error rates are frequently influenced by transient events, such as local thunderstorm activity producing noise on transmission lines, local power fluctuations or outages causing erratic terminal operation, and others. By changing the error thresholds in the appropriate network processors, error messages will not be sent out at such a rapid rate. This allows the terminal involved to maintain a level of access to the network, even if a degraded one. When the transient event clears, the thresholds can be returned to their original state and normal operation resumed.

15-2 DISTRIBUTED SUPERVISORY CONTROL

Larger networks with multiple network processors may find that some form of distributed supervisory control is more optimum and responsive than a single, centrally located implementation. The selection of the control locations may be on some district, regional, or area basis or may be simply those locations where network processors have been placed.

Each supervisory control location must include the logic necessary to handle the control messages that are encountered. Logging of the control message activity may or may not occur at the location, depending on the anticipated volume. For those locations with high control message volumes that are also operator attended, an appropriate control station or terminal is required. The lower volume locations may log their control activity on the supervisory terminal or maintain the log in queue and periodically send it to some location equipped with a logging device.

As in centralized supervisory control, two types of control messages are encountered—those that are entered from a source/destination device serviced by the network processor and those that are entered from the control terminal adjacent to it.

15-3 HIERARCHICAL SUPERVISORY CONTROL

It may be desirable or even necessary in large networks with distributed supervisory requirements to provide some method of controlling the entry of supervisory messages.

The supervisory control function can be organized into three hierarchical levels.

Terminal Supervisory Control

This level includes those functions that can be initiated by terminals in the network. It includes such things as requests for retransmission of a lost or destroyed message, requests to be placed on intercept for paper change and removed when complete, and other similar terminal-oriented activities.

In networks with various classes of terminals or levels of security, it may be desirable to identify subsets of the terminal control functions and only accept control messages within the subset that a specific terminal is assigned to.

Intermediate Supervisory Control

Included in this level are those control functions that are limited to supervisory control stations—they cannot be initiated from a terminal device. Adding or deleting terminals or trunks to the software tables representing the network configuration, requesting a statistical information report, changing a trunk routing table, and altering poll/select sequences are examples of intermediate supervisory control functions. Such control messages are entered from terminal devices that have been identified as supervisory control. Usually these are located at relay nodes in the network where a network processor has been configured, and the control messages are initially received and acted upon by that processor.

The set of functions that can be initiated by intermediate supervisory control terminals usually, but not necessarily, includes the lower terminal control functions as a subset.

Master Supervisory Control

This level of supervisory control includes all lower level functions plus the ability to initiate actions reserved exclusively for the designated master control terminal. The master control terminal is usually located in some central facility or in the corporate headquarters.

The terminal complement for the master supervisory control function in larger networks usually consists of several devices; one or more receive-only devices for activity logs and statistical reports, an active master device for entering control messages, and one or more standby or backup devices for use in the event of failure.

Control functions usually reserved for the master location include the initiation of the network start- and end-of-day activities, changing of security level information in routing tables, and other sensitive activities whose initiation should not be possible by any intermediate or terminal level messages.

As discussed in Chapter 4, larger networks may require a logical subsetting of the supervisory control functions based on departmental, district, regional, or some other corporate organizational boundaries. Those networks shared by entirely separate corporations have a similar subsetting requirement. A similar problem is presented by a cluster of terminals unique to a specific corporate entity requiring supervisory control functions unlike any others in the network.

SECTION V

Information Network Example

This section presents a discussion of an existing information network that embodies many of the concepts and functions described in earlier chapters. The Advanced Research Projects Agency (ARPA), Washington, D.C., was chosen as it: (1) is heavily communications oriented; (2) is nationwide in scope; and (3) has documentation available.

The discussion proceeds in the same basic sequence as the main body of the book—the network or hardware functions first, followed by the control or software functions. Since the ARPA network was designed from a slightly different point of view than would be used by a large-scale business information network user, not all of the functions defined in the tree structure appear in ARPA. Further, some specific assumptions and design goals were adopted in the ARPA network that are perhaps unique in ARPA or ARPA-like networks and would not appear in business information networks.

CHAPTER **16**

The Advanced Research Projects Agency Network

The ARPA network was conceived as a means of providing a resource sharing capability between a number of geographically distributed computer installations engaged primarily in computer research. The resources to be shared include the computer hardware, the software, and the data files at the various locations. The stated goal of the ARPA network was to make every resource at every location available to any user regardless of his location.

The initial configuration included 18 existing computer installations, ranging from MIT in Massachusetts to UCLA in Southern California. The computers at these locations encompass a wide variety of manufacturers' standard offerings and a number of unique machines such as the Illiac IV at the University of Illinois.

The approximate ARPA network topology as of August 1972 is shown in Figure 16-1.

The first phase of the ARPA network which started in September 1969 included 14 of the sites, which were connected and used for initial research and experimentation. In late 1970, a second phase involving extension to over 34 sites and exposure to the external research community was started.

Several basic considerations influenced the

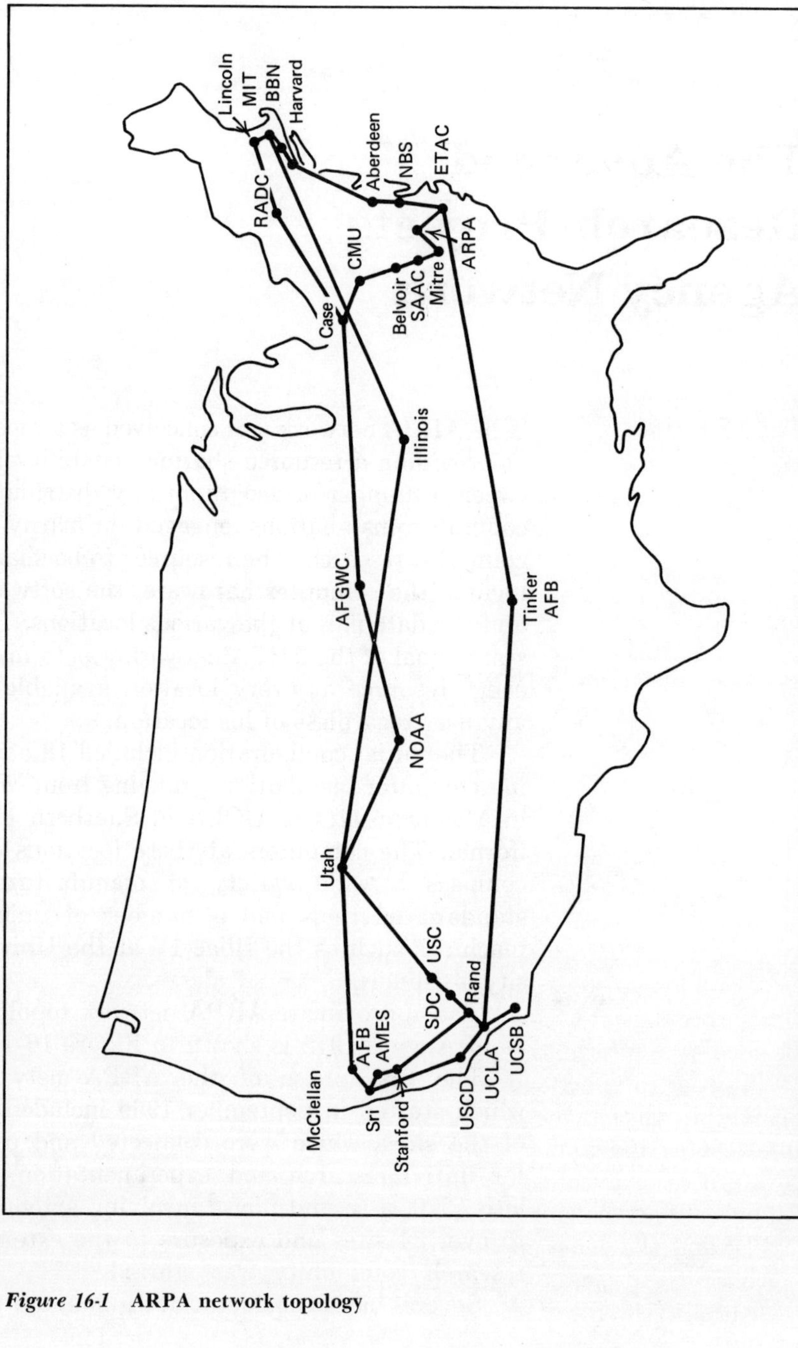

Figure 16-1 **ARPA network topology**

design and implementation of the ARPA network, among which were reliability, responsiveness, capacity, and cost.

Since the network would be heavily dependent on common carrier supplied lines and trunks, it was necessary to: (1) provide the error detection and retransmission capability required to overcome line or trunk induced errors; and (2) configure the lines and trunks such that at least two physically separate paths exist between any pair of nodes in the network.

Since time-sharing or similar interactive access to the network will constitute much of the usage, delays encountered in the network must be kept to a minimum. A response time of .5 second was set as a design goal.

The amount of information flowing in the network of 20 nodes was estimated to be 200–800 Kbps (kilo bits per second) during the peak hours by mid-1971. This means that each node must pass 10–40 Kbps during the peak hours of the operating day.

It was felt that the cost of the communications capability for the network should not be more than 25% of the cost of the connected computing systems in order to be efficient. This is somewhat at odds with the trend evolving in the business data processing community, where the communications equipment cost is rising to meet or exceed the cost of the information processors.

SEPARATION OF FUNCTION

It was recognized early in the design of the ARPA network that: (1) the individual computer centers should not be required to deal with the network processing functions of information routing; and (2) the network interconnecting the computer centers should be independent of the information processing functions performed at those centers. This is precisely the separation of the information and network processing functions that is and will continue to be the key to the success of information networks.

In order to effect this separation of function, it was decided that a small but efficient network processor would be placed at each computer center and would act as its interface to the network. This network processor is called an IMP (Interface Message Processor); the computer it serves is called a Host. The relationship between Hosts, IMP's, and the remainder of the network is shown in Figure 16-2, which represents just a portion of the total network.

Initially, the interface between the Hosts and the clusters of ter-

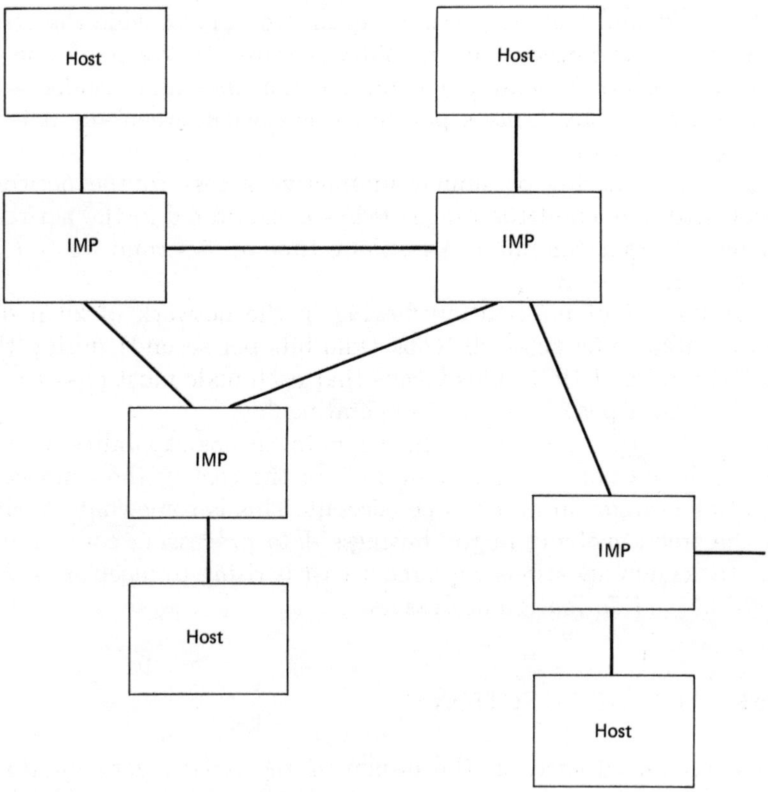

Figure 16-2 **IMP/host relationship**

minals they serviced was to be provided by the Host processors, using equipment and techniques already in place. In this way, information would flow into a Host from a terminal, possibly through a multiline controller, and then be sent by the host to its associated IMP for delivery to the distant computer center being utilized.

Later, in order to make the network and its resources available to more users without adding the increased terminal interface overhead to existing, or possibly additional, Hosts, the use of Terminal Interface Processors (TIP's) was explored. These TIP's perform the same relay node function as the IMP's and, in addition, interface with up to 63 local or remote consoles or remote job entry terminals operating at speeds up to 19.2 Kbps.

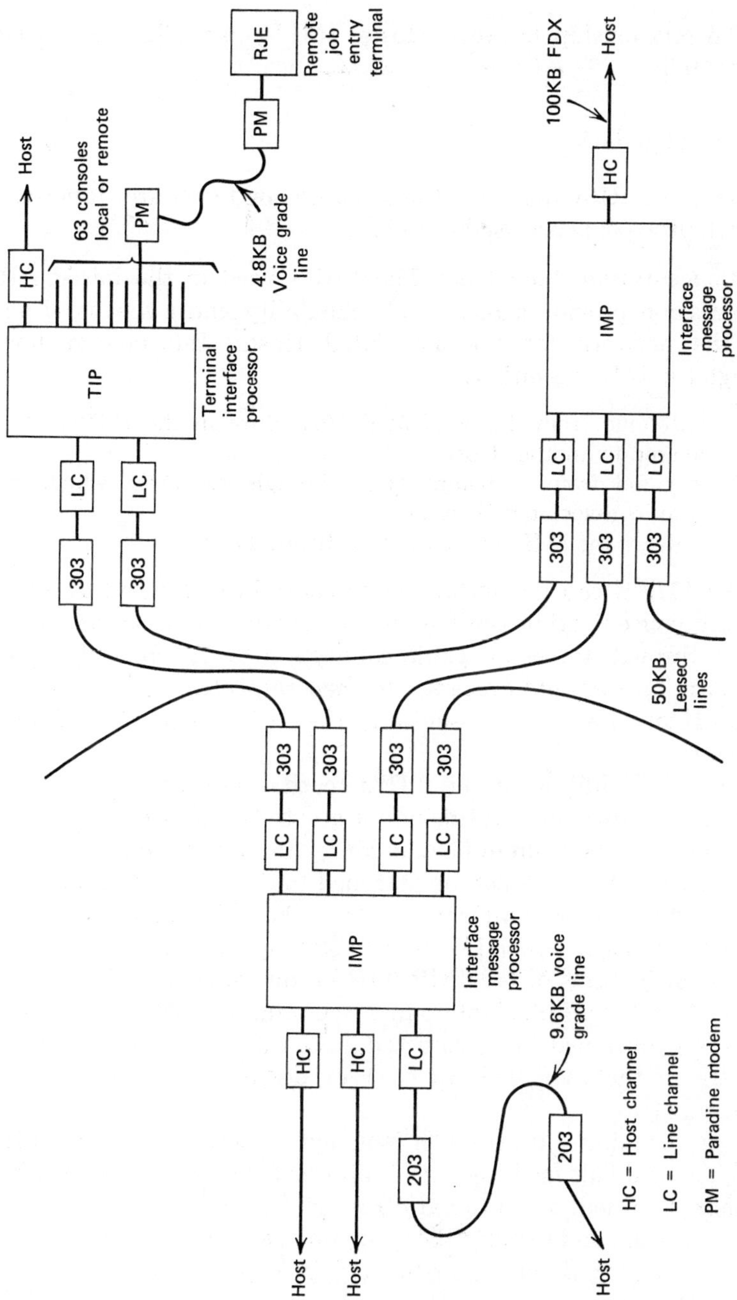

Figure 16-3 **ARPA network**

The relationship between Hosts, IMP's, and TIP's is shown in Figure 16-3.

Network Functions

Within the ARPA network, the network, or hardware, functions of network processing are used as follows.

The Concentration Function. The IMP's used in the initial ARPA configuration provide a relay node capability and a means of accessing the network for the associated Hosts. Information flowing through the IMP's is either:

1. outbound from the associated Host through the IMP to be delivered to another Host,
2. inbound from a distant Host through the IMP, which relays it to its associated Host, or
3. through the IMP on its way to a distant Host.

The IMP'S can be considered as centralized concentrators since they are concentrating the flow of information from several possible sources through the single cable connection to the Host. The IMP's are a form of front-end processor to their respective Hosts. The IMP–TIP-to-Host interface is essentially the "I" configuration discussed in Chapter 5, page 50.

With the addition of the TIP's to the network, the relay node functions are expanded to include a greater level of centralized concentration. A maximum of 63 source/destination devices operating at speeds up to 19.2 Kbps can be attached to each TIP. The TIP's then concentrate the flow of information from these devices over the higher capacity trunks to other IMP's or TIP's in the network.

Several features of the IMP/TIP hardware contribute to its reliability. A 512-word block of memory containing special recovery programs is maintained in a protected status. It is not possible for any software in the IMP/TIP to alter or destroy the contents of the protected area.

A power-failure interrupt is included to permit the IMP/TIP to reach a logical halt in the event of failure of the primary power. When power is returned, an automatic restart feature turns the processor on, cycles it up, and restarts the program.

A "watchdog timer" implemented in hardware transfers control to the recovery software in the protected memory area if the operating software ignores the timer for more than 60 seconds. The restart and recovery functions implemented in the IMP/TIP configuration are covered later in this chapter under the discussion of "Network Integrity."

The Coupling Function. A variety of analog couplers in the form of digital subsets are used in the ARPA network to connect the IMP's and TIP's to the distribution network lines and trunks (refer to Figure 16-3).

The IMP's and TIP's are coupled to the 50Kbps interconnecting leased lines with Bell System 303C digital subsets. The subsets operate in the two-way simultaneous (full-duplex) mode.

In some instances, the IMP-to-Host interface is accomplished using a leased voice band line operating at 9600 bits per second. The couplers at each end of these lines are Bell System 203A series operating in the full-duplex mode.

Remote job entry terminals can gain access to the network through the TIP's via 4800 bit per second leased lines, using couplers supplied by the Paradine Company.

Other source/destination devices accessing the network through the TIP's use couplers appropriate for their operating speed. These couplers range from the Bell System 103 series for devices operating in the 0–300 bit per second range to the Bell System 303B at 19,200 bits per second. This latter coupler represents the highest speed interface possible through the TIP's, with the exception of the Hosts themselves.

The Distribution Function. The selection of the distribution lines to interconnect the IMP's and TIP's of the ARPA network was the result of extensive analysis and comparison of several line types and interconnection possibilities. Included in the list were: 2.4Kbps and 19.2Kbps leased, 50Kbps switched, direct distance dialing at 2Kbps, and 50Kbps leased.

The two most revealing comparisons made were: (1) the cost per million bits transmitted as a function of the delay; and (2) the effective bandwidth as a function of the block size of the information. These studies were made assuming a 1400 mile distance, which is the average distance between pairs of nodes in the ARPA network.

The 50Kbps leased lines were finally chosen as they provide the best performance at the relatively small block sizes where most of the ARPA traffic is expected. Since the 50Kbps lines were obtained by ARPA directly through government purchasing channels, it is not known if they would be the best choice for a commercial business making similar studies using the standard rates.

The Switching Function. Currently available literature does not indicate the use of any form of line-trunk switch or reconfiguration switch in the ARPA network.

Source/Destination Interface. Excluding the interface to the terminals connected directly to the Host information processors and those connected to the TIP's, the source/destination interfaces of major interest in the ARPA network are: Host-to-IMP/TIP and IMP/TIP-to-IMP/TIP.

The Host-to-IMP/TIP interface was designed to operate asynchronously with information flowing in both directions simultaneously. Each IMP/TIP was designed to service up to four Hosts. A portion of the interface hardware is standard in the IMP/TIP configuration, with the remaining portion unique for each different Host being serviced.

The IMP/TIP-to-Host interface is such that the IMP/TIP can continue to function even though one or more of the Hosts is malfunctioning or even down. There is no reliance on the Host for any assistance, such as buffer storage or program reloading in the event of failure of an IMP/TIP. The Hosts cannot alter the operation or configuration of the IMP's/TIP's, thus assuring completely autonomous operation.

Information stored on either side of the interface to be forwarded to the other is under control of the storing processor (IMP/TIP or Host). Initiation of the transfer is entirely under control of the storing processor and does not require any action from the receiving processor.

Since information is passed across the interface in both directions, the processors on either side are simultaneously sources and destinations. These source/destination pairs can be considered as fixed, since neither one of the pair will be moved unless removed from the network.

The information flow rate across the interface is variable and is governed by a "Ready for next bit/Here's your bit" handshake procedure. A manually adjustable delay time between bits is introduced in the IMP/TIP, thereby limiting the maximum rate. This technique allows the flow rate to adjust to the slower of the two processors. A receiving processor can further slow the rate by introducing additional delay in the handshake procedure.

The IMP/TIP-to-IMP/TIP interface includes several features to insure high reliability and accuracy. The hardware itself was ruggedized, although not to complete military specifications. This added approximately 10% to the hardware cost.

Special crosspatching or loop-back features were built into the interface hardware, allowing program controlled connection of specific output lines to corresponding input lines. During the execution of a special test program or the operational program itself, a test message can be sent on the output line and the looped back input line examined to determine of the data returns as sent or has been altered.

Control Functions

Since all Host computers in the ARPA network support research independent of the network and are under a time-sharing discipline as well, the following philosophy was observed in designing the control function software:

1. The independent, decentralized administrative control of the individual Hosts will be maintained. The load received from the network will be handled in the same manner as the locally generated load.
2. Due to the time-sharing nature of the Hosts and the network, the interactive disciplines will be facilitated.
3. The network control functions will not impose any restrictions concerning character sets or programming languages.
4. The design is open-ended to facilitate the inclusion of conventions arising from solid user experience, rather than arbitrarily imposed initially.
5. The various Host operating systems will be changed as little as possible.
6. In support of point 2 above, it is assumed that major network usage will consist of prolonged interactive exchanges, rather than one-shot requests for access.

The control function software in all IMP/TIP processors is identical, with the exception of that which is resident in the 512-word protected memory area. The protected software contains everything that is unique to the IMP/TIP that it resides in, which greatly facilitates the restart/recovery procedure discussed later in this chapter.

Each Host in the network contains a Network Control Program (NCP) that is usually a part of its operating system. The NCP is used by the Host to allow programs or processes within it to communicate with the network. The NCP functions include the initiation of connections, breaking connections, switching connections, and control of the information flow.

Information Routing. Information addressing in the ARPA network is primarily of the explicit form. Terminal users signing on at their Host and desiring access to a distant or foreign Host specify its address explicitly as part of the logging in procedure. Each Host in the network is identified by a unique 8-bit number that becomes a part of the address.

Each user accessing the network is identified by a unique 24-bit number that is recognized throughout the network. This number includes the user's 8-bit home Host designation and a 16-bit number which uniquely identifies the user at that Host.

The sending Host in a transmission is identified by a bit configuration known as a "send socket," and the receiving Host is identified by a "receive socket." This pair of sockets identify a "connection." A pair of these "connections" is required for a two-way exchange of information between Hosts.

It is possible for a user in the ARPA network to have a user number that does not associate him with any particular Host. This capability facilitates the mobile user with no fixed home Host and the user associated with several Hosts. Any processes initiated in any Host or Hosts by such users are tagged with the user number. Virtual networks consisting of processes initiated by these users may span any number of Hosts. These virtual networks allow the user to take advantage of the capabilities of several computers in the network by interconnecting processes initiated in them.

Messages originating in a sending Host are presented to its IMP/TIP in segments which are formed of packets of approximately 1000 bits maximum. These packets are forwarded separately into the network. The receiving IMP/TIP of the destination Host reassembles the packets into a message and delivers them in sequence to the receiving Host.

The trunk routing algorithms used in the ARPA network were designed to provide for the smallest possible in-transit delay times. Paths between pairs of Hosts are not determined in advance and in fact may change several times during a single transmission.

Each IMP/TIP estimates the expected delay for each possible destination on each of its output lines every half second. This estimate is passed on to each adjacent IMP/TIP as well as used to update the estimating IMP/TIP tables. In selecting the trunk to be used to forward information, each IMP/TIP examines its own delay tables and those of its adjacent neighbors, looking for the shortest delay time available.

This form of heuristic trunk routing provides not only the shortest possible in-transit delay but a high degree of dynamic load leveling as well. Congested IMP's/TIP's or those experiencing difficulties are automatically avoided by the adjacent IMP/TIP locations.

A valuable benefit of the ARPA trunk routing algorithm is that each IMP/TIP in the network does not require knowledge of the entire network topology. It is not even necessary that they know the identity of their immediate neighbors. This capability greatly facilitates reconfiguration of the network without requiring extensive changes in the IMP/TIP software.

All information flowing in the ARPA network is treated as having the same priority level. This simplifies the IMP/TIP software by eliminating the need for multiple priority level tables, queues, and routing algorithms.

Rerouting and intercept capability as such are not included in the ARPA network, except within the bounds of the dynamic trunk routing previously discussed.

The interface between the ARPA Hosts and their IMP/TIP frontends takes one of two forms. The "I" configuration is used where the IMP/TIP is providing access to the network for a single associated Host. The radial configuration is used when a single IMP/TIP is providing access for more than one Host. Due to the nature of the information flow and the lack of a requirement for journaling capability, mass storage devices such as disks or tapes were not considered.

A message sent from a Host to its IMP/TIP to be forwarded to a distant Host is received by that Host, and a request for next message (RFNM) is sent back before the sending Host can enter its next message. This mechanism acts to prevent an individual user from overloading a Host or IMP/TIP processor and as such is a form of inherent load leveling.

Each Host in the network contains a software module known as a Network Control Program, or NCP. The NCP in each Host provides it with access to the network and control of the resulting information flow. The NCP thus interfaces with various user software in the Host on one side and the IMP/TIP that is servicing it on the other.

Network Integrity. Numerous features were included in the ARPA design to maintain network integrity. At a high level, the trunks between the IMP's/TIP's were configured such that at least two paths exist between any IMP/TIP and any other. This configuration plus the dynamic routing algorithm already discussed assures that the failure of a single trunk will not cause loss of access to any Host computer.

Integrity of information moved through the network is maintained through the use of a 24-bit checksum that is appended to each block of 1000 bits by the sending IMP/TIP. The receiving IMP/TIP generates its own checksum as it receives the information and compares it with the one appended to the block. If both checksums agree, the information is assumed to be correct in the receiving IMP/TIP and can now be forwarded on the next leg of its journey to the destination. Failure of the checksum to agree after comparing results in the receiving IMP/TIP causes a negative acknowledge to be sent back to the sending IMP/TIP, which responds by sending the block of information again. It is estimated that the undetected error rate in the ARPA network is on the order of one in 10^{12} bits transmitted. This rate equates to approximately one undetected error per year for the entire network.

As mentioned earlier, the IMP/TIP hardware selected was ruggedized and maintains a Mean Time Between Failure (MTBF) of approximately 10,000 hours, which is less than one failure per year per device. The absence of mass storage devices (disks, which usually represent a lower MTBF due to their electromechanical rather than pure electronic nature) on the IMP's/TIP's also contributes to the high reliability of the network.

The lack of mass storage capability contributes to increased throughput and performance of the IMP's/TIP's by eliminating the access, latency, and queue times inherent in their use. However, it is not possible to maintain any long-term message storage at the IMP/TIP locations or to provide any form of individual message accounting.

Failure of a Host results in word of the event being forwarded to all remaining Hosts in the network so that they can suspend requests for access to the failed unit. This contributes to keeping the amount of nonusable information in the network to a minimum.

During idle periods in the network, the IMP/TIP processors exchange special "Hello" messages over their interconnecting trunks. The correct acknowledgement for a "Hello" message is an "I heard you" message, which must be received within approximately 2.5 seconds. Absence of either regular messages or "I heard you" messages for 2.5 seconds causes the associated IMP/TIP to assume the trunk is dead and logically remove it from service.

All information in queue that would have been forwarded on the dead trunk is automatically rerouted on another trunk. The necessary routing tables of the network are also automatically updated to indicate the dead trunk. When the trunk has been restored and is again operational, the IMP's/TIP's that it connects are required to exchange 30 Hello messages before they consider the trunk usable again.

Should it happen that enough interconnecting trunks fail to make it impossible to establish any route between two IMP's/TIP's, they are defined as disconnected and each discards all messages waiting to be forwarded to the other. A similar purge occurs to rid the network of messages destined for dead Hosts. This purge can occur at either the source or destination IMP/TIP.

A valuable tool included in the network design is the ability to trace the flow of information as it moves through the network. Host processors wishing to have a message they are entering traced do so by turning a trace bit "on" in the header. Every IMP/TIP that handles any portion of such tagged messages generates special statistics which are forwarded to a specified Host, where they are printed out for evaluation.

Journaling. As previously mentioned, no provision was made in the initial ARPA design for mass storage devices on the IMP/TIP processors, thus eliminating the journaling capability. The ARPA designers decided that, should journaling or message accounting become a desirable feature, it could be added at a later date by creating a special node in the network.

Message accounting information as well as information that is currently undeliverable (Host down or unreachable) could then be forwarded to the journaling location. This latter use of the mass storage device is an example of an intercept queue.

If the mass storage device were to be used for any extensive journaling, additional studies would be required to determine the load imposed on the network by sending a copy of all information to be journaled to this journaling location. At some level, this load could begin to affect response times and might indicate the need for a distributed rather than centralized journaling capability.

Statistical Information Recording. Various types of statistical records concerning the flow of information and the performance of the network are generated by the IMP/TIP processors. This statistical record keeping is normally performed as a matter of course, but provision is made for turning it on and off from remote locations via a suitable supervisory control message.

All statistics collected by the IMP's/TIP's are sent to a specified Host, where they are evaluated and the corresponding reports produced. The types of statistics collected include snapshots of current queue lengths and routing information, 10-second summaries of information flow statistics, and packet (portion of a message) arrival times.

The snapshots are taken every half second by the IMP/TIP processors. A synchronization technique is used to insure that this event occurs at approximately the same time in all locations. This synchronization is necessary to produce an instantaneous picture of the entire network for analysis by the Host receiving the statistics.

The 10-second summaries are primarily concerned with message counts by type flowing through the IMP/TIP processors, number of retransmissions required due to error conditions, message flow in and out of the associated Host, and other similar statistics.

The statistics reflecting the packet arrival times at the IMP/TIP processors are used as input to various models of line traffic produced and maintained at a specific Host in the network.

The information generated through use of the trace function mentioned previously is also statistical in nature. Each IMP/TIP that handles a packet of information records its time of arrival and departure, how long it was resident in various queues, and other information concerning its handling of the packet.

Statistical information concerning the flow of information in the ARPA network is generated on a distributed basis due to the multiplicity of IMP/TIP processors. These statistics plus the trace function provide valuable insight as to the performance of the network as a whole, as well as the ability to detect existing or potential flow-related problems at a specific location. Variations in queueing techniques or routing algorithms can be tested and evaluated much more effectively than is possible using purely analytic or simulation approaches.

Supervisory Control. Supervisory control of the type most frequently found in business information networks is not used in the ARPA network. Teletypewriters are attached to the IMP/TIP processors but are used only for maintenance, debugging, and system modification.

Many of the functions normally included in manual supervisory control are automatically performed in the ARPA network. Rerouting, load leveling, and intercept are examples. The high level of attention given these functions during the ARPA design and their implementation as automatic rather than manual resulted in a network requiring little, if any, manual control or intervention while running. Malfunction or failure of a network element—line, Host, or IMP/TIP—is handled automatically with minimum disruption or degradation of service with notification of the failure made at the appropriate Host.

Conclusion

The ARPA network represents an ideal proving ground for the design and implementation of information and network processing techniques. Spanning the continental U.S., its topology is broad enough to be representative of most, if not all, networks currently installed or under investigation.

Several problems not previously evident but of growing magnitude in business information networks have been explored and solutions presented. The most significant of these is coexistence in a common network between computers made by several different manufacturers. This is exactly the problem faced by many companies today that are attempting to connect installed computers at distributed locations into a common information network. Obviously, it is desirable to do this in a manner that creates the minimum amount of hardware and software disturbance at each location.

The fundamental design goal of the ARPA network—make every resource at every location available to any user at any location—is similar to the business community's desire to make the computational power of its computers available to ever-widening spheres of existing and potential users.

Setting and meeting a design goal of .5 second response time from any node to any other node in the network, using regular common carrier facilities, has shown that such expectations are not unrealistic. This should go far in convincing the business community that such networks can be extremely responsive to their needs.

The high reliability and availability of the network and its inherent ability to provide access even though one or more elements have failed should instill a measure of confidence in those reluctant to depend on such networks.

Several functions required in business information networks were not included in the ARPA design—multiple priority levels, message journaling and accounting, and others. However, a more than adequate number of functions has been provided to establish the ARPA network as a prophet of things to come. Computer manufacturers and users alike can learn much by examining the existing ARPA network and keeping one eye on its future evolution.

The ARPA Network Related Reading

The following list of reading material relating specifically to the ARPA network is included for the interested reader. A similar, more general list is contained in Appendix B, Related Reading.

1. CARR, C. S., CROCKER, S. D., and CERF, V. G. 1970. "HOST-HOST Communication Protocol in the ARPA Network". AFIPS Conference Proceedings, Vol. 36. 1970 Spring Joint Computer Conference. AFIPS Press, Montvale, N.J. 589–597.
2. CROCKER, S., HEAFNER, J. METCALFE, R., and POSTEL, J. 1972. "Function-Oriented Protocols for the ARPA Network". AFIPS Conference Proceedings, Vol. 40, 1972 Spring Joint Computer Conference. AFIPS Press, Montvale, N.J. 271–280.
3. FRANK, H., FRISCH, I. T., and CHOU, W. 1970. "Topological Considerations in the Design of the ARPA Computer Network". AFIPS Conference Proceedings, Vol. 36, 1970 Spring Joint Computer Conference. AFIPS Press, Montvale, N.J. 581–588.
4. HEART, F. E., KAHN, R. E., ORNSTEIN, S. M., CROWTHER, W. R., and WALDEN, D. C. 1970. "The Interface Message Processor for the ARPA Computer Network". AFIPS Conference Proceedings, Vol. 36, 1970 Spring Joint Computer Conference. AFIPS Press, Montvale, N.J. 551–568.
5. KARP, P. M. 1973. "Origin, Development and Current Status of the ARPA Network". Digest of Papers COMPCOM 73, Seventh Annual IEEE Computer Society International Conference. IEEE Society, N.Y., N.Y. 49–52.
6. McKENZIE, A. A., et. al. 1972. "The Network Control Center for the ARPA Network". Proceedings of The First International Conference on Computer Communications. Association for Computing Machinery, N.Y., N.Y. 185–191.
7. McQUILLAN, J. M., CROWTHER, W. R., COSELL, B. P., WALDEN, D. C., and HEART, F. E. 1972. "Improvements in the Design and Performance of the ARPA Network". AFIPS Conference Proceedings, Vol. 41. 1972 Fall Joint Computer Conference. AFIPS Press, Montvale, N.J. 741–754.
8. ORNSTEIN, S. M., HEART, F. E., CROWTHER, W. R., RISING, H. K., RUSSELL, S. B., and MICHEL, A. 1972. "The Terminal IMP for the ARPA Computer Network". AFIPS Conference Proceedings, Vol. 40. 1972 Spring Joint Computer Conference. AFIPS Press, Montvale, N.J. 243–254.
9. ROBERTS, L. G., and WESSLER, B. D. 1970. "Computer Network Development to Achieve Resource Sharing". AFIPS Conference Proceedings, Vol. 36. 1970 Spring Joint Computer Conference. AFIPS Press, Montvale, N.J. 543–550.
10. ROBERTS, L. G. 1973. "Network Rationale: A 5-Year Reevaluation". Digest of Papers COMPCOM 73, Seventh Annual IEEE Computer Society International Conference. IEEE Society, N.Y., N.Y. 3–5.

Appendixes

APPENDIX A

For Appendix A, see foldout at back of book.

APPENDIX B

Related Reading

The following list of related reading material is presented as a cross-section of currently available material. The list is presented in a free-standing form, rather than keyed to specific chapters of subjects covered in the text.

A separate list of reading material specifically related to the ARPA network follows Chapter 16, "The Advanced Research Projects Agency Network."

ABRAMSON, N. "The ALOHA System—Another Alternative for Computer Communications." *AFIPS Conference Proceedings* Vol. 37. 1970 Fall Joint Computer Conference. AFIPS Press, Montvale, N.J. 281–285.

BECHER, R. W., and AUPPERLE, E. M. 1972. "The Communications Computer Hardware of the MERIT Computer Network." *IEEE Transactions on Communications* Vol. COM-20, No. 3, June 1972.

BELL TELEPHONE LABORATORIES. 1964. "Transmission Systems for Communications." *Western Electric Company, Inc.* Technical Publications.

BENNETT, W. R., and DAVEY, J. R. 1965. *Data Transmission.* McGraw-Hill, New York.

BOWDEN, E. 1969. "Priority Assignment in a Network of Computers." *IEEE Transactions on Computers* Vol. C-18, No. 11, November, 1969.

DAVENPORT, W. P., *Modern Data Communication.* Hayden Book Co., Inc., New York, 1971.

FARBER, D. J. 1972. "Networks: An Introduction." *Datamation* Vol. 18, No. 4, April 1972. 36–39.

FARBER, D. J., and LARSON, K. C. 1972. "The System Architecture of the Distributed Computer System." *The Communications System Symposium on Computer Networks.* The Polytechnic Institute of Brooklyn, April, 1972.

FORD, L. R., and FULKERSON, D. R. 1962. *Flows in Networks.* Princeton University Press, Princeton, N.J.

FRANK, H., KAHN, R. E., and KLEINROCK, L. 1972. "Computer Communication Network Design—Experience with Theory and Practice." *AFIPS Conference Proceedings* Vol. 40. 1972 Spring Joint Computer Conference. AFIPS Press, Montvale, N.J. 255–280.

HEAU, E., and McNELIS, D. 1968. "Principles of Data Communications for Professional Programmers and Systems Analysts." *Computer Methods Corporation* N.Y., N.Y.

HILL, M. F. 1972. "The World of EDP Standards." *Control Data Corporation Tech. Memo TM4.* Control Data Corporation, Minneapolis, Minn.

KAHN, R. E. 1972. "Resource Sharing Computer Communication Networks." *Proceedings of the IEEE* November, 1972.

KAHN, R. E., and CROWTHER, W. R. 1972. "Flow Control in a Resource Sharing Computer Network." *IEEE Transactions on Communications* Vol. COM-20, No. 3, June, 1972. 539–546.

KLEINROCK, L. 1970. "Analytic and Simulation Methods in Computer Network Design." *AFIPS Conference Proceedings* Vol. 36. 1970 Spring Joint Computer Conference. AFIPS Press, Montvale, N.J. 569–580.

MARTIN, J. 1968. *Telecommunications and the Computer.* Prentice-Hall, Englewood Cliffs, N.J.

MARTIN, J. 1970. *Teleprocessing Network Organization.* Prentice-Hall, Englewood Cliffs, N.J.

MARTIN, J. 1971. *Future Developments in Telecommunications.* Prentice-Hall, Englewood Cliffs, N.J.

MARTIN, J. 1972. *Systems Analysis for Data Transmission.* Prentice-Hall, Englewood Cliffs, N.J.

MATHISON, S. L., and P. M. WALKER, *Computers and Telecommunications Issues in Public Policy.* Prentice-Hall, 1970.

ROBERTS, L. G., and WESSLER, B. D. 1970. "Computer Network Development to Achieve Resource Sharing." *AFIPS Conference Proceedings* Vol. 36. 1970 Spring Joint Computer Conference. AFIPS Press, Montvale, N.J. 543–549.

RUSTIN, R., *Computer Networks.* Prentice-Hall, 1970.

STIMLER, S., *Real-Time Data Processing Systems.* McGraw-Hill, 1969.

WALDEN, D. C. 1972. "A System for Interprocess Communication in a Resource Sharing Computer Network." Communications of the ACM, Vol. 15, No. 4, April, 1972. Association for Computing Machinery, N.Y., N.Y. 221–230.

"Computing Networks from Minis through Maxis—Are They for Real?" Digest of Papers Presented at COMPCON 73, the Seventh Annual IEEE Computer Society International Conference. IEEE Computer Society, N.Y., N.Y.

APPENDIX C

Standards

Early users of computers had a very simple problem in relation to standards, compared to a large distributed user today. A user with a single machine, supplied and maintained by one manufacturer, could simply adhere to the "standards" or "conventions" for that particular machine. The fact that other computers supplied by different manufacturers operated with somewhat different "standards" was not a problem, as there was no exchange of information between these machines.

The first information "media" used for exchange between different computers was the 80 column punched card. The basic format for the punched card was set down over half a century ago, and probably became the first computer standard. (The use of punched paper tape as an input/output medium evolved at or about the same time, and in some instances may have preceded the punched card as an exchange medium.)

The large computer user of today faces a complex, bewildering problem concerning standards. Frequently, in his efforts to incorporate his existing computers into a common network, the need for information exchange between a variety of different machines arises. Most commercial information networks designed today revolve around the consolidation of existing, installed equipment, rather than a complete "ground zero" design where a completely homogeneous hardware and software complement could be selected.

Many users are faced with this problem as the result of corporate mergers and/or acquisitions. Each party to the merger may bring his own, frequently different, hardware and software complement into the new organization. In each case, the differing systems are already operational, and each represents a substantial investment in terms of man-years of systems design. Rather than scrap one or the other of these systems and face the resulting conversion problem, the user seeks a way of integrating the two (or more) independent systems into a common information network. At this point, the standards problem assumes an order of importance that was previously, in many cases, unsuspected.

Standards, like the networks themselves, fall into two broad categories —physical standards concerning the interconnection of the various hardware elements, and logical standards concerning the flow and control of information in the network.

PHYSICAL STANDARDS

The need for physical standards covers the entire range of hardware elements. Several of the more obvious areas where standardization would facilitate the network designer's task are outlined briefly in following paragraphs. Many of these areas are being addressed by standards committees today, with some success. The relatively large number of different manufacturers supplying hardware elements, each with his own ideas as to what the "standard" should be, makes a universal set of agreed upon standards (physical and logical) a distant goal rather than a current reality.

Terminal devices present a large number of variables concerning their physical access to the network. The more obvious are the code set(s) used ,the line speed(s) the unit is capable of, the line length possible, the direct-connect or analog couplers that can be used, and the control character sequences that cause the device to perform various functions. Others include answerback devices that identify the terminal with a coded response when queried, "stunt boxes" that cause the terminal to react to various poll and select sequences, switches for access to back-up couplers, lines, and trunks, and various "pluggable" options available from the manufacturers. These options can control many combinations of the above physical parameters, thus presenting an even greater number of different physical devices.

Coupling devices produce an equally large but different set of standards problems. The coupler must interface on one side with the terminal device and on the other with the selected line or trunk. Since the greatest majority of lines and trunks are still supplied by the common carriers, a level of standardization exists already for that interface. Similarly, a standard plug or connector is available for interface with the terminal device.

Couplers supplied by non-common carriers present a different situation. While they will interface with the standard lines and trunks on the one side, the terminal interface side can assume a much wider variety of forms. These forms may be the result of terminal designs for specific applications, or may include optional capabilities (within the coupler) that are not available on common carrier supplied couplers. Examples of this would include channel loop-back or test and diagnostic capabilities.

Network processors must interface with the lines and trunks of the network, and thus have a coupler problem similar to that just described. Those network processors configured as front-ends to information processors incur a different level of interface standard problem. Those front-end network processors that use a common carrier supplied line or trunk to access the host information processor use an appropriate coupler. Those front-ends that use a direct port to host memory type of access have a more significant problem.

If the front-end has been supplied by the same manufacturer as the host information processor, the access methods and combinations thereof are usually fairly rigidly defined, as is frequently the case. However, the front-end network processor may be supplied by a different manufacturer than the host information processor. In this case, the interface will require physical change on either or both sides of the interface. Usually, the network processor manufacturer will make most, if not all, of the hardware changes required. In this way, the front-end can be made to conform to an already existing interface on the host. Frequently the front-end will appear as an already known device to the host, such as a magnetic tape or disc file controller. In this way, hardware and software changes in the host in order to accomplish the interface are significantly reduced or eliminated. In some instances, the front-end will access a port directly to memory of the host, and will be recognized specifically as a front-end.

The foreign front-end to host interface problem lies in that there exists little, if any, agreement between manufacturers concerning "standard" interfaces to memory ports or peripheral subsystem ports. In fact, manufacturers perpetuate these differences as a means of assuring that foreign peripheral subsystems and/or front-ends will be difficult to interface to their host processors. This, in turn, insures the sale of more of their products. This position, while understandable from a manufacturer's point of view, creates significant problems for the user not entirely satisfied with one vendor and wishing to use other vendors' front-ends and/or peripheral subsystems.

Other physical elements in information networks produce similar interface standard problems. These include passive elements, such as time and frequency division multiplexors, line and trunk switches, reconfiguration switches, non-common carrier supplied lines and trunks, in-plant distribution facilities, and others. These will not be discussed in depth here, but are mentioned to avoid the implication that they are not subject to the same kinds of problems described earlier for other elements.

LOGICAL STANDARDS

Logical standards involve those sequences or procedures required to control the flow of information through the elements of the physical network. Most of these procedures are executed by the network processor(s) of the network, acting either as a front-end to an information processor or as a remote network processor. Obviously, for exchanges between a host and its front-end, a portion of the procedures must reside in the host.

Examination of the routing function suggests several areas where standardization would greatly facilitate the integration of previously independent networks. In most cases, the addressing technique employed in one network makes no sense at all to the network processor(s) of another. Frequently, in an effort to retain a level of meaningful symbolic addressing, little if any information exists in the destination codes that could be used by a foreign network processor in directing the information towards the intended destination.

Even though elements in a destination code that would locate the device in the network's topology tend to detract from the meaning of the symbolic code, some use of this technique seems appropriate. Time zone, state, or other regional distinctions would aid in the development of destination code or addressing schemes that would lend themselves to standardization.

These destination codes could then be used to develop routing algorithms that would enable independent networks to intersect for the exchange of information between interested source/destination devices.

In obvious conjunction with the addressing and routing schemes is the need for uniformity concerning message formats, lengths, blocking factors, priority designators, security clearance, and many others. While expecting industry standardization to this level is probably irrational, a higher level approach to the definition of such parameters may prove of considerable value. In other words, standardize the way in which the parameters are defined, rather than attempting to standardize the parameters themselves.

An agreed upon "language" for describing the parameters, and a format for the language would enable independent but intersecting networks to exchange information. This language may define or imply a "canonical" form that is to be used for such interchanges. This form would be understood by both networks, and would contain, in standard format, the parameters necessary to convert from the network specific formats to the canonical format and back.

The more immediate problem of logical standards within integrated networks consisting of different manufacturers' equipment (as opposed to independent but intersecting networks) presents the following types of problems in addition to those already mentioned.

The integrity functions, including error detection/correction, retransmission, and continuity maintenance, usually differ widely between manufacturers. Similarly, the fail soft/backup, restart/recovery, and test/diagnostic procedures are at variance. Journaling formats, media, and searching algorithms must be agreed upon if the journals are to serve their intended use.

The types of statistics, the collection frequency, reporting, and evaluation criteria must also be standardized if a true perspective of the operating network is to be obtained. Similarly, the "set" of supervisory control functions, their execution, and their effect on the network's operation must be standardized. This is necessary if the specified level of control is to be maintained along with the network's ability to react to the many exception events that can and will occur.

STANDARDS ORGANIZATIONS

The following list of standards organizations is provided as a source of reference for interested readers. Comprehensive coverage of standards activities can be found in "The World of EDP Standards," by M. J. Hill.[1]

International Organizations

1. International Electrotechnical Commission (IEC)
   National committees in participating countries working toward the unification and coordination of national electrotechnical standards.
   Founded in 1906.
2. International Federation for Information Processing (IFIP)
   An international organization concerned with all aspects of information processing, including both hardware and software.
   Founded 1960.
3. International Organization for Standardization (ISO)
   An international organization promoting standards for exchange of products and information, and the development of intellectual, technological, economic, and scientific cooperation.
   Founded 1946.

European Organizations

1. European Computer Manufacturers' Association (ECMA)
   An organization promoting the standardization of methods and procedures used in data processing systems.
   Founded 1961.
2. European Standards Coordinating Committee (CEN)
   One of two committees for standardization among European countries. CEN is responsible for all industrial fields except electrotechnical (see CENEL).
   Founded 1960.
3. European Electrical Standards Coordinating Committee (CENEL)
   The other of two committees for standardization among European countries. CENEL is responsible for electrotechnical fields.
   Founded 1960.

[1] See Appendix B—"Related Reading"

4. International Committee on Rules for the Approval of Electrical Equipment (CEE)
   An organization defining compliance standards for electrical equipment, to protect users from electrical hazard.
   Founded 1926.

National Organizations

1. American National Standards Institute (ANSI)
   An organization of trade and professional associations, companies, and governmental departments and agencies coordinating the development, approval, and issuance of national standards.
   Originally founded in 1918 as the American Engineering Standards Committee (AESC).
   Current name adopted in 1969.
2. Electronic Industries Association (EIA)
   An organization directed by a board of governors coordinating the advancement and progress of the industry, the industry's interface to various legislative bodies, the interchange of information between industry members, and assisting the federal government in obtaining advanced, reliable products.
   Originally founded in 1924 as Radio Manufacturers' Association.
   Current name adopted in 1957.
3. National Bureau of Standards (NBS)
   Originally established as part of the Department of Commerce in 1901. Computer system involvement began in 1946—concerned with hardware and software standards for the industry and federal government, assistance to government agencies in efficient use of computers, related training and information services, and computer services to government agencies.
4. Underwriters Laboratories Inc. (ULI)
   An organization for the independent examination and testing of devices, systems, and materials, and the development of standards relating to the testing and use of such devices, systems, and materials.
   Originally founded in 1894.

Index